SOLITAIRE

SOLITAIRE

The Intimate Lives of
Single Women

Marian Botsford Fraser

Macfarlane Walter & Ross
Toronto

Macfarlane Walter & Ross
An Affiliate of McClelland & Stewart Ltd.
37A Hazelton Avenue
Toronto, Canada M5R 2E3
www.mwandr.com

National Library of Canada Cataloguing in Publication Data

Fraser, Marian Botsford, 1947–
Solitaire

ISBN 1-55199-064-4

1. Single women — Canada — Interviews. I. Title.

HQ800.2.F73 2001   305.48'9652   C2001-901889-4

Excerpts on pages 36-45 and pages 189-90 are reproduced by permission of Chatelaine Magazine.

Macfarlane Walter & Ross gratefully acknowledges support for its publishing program from the Canada Council for the Arts, the Ontario Arts Council, and the Government of Canada through the Book Publishing Industry Development Program.

Printed and bound in Canada

For the women in my family:

my mother, Katherine Louise Botsford
my sister, Sara Louise Botsford
my daughter, Katherine Jane Fraser

Contents

SOLITAIRE

Prologue

The game of solitaire, the game of being a single woman, plays out differently every time you turn the cards, every time you think it through. You win, you lose, you win again. You love your life, your hard-earned independence, your big brass bed. But you would kill for sex, for someone to help clean out the basement, for an unhurried, murmured conversation. You feel strong and alive and exuberant; you feel lonely and isolated and selfish.

You are dealing your own hand, but the cards you play with carry a long history of contradictory icons and ideas about single women and their role in society. Remember the child's pack of Old Maid cards, she of the wizened turnip face, or tales of the goddesses of Greek mythology who were, with one exception, all gloriously independent women, or the mysterious Amazon warriors who marched defiantly alone? For Canadian women, those ideas sit alongside 18th- and 19th-century European traditions of marriage and family, the social-security state that evolved in Canada in this century under the watchful eye of a very maternal, family-based feminism, and the mixed bundle of cultural assumptions that have informed North American society since the Second

World War. At the beginning of the 21st century, the lives of Canadian single women are affected by all of these influences.

There are over 4 million single women in Canada, ranging in age from early 20s to late 90s. A single woman may be unmarried (so far or never), separated, divorced, or widowed. She may be childless or a single mother of children young or grown; or she may find herself still defined as the unmarried daughter of aging parents. She may be temporarily single or permanently alone; she may be heterosexual or lesbian, sexually active or celibate. She may be wealthy or on welfare, a pensioner or a prostitute.

Single women are potentially a powerful socio-economic group. Almost a million single women are identified by Statistics Canada as "heading households" in Canada. They make economic and political decisions, spend money independently and on behalf of dependants, run households, pay taxes. As they age they become a majority, outliving the males of their cohort by a considerable margin. The circumstances of single women today differ dramatically from those of even 40 years ago, when women were financially dependent, rarely lived alone or owned property, and were forever Miss.

But single women are still widely perceived as disadvantaged or insignificant, subordinate or invisible. The term "spinster" is rarely uttered without a smirk. Even as we turn the corner into a new century, with flexible and dynamic definitions of family, household, and couple, a single woman remains a woman without a man, poor thing. Most women will be single for more than half their lives, and yet being single is considered an anomalous state. In a society governed by implicit assumptions, married or coupled is "normal"; single is "other."

Remaining single or reverting to single status is one of the choices available to women now. But it is a state of enormous ambivalence: freedom and serenity and independence on one hand,

and on the other, a sense of failure, a lack of fulfilment, an unsettling physical imbalance in a life without intimacy, and the anxiety of financial insecurity.

I have been single for almost a decade, after a comfortable 20-year marriage and one child. Even now, I stumble over the word "divorced"; I am never sure how to refer to the man I was married to and still care for profoundly. Is he my former husband, my one and only husband (now someone else's husband), the man now best identified as the father of my daughter, or – another term I dislike – my "ex"?

All this uncertainty from a woman who chose, for a number of reasons, to step outside the box after two decades of marriage. In part, this book is a reflection on the choice that I made, my own personal journey to this point. It is also a journey across the country, an inquiry into the lives of single Canadian women, in many different circumstances.

During the past three years I have corresponded with and interviewed more than 150 single women. I placed an ad in the *Globe and Mail*, and about 75 women responded. I did a brief interview on CBC Radio's *Richardson's Roundup* one spring afternoon, and the next day there were almost 40 e-mail messages waiting for me. I travelled from the Gulf Islands in the west to the outports of Newfoundland in the east. I spoke to women in cities, suburbs, small northern towns, on farms, in villages. I tried to cover a broad range of ages, economic and personal circumstances, ethnic and religious backgrounds. I interviewed women under the age of 30 but for the most part focused on those over 30 (the oldest was 94), those who are confronting the issues. Younger women are . . . well, young; they are not yet defining themselves as single.

I spoke to a number of women who are either lesbian or open to the idea of relationships with women. It is surprising how often books about single women do not include lesbians, thus reinforcing the stereotypical notion of heterosexual relationships as the norm.

There are some specific situations that this book could not address. I did not talk to women whose single state is part of a larger, more complex scenario: for example, women who are physically or mentally disabled, or women in Canada on work permits as domestics and perhaps only temporarily or theoretically single, or women who are new immigrants, whose marital status is a central piece in their immigration story. Constraints of time and space prevented me from exploring the changing community of the convent or the realm of prostitution, although I did meet women who had resided for a time in one or the other of those worlds.

Women introduced me to other women or helped spread the word. You really should talk to my mother, some said, or to my great-aunt, or to the woman who lives by herself in the little clapboard house in the village. Would you like me to call a few of my friends and we can get together as a group? Would you like to come for dinner, spend the night, stay for a few days?

But even more extraordinary than their hospitality and support was the gift of their lives. One day in Ottawa, as I went up in the elevator to call on a 65-year-old woman who had answered the newspaper ad, I wondered, Why is this woman, with whom I have exchanged two letters and one phone call, receiving me? Why is she opening her door to a complete stranger, who wants to interview her about the most intimate details of her life?

The answer was simple and almost universal. Single women are very interested in other single women's lives. They tend to have a network of like-minded friends, but they don't see themselves mirrored in books, films, or television shows, where they are frequently portrayed as sex-crazed, hysterical, anorexic urban professionals. In books about issues affecting women – books on sex, hormone replacement therapy, family history, family therapy, financial planning – they seek in vain for full-length, thoughtful discussions about single women. They wrestle alone with their doubts and fears, which they often see as peculiar to themselves, in a society overtly dedicated to the preservation of the family – meaning the heterosexual, married couple with children.

In order to find out how other single women think and live, they were happy to share their own experiences. This combination of curiosity and generosity made women trust the process. They answered my questions with honesty and self-awareness. They told me the very best and the very worst things that had happened in their lives. They spoke frankly about virginity, celibacy, masturbation, money, abuse, secret sex lives, and fear of illness and death. You are writing about *me*, they said, and they acknowledged that this was a rare and valuable form of validation of their lives. It was comforting for people to simply hear the words "You are not the first person who has said that."

Whenever possible I spoke to women in their homes. Sometimes, as we sat together in late-afternoon light in a modest apartment, or in the deep gloom of a house almost pulsing with sorrows, my tape recorder running silently, feelings would erupt into tears. I was conscious of opening doors that had long been shut or scraping the scar on a wound that had barely closed. Often, women were quite clear that they had chosen to talk to me as a way of dealing with unfinished business; they had stories they needed to share and could do so with a stranger; healing required telling. Often I carried away their burden of grief.

There were also moments of great pleasure, instant recognition, an interview that stretched from one hour to two, with neither of us budging from our chairs. There was laughter, there were goofy dogs and cranky cats; there were cups of coffee on the porch in the sunshine, an immense glass bowl filled with daffodils on a coffee table catching the light, an unexpected rapport with a woman completely unlike myself.

At times I had to consciously resist offering anything more than sympathy with my questions. I wanted to say, "Get the breast reduction, it will change your life." "Don't even think about going back to him, he's a nut case." "Of course you should move/change your job/have an affair with a woman." But I mostly resisted these impulses, and I hope that I was provocative only in a supportive or helpful way.

The interviews were conducted in confidence, so I have changed names and identifying details. While particular individuals may not be recognizable, their stories will be. This was not a scientific research project; the evidence is anecdotal and unverified. I have no sense of these women as a representative sample in social science terms, although I believe absolutely in what I learned as true and significant. I also read widely on subjects that came up during conversation and reflection, but my approach was neither academic nor definitive.

This book is about the choices that women make to be or become single. It is about the rules they live by and the passions and ambitions that play havoc with those rules. It is about the face they see in the mirror, and the face they present to the world. It is about how they play out their game of solitaire.

From the Diary of a Single Woman

A man, a complete stranger, asked me at a public event last night if I would make the same decision again, to leave a 20-year marriage. I said yes, although I have asked that question of myself innumerable times. He told me he could not imagine being alone, that he has made himself fantasize about it: his wife gets cancer and she dies and then he . . . but he can never go farther with the fantasy. He said, Or what if she were to leave me for a younger man; I can't imagine that either. When I asked him which he would prefer, his wife leaving him for a younger man, or his wife (who was sitting at the table, a calm and exceptionally lovely woman) dying of cancer, he said, Oh, definitely the latter. He did not contemplate, nor did we discuss, what for some men is equally unimaginable: the wife who leaves a marriage not for another man at all, but for herself. Or the woman who happily never marries at all.

At the end of the evening, all the couples drifted away. I found several single friends to have a last drink with, and then we too went our separate ways. I took a taxi home.

I lit a fire, put on some music. Resisted the game of computer solitaire I sometimes play as a way to start writing, like the scales I used to play at the beginning of piano practice. Limber the fingers, settle the mind. Instead, I called my friend Suzanne and told her about the man who would rather see his wife dead than happy. Really!

CHAPTER 1

That Spinster Word

*W*hen I was nine, I took Robbie Cook as a lover. I chose him because he was handsome, distant, and older. I had taken baths as a five-year-old with his younger brother Teddie, who in no way interested me romantically. Even then, there were rules.

In northern Ontario in the mid-1950s, when we were little and it was girls only, play consisted mostly of dress-up. At an earlier age, my best friend, Susan, and I had played Roy Rogers and Dale Evans, which involved a lot of galloping around the backyard and down the townsite trail with brooms between our legs, wearing cowboy hats and vests and toy guns in holsters. We switched roles every day, but on your birthday you always got to be Roy. We played with our brothers and drove trucks up and down the sandpit behind the house and built forts in the bush or in the snow.

But when we were nine, we put aside trucks and guns and our brothers and their friends. We donned cast-off clothes from our mothers' closets and whatever we could beg in the way of costume jewellery and high-heeled shoes and bright used lipsticks. I remember a full, vibrantly printed cotton skirt that would stand out in a full circle when I twirled. There were hours of twirling, on long, hot summer days and evenings on the front lawn of our house, as we danced with our imaginary boyfriends and then pressed ourselves against the birch trees in murmuring, passionate embraces. We never married the objects of our desires. Our fictional heroines – Cherry Ames, Nurse, and the more pallid Vicky Barr, Stewardess – were partly to blame for the lengthy, unconsummated courtships we favoured.

Robbie Cook did not know I had chosen him as the partner in my romantic fantasies. Only Susan knew. Susan had already chosen an airline pilot as her imaginary lover; she had travelled to Newfoundland with her family and been taken up to the cockpit, and there he was, the Man of Her Dreams. When she came back, triumphant, brandishing this gorgeous persona like a trophy from the Crusades, it became a matter of urgency that I too find a man. Someone similarly attractive and impossible. None of the boys in Dobie would do. In any case, by then I had humiliated myself by passing a love note to a townsite boy named Dennis one wintry afternoon while skating on the outdoor rink beside the curling club. He had responded, to my mortification: "Dear Mush-Mush, When shall we plan the wedding?" No, I needed a partner who was more compliant, and besides, Dennis was short.

Susan and I agreed that when my family went for a weekend visit to the Cook family, who lived two hours' drive to the east, I would check out 15-year-old Robbie. It was that cold-blooded, this exercise in matchmaking; all that mattered was that he be cute and tall. He checked out, although I doubt that we even spoke as I tobogganed with Teddie.

Even at that age, men could be mere objects. They had to conform to the cut-out image in our minds: tall, dark, and handsome, engaged in exotic careers, doctor or pilot, or vaguely rich. They certainly didn't work underground or run small businesses or drive a bus, like the real men around us. They were the precursors of Ken, the smooth-groined boy doll that came along a couple of years later. They were the paper dolls that my second-best friend, Barbara, and I played with, after Susan moved away.

I do not recall dressing up as a bride; we preferred nuns to brides when we got bored with the men. We wrapped ourselves in billowing white sheets held together with big safety pins and floated around the lawn, holding candles and flowers and a small white plastic cross that glowed in the dark. Then we would kneel in front of the birch trees to pray and sing our United Church hymns. We were little WASP girls, after all, who attended painfully austere Sunday services in the one-room schoolhouse where we went on weekdays.

We had no knowledge at all of nuns, except for Sister Lucie, who gave us piano lessons at the convent in Kirkland Lake. Once a week, waiting to be summoned, we sat in awe of the large statue of Mary in her chipped blue plaster robes, smelled the peculiar sweet odours of the nuns' supper cooking behind doors that never opened, and finally went into the small piano room with Sister Lucie. She was warm and laughed hugely, and she openly envied the white, short-sleeved Terylene blouse that I sometimes wore. In her heavy, black caped gown and stiff white guimpe, she would rub the Terylene between her strong brown fingers and wish out loud that it were the stuff of habits.

We loved Sister Lucie in the same way that we loved some of our unmarried women teachers. We were excited, in ways we did not understand, by women who did not walk in the shadow of husbands. We understood that the rhythms of their lives must be completely different from those of our mothers and we wanted to know more. But we dared not ask. We were pretty sure we would not become nuns, but we certainly took the measure of the women teachers who stood before us in that one-room schoolhouse. There I took Grades One through Six, moving year by year from one row of desks to the next, under the bemused eye of Her Majesty the Queen. All my teachers were single women, culminating in the formidable, challenging person of Pat Madden, who landed in our midst like a great peregrine falcon all the way from Wales.

Miss Madden had blazing eyes and short hair that she somehow managed to toss; she wore bright, polka-dotted cotton dresses with full skirts and wide belts and sleeves that could be rolled up dramatically, a gesture with great effect because of the clattering bangles on her wrists. I recall chiffon scarves streaming from her pockets or sleeves, and high-heeled pumps, the highest imaginable, in colours that matched her frocks. She spoke beautifully, her precise and complex sentences laced with a delicate accent and a mostly delicate irony; the latter would sharpen somewhat if she was displeased. Her age we speculated on endlessly, fruitlessly.

Miss Madden was witty, flamboyant, and very clever, the most interesting person I had yet encountered. She raised the expectations of her students; she is the reason I became a writer and my sister an actor. She continued to be a presence in my life through high school, where she taught English, coached drama, and mounted brilliant productions of Gilbert and Sullivan. She lived in a tiny house with her aunt and her beloved cousin Margaret, then just with Margaret, and after Margaret's death alone. She was Miss Madden then; she is Miss Madden still. In the European tradition from which she came, the tradition that firmly underwires historical and contemporary ideas about women in this country, she would be deemed an old maid, a spinster.

"Despicable creatures, called Old Maids"

I write of the High Priestess of Society. Not of the mother of sons but of her barren sister, the withered tree . . . of the Spinster I write . . . She, unobtrusive, meek, soft-footed, silent, shamefaced, bloodless and boneless, thinned to spirit . . . moulds and fashions our emasculate society. She is our social nemesis . . . She haunts every library . . . In our schools she takes the little children, and day by day they breathe in the atmosphere of her violated spirit. (*Freewoman Magazine*, 1911)

The stock figure of the old maid or spinster is a constant in our inherited history, and her characteristics are still invoked in discussions about single women at the beginning of a new century. For a woman to be uncoupled, childless, even widowed has always been, in most societies, a compromised status. As early as 1673 in England, an old maid was seen as "the most calamitous creature in nature" even though this was a time when patriarchal, extended-household models of the family were prevalent. Before 1700, lines were not so clearly drawn between the married and the unmarried; most households, in which the eldest male was the only legal entity, embraced several generations. Unmarried women, described from the early 1600s as "spinsters" in census records, had child-minding or household functions such as weaving or farm work that were essential to the family's well-being.

But even then, the emphasis on women's domestic duties, the derision of their weaknesses (of intellect or moral fibre), and a resolute division of public and private spheres (dominated respectively by men and women) established the framework within which unmarried women either acquiesced or rebelled. In the courtly debate known as the *querelles des femmes* – What is her Nature? Can she be educated? – carried on in northern Europe from the 15th to the 17th centuries, women were assigned vices such as insatiable lust, greed, gluttony, and cowardice. Women who argued against the characterization of their sex as weak and evil often identified marriage as the enemy of women.

The 18th century saw the burgeoning of a middle class and the emergence of new ideas about marriage and households. With England's formalization of legal marriage, condoned by both church and state in 1753, and the focus on the couple as the foundation of the family, the figure of the unmarried woman became more iso-lated. The first use of the word "spinster" to describe not just an unmarried woman but "an unmarried woman beyond the usual age for marriage" occurred in a short-lived, mid-1700s satirical periodi-cal called *The Spinster*, written by Sir Richard Steele under the slightly smirky pseudonym Rachel Woolpack. Steele's more famous journal, *The Spectator*, consistently celebrated the fully domesti-cated woman. Indeed, mid-18th-century England is notable for the emergence of women from the home into intellectual and literary public life, and the simultaneous denigration of women who thus broke the domestic mould, usually by being both clever and single. Both "bluestocking" (a previously non-pejorative term for women interested in learning) and "spinster" were thereafter terms used mockingly, not just descriptively.

Women who chose not to marry were expected to earn their keep in a womanly fashion, even if they had intellectual aspirations. The English bluestocking Elizabeth Carter, a contemporary of Steele's and a classic upper-middle-class spinster, was a scholar who took in sewing. Called "Mrs." as a sign of respect to her years, she was patronized for her brains and admired for her household skills: "My old friend Mrs. Carter could make a pudding as well as trans-late Epictetus from the Greek and work a handkerchief as well as compose a poem," wrote Samuel Johnson. Meanwhile in France, Diderot and Rousseau glorified motherhood and breast-feeding. In Germany, Kant decried intellectual women as manly. In public dis-course, literature, and drama, the smart woman not interested in marriage was cast as unnatural and unwomanly, a threat to the social order.

By the end of the 18th century, and through the 19th, properly married women with no unsettling public or intellectual ambitions became imbued with moral purity through housewifery and mother-hood. This ideal culminated in the late-19th-century vision of the "Angel in the House." Gradually, married women seized upon their undisputed authority in the private domain as a way to extend their influence publicly through charities and religious organizations, taking up causes such as improving the lot of poor children and working mothers, banning prostitution, and campaigning for female suffrage.

In this milieu, the spinster was by turns the object of ridicule, pity, contempt, compassion, or fear. She embodied, willingly or not, the qualities of the outsider. When the unmarried woman was middle-class, she was assigned the responsibility of caring for aging and ill relatives and rarely left the family home. When she was working-class, or an unmarried mother, she was judged by the values of the middle class and punished or pitied. It was better to be widowed than deserted, and to be an unmarried mother was to be morally unfit. If the spinster had intellectual interests or career ambitions other than marriage, she was queer. If she actively challenged marriage as a repressive institution, she was an outlaw.

There have always been women who made themselves exceptions, through force of intellect and personality and talent, and there were circumstances under which the rules were briefly suspended, mostly during wars. And there have always been women who deliberately exploited their outsider status to question and disturb the status quo. Wherever you turn in the history of women, you hear the insistent voices of solitary women demanding better education, arguing for equality between women and men, questioning the patriarchal assumptions of laws and customs. Few such women were happily or conventionally married. They were spinsters or widows, religious or convent women, or courtesans; they were women with lovers, male and female.

Women as different as Hildegard of Bingen (12th-century Germany), Christine de Pizan (15th-century France), and Mary Wollstonecraft and Hannah More (18th- and 19th-century England) lived lives that did not conform to the strictures of marriage and family that were hardening around them. Mary Wollstonecraft was resolutely single for a good part of her life, took lovers, and bore an illegitimate child. When she finally did marry William Godwin, they maintained separate residences. Writers like Jane Austen, the Brontës, George Sand, George Eliot, and Colette were either unmarried or highly unconventional in their couplings. In the great campaigns of the late 19th and early 20th centuries for women's independence, education, and suffrage, those in the forefront in Europe and North America were very often spinsters, sometimes defiantly celibate or sometimes involved in relationships with other women: Florence Nightingale and Christabel Pankhurst in England, the Americans Susan B. Anthony and Frances Willard, the Canadians Clara Brett Martin (a lawyer), Agnes Machar (a writer), and Carrie Derrick (a scientist).

The evolution of Canadian society occurred within this context. European women who came to Canada from the 1600s onwards brought considerable cultural baggage in their bundles of personal belongings. They came mostly to marry, to provide the necessary glue of a new society – families and children – in both New France and British North America. They did not aspire to spinsterhood or the solitary life, unless they belonged to a religious order. The early history of the nation is a history of family-making and community-building inside the larger, noisier contests for territory and goods.

It is not surprising that the family became both the foundation and the battleground for Canadian social policy. The family was the main unit of immigration upon which the country was claimed, cleared, and settled. (The family unit is still the problematic basis for Canada's immigration policies.) To reinforce the first settlers in New France, single women were brought in for the express purpose of marrying (the *filles du roi*), or they were indentured as servants or members of several orders of nursing, missionary, or teaching nuns. Migration under British rule began with families from the American colonies and shifted to families from the British Isles in the mid-1800s. As in New France, boatloads of single women were imported as potential wives. The shortage of women in the colonies conveniently coincided with an abundance in Great Britain, where "surplus" women were considered a significant problem in the 1860s: "The first difficulty is chiefly mechanical . . . To transport the half million [women] from where they are redundant to where they are wanted . . . would require 10,000 vessels." (W.R. Greg, *National Review*, April 1862)

The sparseness of settlement across a vast and inhospitable landscape and bitter struggles to establish homesteads, villages, and viable communities have undoubtedly imprinted Canadians with a profound anxiety about their survival as a nation, which historically has translated into family-based politics and policies. At the turn of the 20th century, when there was agitation in most Western democracies for women's advancement, a strong form of "maternal feminism" took hold in the dominant Anglo-Canadian middle-class culture.

Maternal feminism was championed by women, married and otherwise, who believed in marriage and the family as the foundation of society. Women were to bring the same order and discipline to society that they administered in the home. As a socially affirmative ideology, maternal feminism joined comfortably with other conservative forces to create the sturdy father-as-breadwinner model for social policy that still informs Canadian legislation. Through church groups, benevolent and missionary societies, the Temperance Union, and the YWCA, married women seized the social agenda. Their focus on poor children and unwed mothers was broader than that of the spinsters of an earlier generation, whose interests were professional and academic. In retrospect, it looked like a successful strategy, except that it implicitly accepted limitations on women's rights and public role and entrenched assumptions about race and class.

Between 1880 and 1940, urbanization and industrialization dramatically altered workplaces, living conditions, and family dynamics. But even with women streaming into the workforce as factory and clerical workers, as teachers and nurses, the notion that man was the provider and that woman's primary role was as wife and mother did not change.

In 1902, only 2 percent of Canadian working women were married. It became normal for young women to work before marriage, but rarely afterwards; in some sectors, such as teaching, women were forced to resign when they married. Women were rarely designated as "skilled" workers and were paid significantly less than men in all instances. Legislation controlling the working hours of women and children was inspired by concern for women's child-bearing capabilities. Financial assistance from the state for women, such as that provided through the Ontario Mother's Allowance after 1920, was not quite enough to actually support women, and it was always subject to a moral means test, made available only to women who were genteel, which usually meant widowed and white.

In many cases well-meaning and socially beneficial measures did improve the lot of women within marriage. At the same time, it became extremely difficult to choose to be or to remain single, or to admit to being single. The place of women in the workforce, for example, was subject to the vagaries of economic conditions and the needs of the nation: "To women workers: . . . The war is over . . . Do you feel justified in holding a job which could be filled by a man who has not only himself to support but a wife and family as well? Think it over." (Ontario Department of Labour circular, 1918) Hired or enlisted in war; fired or replaced during depression; called into service again in another war; yielding again to the returning soldier. The focus of labour, economic, and social legislation shifted over the first half of the century from the protection of children, deserted women, and widows to policies that confirmed and celebrated the conventional family unit, protecting the male breadwinner's wage and encouraging jobs for men. A marriage of interests was arranged: families provided workers and soldiers for the state; government implemented legislation in support of the family.

The single woman was invisible in this union of state and family, except as the occasional grateful recipient of mother's allowance. Single working women resented the presence of married women in the workforce because women "with homes" accepted lower wages. During the Depression, unmarried mothers were denied relief because they could not prove they were employable. The 1940 Unemployment Insurance Act provided assistance only for skilled workers, and by then, most of the work done by women had become defined as unskilled. Income tax policies were used to encourage married women to work during the war and to discourage them when the war was over.

Eventually, married women formed increasingly larger percentages of the workforce; by 1961, there were almost equal numbers of married and unmarried working women, despite criticism and disapproval. And when feminism stirred again in Canada, in the 1960s, its first impulses were towards equal rights for women in the workplace and in family legislation. For the most part, the emphasis was on the rights of married women.

The 1970 report of the Royal Commission on the Status of Women targeted four issues: employment outside the home, shared responsibility for children, maternity support, and the need for short-term, special treatment for women to reverse the effects of discrimination. It took the abortion campaign to galvanize the women's liberation movement in Canada, an issue that finally crossed marital, class, race, and age boundaries.

The central position of the family and the activism of women in shaping public policy have contributed greatly to the national character and to the liberal, community-based, and consensus-oriented nature of our politics. But public discourse and the legislative framework are still linked to an oversimplified notion of family: a white, middle-class, heterosexual triangle of husband-wife-children that does not include other realities in a legal sense or honour them in a social sense.

Today most single women are not comfortable with the word "spinster" and would never use it to describe themselves. Happy to obscure their marital status, as are many married women, with the use of Ms., they have chosen not to reclaim "spinster" or to divest it of its negative, prissy connotations.

But are there women who fit the old-fashioned spinster profile? Yes, there are. I spoke to a number of women between the ages of 40 and 75 who resolved early in their lives not to marry and never have. They come from different cultural backgrounds, but all have been caregivers for ailing and aging parents. They express little or no interest in sex, although several either are in conflict about their sexuality or have secretly explored relationships with women. Some are cheerfully celibate, in a few cases virginal; others may have had one or two dismal experiences with sex. Their values are more conservative than radical, and a significant number are either active in a church or quietly religious.

As with many single women, there is something in their life stories – a strained relationship between their parents, an obviously unhappy mother, for example – that they connect with their decision to be single. Something about the tenor of their childhood brought them to a moment of clarity concerning marriage. It defined how they charted their lives, and it is the factor they can pinpoint when they look back and tell their stories. This self-awareness is something that artists also identify; it is as deeply felt as a need to write or sing or paint. But when it defines a choice to be single, it is not generally recognized as interesting or honourable, simply peculiar.

The significant difference between these women and the stereotypical spinster is that they are socially integrated and often materially successful; they enjoy a high profile in their communities;

they are leaders in their professions. They live well and are comfortable with their status and their lives.

Alma

"There's nothing particular about myself. I think it's just my own personality. I've never thought of myself as a spinster. I don't think in those terms."

Alma, 65, is a retired senior civil servant. She owns a large apartment in downtown Ottawa, reads seriously, loves music, especially opera, and travels a great deal. There was a huge stuffed bear on one of her living-room chairs, which she thought of hiding before my visit but didn't. Her nieces and nephews adore this toy. The furniture is old-fashioned, European. Alma describes herself as traditional; she says she dresses as she did in high school, in skirts and button-up blouses and "shoes that tie."

As a girl, Alma never imagined that she would marry. "It just didn't seem very important to me. I think I knew by the time I was seven that I really wasn't interested in domestic things, you know? I saw people with babies and it didn't stir anything in me. By the time I was in Grade Four I was thinking of travel.

"I've been very fortunate. The people I went to school with, a lot of them didn't get anywhere. They dropped out at Grade Eight and went to work, either in restaurants or in what we called the Fifteen-Cent Store. Some went to Grade Ten and then got jobs as typists in the government. My mother used to say to me – I was over at Lisgar for Grade Ten – Why don't you quit and go to work? Like such-and-such girls down the road. No, I said, I haven't finished. My father understood why I wanted to stay. I was a good student."

Alma has a calm, alert demeanour, and she offered carefully considered, articulate responses to my questions. She was modest about her career but said enough to convey her rise through the ranks of bureaucracy and her influence as a civil servant, instrumental in an unacknowledged way in the formulation of important social policy. When I asked, "Were you exceptionally bright?" she replied easily, "Yes, I was. From my early years I observed and understood very well what was going on around me, what was going on in the neighbourhood I lived in, and in the homes of my friends. I saw families where there was drinking. I saw families where there was abuse, spousal abuse. I was very little, but I saw it all. I realized then that women were not in the top position, that, generally speaking, women couldn't look forward to as good a life as men. That's the way I saw it. I can't imagine being in a home with little kids, with a husband, having to do all those domestic duties. And raising the children. I just don't understand how people do it. And *why* people do it."

For a time, Alma fell into a way of life that is familiar to people from small towns, especially those with struggling immigrant populations. It just happened that she grew up in Ottawa and the local employer was government, not a factory. Girls did not leave home. They finished their schooling and found jobs and remained in their childhood bedrooms. "I was actually with my parents until I was . . . let's see, was I 40? My father preferred to have me at home, because my mother was rather difficult to get along with. But finally the point came; they were shifting homes, and I said to my father, I won't be coming. Mother is difficult, and I find her difficult too. I just feel that this is a good time for me. I thought, If I don't get out now, when am I going to have the opportunity? So I did."

As the oldest child and the unmarried sibling, Alma ended up with responsibility for her parents. "My father died in 1990, of cancer. And Mother felt she would carry on on her own and stay in their home. But by '91 it was obvious that things were going badly. I didn't live with Mother, but I had a nurse [for her] 10 hours a day. I spent the entire weekend there and I couldn't go anywhere, except to get the newspaper at the corner. My sisters conveniently decided that they had to look after their retired husbands. And none of them were working. Eventually I had to place Mother in – well, actually, it was what she wanted – in a home."

Alma has been celibate all her life. "I've had an affectionate relationship with a few people. I mean, you know, I get on with them, but I'm really just not interested. I think they call that low sex drive. I can certainly feel affection for a male. I just don't feel that I would want to be stuck with somebody 24 hours a day. I've avoided the opportunity."

She has never regretted the decision not to marry and does not think her choice resulted in prejudicial treatment by her family. "No. Like even this minute, no. I see that it's suited me very well . . . I think because I've been involved with all the children in the family. All the children are very fond of me. Anyway, *this*" – she gestured towards the huge stuffed bear – "lives here. Would it be all right if I gave Winnie away? Oh no! the 14-year-old said. Winnie lives here!"

Beneath Alma's delicate facade and quiet voice, there is a spine of iron, a razor-sharp intelligence. At the same time, I sensed a distancing disingenuousness in her serene rejection of the spinster label. When I asked how her friends would describe her, she said, "I think they will say I'm eccentric. But I'm not quite sure why I'm eccentric. I never felt unusual."

Women are readily admired for focus and determination in their quest for a successful marriage: "She got her man." Alma got her life.

Wanda

"Everybody asks me, am I lonely? And I think, really telling the truth, I'm not! I think if you're satisfied with what you're doing, if you're happy with your life, you don't need to feel that."

Wanda is 49, Chinese, tiny, with short shiny hair and glasses, wearing a trim navy blue suit and floral blouse with beautiful dark blue shoes. A senior hospital administrator in southwestern Ontario, she has a professional manner and speaks quickly, her speech edged with Chinese inflections. She is not especially reflective about her life; it seems her choices were shaped by her family situation, and she made the most of them.

"My grandfather came to Vancouver in 1908, and then he made his way right across Canada. And he went to North Bay, and then he moved down here and opened his own business. And then my father came [to Canada] in 1956, and we came in 1959, December. So we've been here 40 years now. I have eight brothers and sisters. Six of them born in Canada." Her parents ran a small, main-street restaurant – as Wanda said with a laugh, "the same one you find in every little Canadian town!"

"My mother was sick after she had the twins, quite late in life, unfortunately. And then my father was sick. And then somebody had to take care of the business. My older sister was married at 21, so she was gone. I guess I was carrying the family. When my father died, he left six children [at home], and the twins were only 13. And my mother doesn't speak a word of English. I was always responsible for her even when I was younger, 'cause she was always sick. She was only 56 when my father died. She's 74 now.

"I was going to university, managing the business, working full-time. I always tried to keep myself upgraded. I always was into the business world. I think that was from our upbringing. My father said, in order to get somewhere in this world, you have to be a step ahead of everybody."

In the Chinese community, a son would normally take up the caretaker role, but the first son was much younger than Wanda. "And he married a Canadian, so the tradition has gone out the window. I'm sure if he would have married a Chinese, that would be the tradition."

Wanda has, at times, considered marrying, and she has had opportunities. "I do have some friends that are male. Like not sexual relationships, but you know, you could have some male friends. They're actually better than girlfriends. You can talk to them about anything!" But, as she said cheerfully, "who would take this big package? Mother and kids and business? I'm sure if I get married, she would just come with me." Wanda has never wanted children: "Not after I raised those six sisters and brothers. With the twins, I looked after one for the longest time, and my mother looked after one. So I think I have enough."

Her only regret, it seems, is occasional and social. "If there's any function, you like to rent a man to go with you. Like for weddings! But a family gathering is not a problem. You can go and they know you're single and they don't expect you to bring somebody. I'm used to it though. I travel by myself, it doesn't bother me. And you get a kind of high, you want more, you know? You're kind of a career woman, just looking forward to do more."

Wanda has a remarkable air of self-satisfaction that is not at all smug. She has found a way of combining her familial duty with her professional life. She sparkled when she talked about her hospital work, and she carefully separates her two worlds. We met at her workplace, and in passing she said she would not have met me at home, because her mother would have been puzzled and confused by my presence.

Marie

"I guess there are many reasons why I'm not married. When I meet a new man, they'll often say, Well, why aren't you married? Is there something wrong? I say, Well, I'm not married because I said no!"

Marie lives beside a river, not far from the rural northeastern Ontario French Catholic school where she is the principal. She is energetic, warm, pleasant-looking, speaking in lightly accented English and at great length. She has moved up with ease through the separate school system; she travels a great deal and is carefully restoring her modest house, the third one she has owned. Several cats observed our conversation, unblinking.

Marie is francophone, born near Rouyn-Noranda, Quebec, one of four daughters of a father who was a machinist. "Dad's always had a love for the land. Mum we liked to tease that she was a city slicker. She really wasn't, but she wasn't into farming. Mum and Dad bought a property that was only six and a half acres, but he was in his element. There were fields all around, and whenever they would spread the manure, it wouldn't bother him at all. My poor mother would have major problems with her stomach.

"Mum had worked before she was married, and a little bit after until I came along, and then she was an at-home mom. She at one time really wanted to work at a local school that was down the road when we moved out to the country. Dad just didn't like that whole idea. She was in her middle to late 30s when she was married, as was Dad."

When she was 20, Marie had a boyfriend. "He was very nice, and we got along very well. But as a teenager growing up, I went to all the Elvis movies, right? I had this romantic idea that I would be swept completely off my feet. I would know this was the right person for me. And I didn't feel that! So I thought, Well, no. I don't think this is what I want to do.

"But of course, you get teased, and especially when you come from a French-Canadian background, the assumption is that you're going to get married and you're going to have lots of kids! And that wasn't happening, so I realized that I needed to have a sense of humour about it. My students will ask me, Well, don't you have a husband? And I say, Oh heavens, no, I'm much too young to have a husband!

"I did have a male friend, about seven years ago. We were romantically involved, and he came to live with me. But we really weren't cohabiting. We would date, and every once in a while, there would be a bit more than just a date, but it wasn't what I would consider a strong relationship. He did his thing, I did mine. He's a confirmed bachelor. He told me I was making a big mistake being romantically involved with him, and of course he turned out to be right."

Marie has had two sexual relationships, one of which she sought in her 40s, after a hysterectomy, just to have one good sexual fling. Today she is content to be on her own, partly out of inclination and partly because she is not likely to meet eligible men. "It's very limited. Anybody that I teach with, or work with, the majority of those men are married. The church that I attend – again, there are not many single men. I don't frequent bars. I've never been comfortable with the meat market situation. Plus there aren't that many meat markets around here! I've met some wonderful gentlemen when I've been travelling, and kept in contact for a little while, and then they'd be in the other part of the world, or the other part of the country. And that sort of peters out."

"Did you ever want to have children? Did your body ever say to you, Now you've got to have children?"

"No. I don't know why. I often thought that I was the type of person that matured later. It wasn't until I was in my 30s that I was really interested in guys. But to say that I wanted children, and had this urge to carry a child in my womb, that was never there. I guess the closest I came to it was when my second sister had a child. I got some time off work to go down to Ottawa to spend time with her and the baby. It was funny: when he started to cry one night, I started my menstrual period, and I wasn't due, and I thought, What is going on here? Because I'm hearing a baby cry? I never felt anything like that before or since."

"Have you ever thought about having a relationship with a woman?"

"I have, because I have friends who are gay and of course it's crossed my mind. You know, why am I not in a relationship with a man? Maybe I am lesbian! But I've never been in a situation where I've wanted to be intimate with a woman. I've thought about it, I've never acted on it. I have a good friend who is lesbian, and she has told me that she loves me. And that's where it stayed. She said, I will never touch you, because that would be the end of our friendship. And I said to her, Yeah, it probably would, because it would make me feel bad that I can't relate to you the way you want to relate to me."

Marie's parents still cast a strong shadow on her life. Her father dallied; her mother drank; it's not clear which came first. Marie became the support of her mother, a heavy commitment when her mother was hospitalized. "I didn't realize until after she passed away how much time that was taking. We had had a very rough relationship when she was still at home, because she was depressed and she was drinking a lot. I had no patience with that. And then when this situation happened with Dad, I became her confidante; I was her daughter, yes, but I became a friend.

"I went through a period of being depressed, and I could never pinpoint why. If I was with people, I wanted to be alone. When I was alone, I wanted to be with people. Eventually it ended. I've had small depressions since, but what gets me through is knowing it won't go on forever. Mum was depressed a lot of the time. She didn't have a whole lot of energy. I could remember Mum being angry, so angry about things. And I thought, Is this me? Am I becoming my mother?"

Marie was wearing her mother's wedding ring, which she polished gently with her thumb as she spoke. She and her married sisters share the ownership of this ring, which they all treasure. Marie has it for three months of the year; it was almost time for her to hand it off to one of her sisters.

"They're all happy and not happy in their situations. I just shake my head and I said to my youngest sister, Well, you know, Hélène, it could be worse – you could be single. She said, That's worse? We had a good laugh."

Maureen

"At 15, I said, God, I'll do anything for you, but I don't want to get married. I just felt that was something good to do, to devote yourself to the Lord. That was the way I could serve people best. And I wasn't Catholic, I was Protestant."

Maureen is 43, of German-Canadian farm stock, short and heavyish, though she doesn't seem bothered by it. Short hair, open face, blue eyes, pink sweatshirt, blue jeans. She lives in a three-storey walk-up, a simply furnished, one-bedroom apartment in south Winnipeg. She apologized for the size of the television, a large-screened model given to her by a gay male friend. We sat at a small table in the kitchen, for two hours. I wondered why she had committed herself to the spiritual choice at such an early age.

"I felt a really deep love for Christ. I felt he cared for me, and that my identity came from who God said I was. And this is not a choice that was easy in my family. There is no other woman on either side that didn't get married. Out of 42 cousins, I'm the only single woman."

Maureen has never had a sexual relationship with a man, although she admitted to having been in love with someone, from childhood, but their lives and spiritual interests diverged. But as for sex? "No, not at all. It's not that I don't like sex, or don't fantasize about it. And sexually I'm geared towards men. But for emotional closeness, I would lean towards women."

When she was 25, she began an intimate relationship with a woman that lasted five years. "I didn't see her that often, but it was highly sexual, and when I, because of my beliefs, said, I don't want to do this any more, I lost her as a friend. I met her at Bible college – you know, the roommates thing? But I felt guilty and I don't usually have a problem with guilt. It was not that I broke my relationship with the Lord, but I realized I wasn't being loyal and focused and devoted.

"I came to the city, took a creative writing course, and wanted to get my head together. Then I met a lesbian from Australia. She said she had been married. I didn't realize she had been married to a woman in her mind for six years! So I got involved with her briefly, three times. We were not compatible because of the things she wanted me to do. I was not into oral sex; with the first one it was more mutual masturbation.

"I told her about my past, and she says, You know, you're really a latent lesbian. So I talked to a friend and she said, When you're walking down the mall, do you notice men or women? And I said, I notice men. She said, Who do you fantasize about, men or women? I said, Men.

Maureen spoke quietly, calmly about all this, comfortable with who she is. I was puzzled by her determination to be single. "Why, if you are attracted to men, are you sticking to that decision to remain single? Why would that jeopardize your faith?"

She smiled. "Oh, I don't think it would jeopardize my faith. Sex alone is not a great reason to get married. My counsellor says [my choice] is a contradiction. She says, you love commitment, you love forever relationships, and you like intimacy, and you love sex! So I put an ad in the paper and it was fun. Christian woman looking for male friend. But it was just fun. It wasn't something I'd want to really give my heart to. It was more a friendship thing."

"How would you describe the connection between your spirituality and your singleness?"

Maureen thought briefly, spoke slowly. "My beliefs, my Christianity, give me my identity and my values. I'm loved and I'm understood and I'm accepted. By God. Although the church isn't doing a great job with singles. We are seen as a bit odd, there must be something wrong with us. This is more so for men. Either that, or they see you as so highly committed, your standards are so high, that no guy is good enough. That's why my friends and I started a care group. We have similar beliefs, but we're not from the same church."

Maureen's Christian singles group has seven members, all professional women who have never been married. "I would say five out of the seven really want to get married, but it hasn't worked out. We get together for an inspirational reading and we talk about it briefly, and then we share our needs and pray for each other. We'll go out to the park; we went on a trip together once for three days.

"I think my spirituality helps me to be happy single. Gives me a feeling of security. Gives me a purpose too, because one reason I want to remain single is that I feel I am available to more people. If you're in a family situation, your energy will be taken up by your husband and your kids. I work with a number of people who are mentally ill and have terrible backgrounds and aren't adjusted well to society."

"So what do you do about the fact that you have strong sexual thoughts and desires?"

She laughed. "For me that's the toughest part of being single. What do I do? I masturbate. I used to once about every 10 or 14 days, which I see as normal. But I find the more intensity there is in my life, the more I will do it. When I'm feeling great about myself, I see it as a celebration of sexuality."

"So masturbation is not immoral? Aren't there Biblical proscriptions against it?"

Maureen was firm. "There's nothing in the Bible. There's something about Onan spilling his seed on the ground, but that was because God wanted him to impregnate somebody – the dead brother's wife. There's a difference between a natural desire, being human, and lusting. I did have a problem when the guy I loved got married, because that's who I'd been fantasizing about. And in my mind, that's adultery. So I had to retrain my thinking.

"I see myself as a sexual being, even though I'm single. That's probably one of the reasons I'm happy too, because I don't feel at all abnormal that way. I feel good about myself as a woman.

"But I haven't had much affirmation along the way for my choice. People say, Well, it's kind of selfish. You're not having to wake during the night, looking after a baby, and your money's your own. You don't have to sacrifice for the kids. Singles are still in some ways a lower status socially. The way that even numbers of chairs are set up around a banquet table . . . We singles think of that: who are we going to sit with? In the group home agency I work for, some think I must be lesbian, because I don't date. I have my hair very short and maybe have a bit of the butch look. It doesn't bother me. My close friends know who I am."

It was not easy for Maureen's family, first-generation immigrants from northern Europe, to accept her decision. "I had to have it out with my dad. I sat him down and said, Dad, I know I've really disappointed you. I know you wanted to walk me down the aisle. He said, I'd really thought when you were young, you looked so good I thought you'd get a handsome, rich guy. A couple of years later I asked both of them at the kitchen table: of the three kids, who do you think is the happiest? They both said me, I was the happiest."

"Do you get lonely?"

"No, very rarely, and this is also unusual. A lot of my single friends really feel lonely a lot. They feel an emptiness. I can't explain why I don't feel lonely more often. If I'm down, it's four hours or so. Maybe it's my training in counselling. I can get myself out of it."

Maureen has a quiet sense of vocation, what she sees as a gift for working with and caring for people. She consciously lives simply and saves for a time when she won't be working. She showed me a few treasures, some photos, cards, poems. She is a neat, serene, confident person.

"You know, I love weddings. I enjoy weddings. I celebrate with them, and I come home and I'm usually whistling. When I come home to my empty apartment, I just feel so good. I feel like – they can enjoy each other and they can be happy, but this is me. This is me. In our care group we're discussing what we're passionate about, what we're gifted in, and one gal says, Maureen, you're really passionate about singleness. I hadn't thought of that. I could almost say this is a God-given gift, my singleness. How would I enjoy it like this, otherwise?"

I asked Maureen if there is anything in the Bible that speaks to being single. She immediately cited 1 Corinthians, one of the apostle Paul's letters to the persecuted Christians of Corinth. Chapter 7 contains the famous words "Better to marry than to burn" (to avoid fornication) and carefully balanced advice about virginity, circumcision, the duties of husband and wife to each other, and the circumstances under which husbands or wives may "depart." Paul pronounces the unmarried state good, especially in the "present distress." He believes that both men and women serve the Lord better if they are single, because their devotion is not divided between matters of the world and matters of the spirit. But Paul is a realist, and he reluctantly accepts marriage as a necessity to contain the fierce temptations of the flesh. I could see how Maureen would draw comfort from Paul's preaching, but it seemed a small comfort, a frayed scrap of theology to wave at a church much invested in the institution of marriage and the conventional family.

Maureen's faith seemed stronger than the church in which she worships. But there are many single women for whom the church is the centre of their community. It is where they find like-minded people and the satisfaction of good works. It is one of the few public places in which solitude and silence are honoured.

Finally I went back up to northern Ontario, where I visited Miss Madden. The door of her little house was open; I knocked. It was Sunday morning. She recognized me instantly; I had last seen her 12 years earlier during a high school reunion. We embraced.

She was as striking as ever, her hair in a loose coil at the back of her head. She wore a long, flowing bronze silky top over pants. Her house was full of Christian imagery and reading material; since her retirement from teaching she had become deeply religious, something I could not have predicted her doing. She had abandoned the austere Anglican church for the impassioned Pentecostals. "They feed me," she said, with a flash in her eyes, holding before her a well-thumbed Bible. "They feed me the Word." She lamented the years she said she wasted before she found God; I could think only of her devotion to teaching and literature, and the gifts of theatre and poetry she brought to a small northern community. She would not tell me how old she was – "Don't be impertinent, Marian" – and I was 10 again.

I wanted to ask her more, lots more, about the ups and downs of her life, and about coming to Canada alone as a relatively young woman. And where did she get those wonderful clothes that had so impressed me when I really was 10, and which were like nothing no other woman in northern Ontario wore. And how had she nourished herself intellectually and creatively over those years and years of teaching and producing. And who had she loved, apart from her family. But her focus was intent upon worship and prayer.

It seemed to me that she was a woman who needed the fire of an imagined drama to fuel her, and that when she was no longer the teacher who could turn the sons of miners into the lords of the court of the Mikado, she turned to the theatre of religion for acts of transformation and fulfillment.

I drove her to her church service at the modern Pentecostal house of worship out on the highway. She hugged me hard again and hoped that I too would find Jesus. She walked away from the car, holding her Bible, straight-backed, her loose garments fluttering. As she reached the entrance, she paused, turned, and gracefully waved, for all the world like Katharine Hepburn.

Barbara and I always sat on the floor in her bedroom to play paper dolls. We opened up the folders and chose which dolls we would somehow be, setting them out on the twin beds, dressing them in perfectly accessorized, neatly tabbed costumes that we had already cut out, taking them through a highly charged, whirlwind romance to a formal wedding, complete with top hats and veils, and bouquets that fit into their slotted hands. We hummed snatches of wedding music – dum, dum, da dum – and recited what little we knew of the wedding vows. Then we made them dance.

The end of the game was anti-climactic and aesthetically unnerving; we stripped the dolls down to their decorous, painted-on underwear or swimsuits, placed the male paper dolls face down, cardboard buff side up, on top of the females, and then ran downstairs to the living room for puffed rice cereal with white sugar and milk.

CHAPTER 2

A Matter of Choice

$\mathcal{A}$lthough we mark the end of the 1950s as a breaking point between old ideas of marriage and new, and as the time when the notion of choice first entered the minds of young women, those who grew up in that decade were not the first generation to want to do things differently. My mother and her friends were women who left home not for marriage but for careers: they were nurses, teachers, secretaries, or active in the services. Many married late, in their early 30s, their men bruised in some way by war. (This was never spoken of, the uniform mothballed in a trunk in the basement, the medals tucked away in a corner of the sock drawer, not far from the condoms.) They had their children quickly and then zipped themselves into that tight, bright '50s sitcom that their offspring would later flee.

In the shock of the post-war period, which stiffened into the prolonged uncertainty of the Cold War, security was surely the paramount concern, politically and personally. (I remember crying as a 10-year-old after hearing on the radio that everybody should have a bomb shelter; we didn't.) As a middle-class wife in those years, my mother was able to create the perfect house, cook superb meals, and dress her children beautifully in garments that she had made: angora bonnets and matching mittens, intricately smocked cotton dresses with extravagant sashes, even pleated kilts and matching blazers. Once a year she took the Ontario Northland train to Toronto, stayed at the Royal York or the King Edward, and bought ensembles from the Room at Simpsons.

I always believed that my mother was trapped in a role at which she excelled and which she hated at the same time. She subverted her considerable energies into smocking and knitting, a freezer full of green beans and carrots from my father's vegetable garden, and three children she loved madly as babies but couldn't cope with as they grew older. She burned through library books almost as fast as cigarettes. She donned hat and gloves and bone-coloured shoes with matching handbag and went off to manage church bazaars and the hospital auxiliary. She looked after the children in the townsite when they got impetigo and chicken pox. She cooked for anyone who was sick. She was a generous and kindly employer of women who came once a week, on Fridays, to clean. On one hand, my mother fulfilled absolutely the criteria for "Mrs. Chatelaine," that crown of homemaking awarded annually to the winner of a nationwide contest sponsored by *Chatelaine* magazine. But there was always the other hand, the one holding the martini in the perfection of the living room at twilight.

> The chief concern of society is with nests and birdlings . . .
> If civilization is to endure, we must preserve marriage.
> (*Chatelaine,* May 1928)

Every month the authoritative voice of successful domesticity in Canada arrived with a thud on front porches across the country. *Chatelaine,* the only purely Canadian women's magazine, was for at least four decades a barometer and a bible for Canadian women. It both soothed and confused, counselled and lectured, provoked thought and aroused fears. Taunted us with romance and weddings, dealt for us the cards of our chances for failure. Dressed us up and dressed us down. Canadian girls grew up under the influence of *Chatelaine*, and later *Miss Chatelaine*, and American equivalents, which in my household were *McCall's*, *Ladies' Home Journal*, and sometimes *Good Housekeeping*. (Never *Seventeen* or *Redbook*, which my mother said were cheap.)

As girls, we read these magazines lying flat on our stomachs on the living-room floor. Our mothers read them in their favourite chairs while they knitted or darned – never a moment wasted – or drank a cup of tea in the afternoon. They cut out recipes for thrifty casseroles and instructions for decorated candles; they absorbed ads for Lysol as a vaginal disinfectant and Zonitors, "greaseless suppositories for intelligent and exacting women." They occasionally ordered patterns or service bulletins and took note of innumerable household hints: "If you are having a Saturday night Canasta party, remember that a few drops of perfume in an ashtray help deaden stale tobacco odours." (*Chatelaine*, April 1951) I don't think my mother took seriously the beauty advice guiding her into "old-fashioned loveliness," and she never admitted to reading the fiction. We certainly never talked about the "Can this marriage be saved?" articles that have prominence in my memory. The subtext, for girls sprawled on the rugs in the glimmering late-afternoon light, was, of course, Can our parents' marriage be saved?

From its maiden issue, in March 1928, *Chatelaine* expressed and exacerbated the secret anxieties of its readers. The editorial and advertising policies of the magazine were often in direct conflict; no wonder women were confused. *Chatelaine* set florid romantic novellas alongside stern editorials. It featured thoughtful pieces on marriage, divorce, women's work, and wages alongside makeup tips, knitting patterns, and instructions for preserves. The editorial bias of the magazine was conservative more often than not, and the editors were quick to signal when they did not approve of the content of a feature piece.

The single woman was often the foil, or the fool, in *Chatelaine*'s customary paean to marriage as the ideal career and life choice for women. Her familial role was defined and celebrated in a 1929 editorial.

> It has always been the lot of the spinsters in a family to care for parents and relatives and younger children, and with all our much vaunted women's freedom, I doubt if there will ever be much of a change in this situation. I doubt if there ever should be . . . For what else . . . is there in life greater than that glorious sense of being absolutely necessary to someone? That, oh that, gives a meaning to life! (Byrne Hope Sanders)

The single woman was used to advertise products like menstrual relief potions and deodorant soap. "What's become of the Superfluous Woman?" asked a January 1929 ad. "These were the women that the census taker used to put down as Females without Occupation. You know. Old-maid aunts . . . the familiar ailing relatives that had to be supported by some other member of the family . . . You hardly ever meet one any more . . . They'll all tell you they take Nujol regularly." In a May 1934 ad for Lifebuoy: "A Bachelor Girl's Romance . . . B.O. [is the] Odour of Loneliness . . . B.O. Gone . . . her bachelor days are over!"

Almost all of Chatelaine's fiction was devoted to the happily-ever-after theme, embellished with drawings of women in extravagant bridal gowns, arms outstretched towards handsome men, fingers flashing diamond solitaires. The single women in *Chatelaine*'s short stories wanted one thing: marriage. If they were involved

with married men, they were sad and they were punished. If they
were actually spinsters, they were "characters," idiosyncratic loners
with hearts of gold and a long-forgotten love interest.

> Mariana was queer. There was no doubt of that . . . She
> had a fondness for cats, and admitted having no regrets
> for her childless condition. She was very neat and clean
> but, having quite a squint and a curious way of sniffing,
> she was never much for looks . . . And it is quite true she
> had a scandalous way of talking to her pigs. (Laura
> Goodman Salverson, "Little Souls," *Chatelaine*, October
> 1928)

Throughout the 1930s, *Chatelaine* continued to portray marriage as the highest achievement for women and success in marriage
as the responsibility of women alone. In the May 1934 issue, a
father wished for his daughter:

> . . . the realization that the success or failure of the mar-
> riage business is essentially her business . . . She has the
> greatest stake in any marriage venture because she has
> more to lose by its failure. The man has his interests apart,
> his activities, his friends . . . [He can] fall back entirely on
> this side of his life. For the wife, there is no such secondary
> outlet. Her interests, her activities, her friends, her social
> status, focus entirely about her married life.

In the same issue, while acknowledging the growing role of
women in the workplace, *Chatelaine* decreed:

> Success in marriage is as great an achievement for
> women as success in business is for men . . . Women
> are still looked on as birds of passage in business. They are

expected to marry and leave. If they remain single, public opinion is still against them . . . The woman who reaches middle age without being promoted to wife- hood faces a subtle suspicion of failure . . . If, on the other hand, she marries, she has at once a fairly assured life competence . . . Her work will be woman's work, respected and esteemed. (Constance Templeton)

But the diamond-bright promise of marriage was being under- mined by social currents of the mid-1930s. This was acknowledged in *Chatelaine* by the activist and politician Nellie McClung, whose remarks, in 1935, not only ring with the conviction of a widely held sentiment at that time but would be echoed 10 years later at the end of a second war:

The war struck a terrific blow at marriage in taking away the cream of our young manhood, and sending back those who did escape physical injury restless, dis- turbed and distraught. Then, too, it opened a new door to women in industry . . . I am not going to argue that women who have worked outside the home are more likely to make a failure of marriage than those who have led a more sheltered life; but I do believe that a woman who has earned her own money and knows she can do it again is less apt to endure conditions that are distasteful to her.

Thus even while marriage is celebrated, it is seen to be threatened by change.

Chatelaine's wartime messages were mixed; women were incited to support the war effort, to take jobs, to enlist in the Canadian Women's Army Corps. "This is our battle too! Join the CWAC and become a member of this sorority which proudly wears the King's

uniform." *Chatelaine* featured women looking smart, even glamorous in military dress. But *Chatelaine* also reported the true desires
of women in service.

> *It is conceded that more than 90% of the girls in uniform*
> *rate as their first job preference: matrimony!* And they
> want to make it an all-out, full-time business, with
> plenty of dividends of the pram and diaper variety . . .
> But unfortunately it is probable that many of them will
> be forced to trade rose-cottage dreams for commercial
> realities, for the simple reason that there won't be enough
> men to go around as husband material. (Lotta Dempsey,
> December 1944)

Another threat was identified in 1944: "There will be such a
boom in the divorce market after the war as the world has never
seen." Women were advised to be pragmatic and supportive.

> If you want to make a go of your marriage, wake up . . .
> Take your husband 'as is.' After all you picked him out
> yourself, so stick by your bargain . . . Every successful
> marriage has as its central figure a woman who knows
> how to cook, who is a thrifty manager, and who makes a
> home that is a place of comfort and peace and rest to
> which a tired and nerve-worn man can go at the end of a
> hard day's work. (Dorothy Dix, December 1944)

In August 1945, *Chatelaine* offered a cautionary editorial on
the post-war woman.

> Would she stay stubbornly on the job or would she go
> home peaceably? . . . The facts are reasonably reassuring
> to all parties . . . The great majority of women in overalls

and bandanas are going home . . . The reconversion of
womanpower has been achieved without tumult or shout-
ing or cause for alarm. But the story is far from finished.
The economic independence . . . will not easily be forgot-
ten. The profit motive is a powerful factor for individuals
as it is for Big Business . . . The time may be near when the
old conservative cliché, "Woman's place is in the home,"
may be dropped as useless baggage. But how the individual working mother will stand up to the double life of
home and job, year in, year out, giving her best to each . . .
is a problem that awaits complete solution.

And directly opposite this editorial, the table of contents set
out *Chatelaine*'s post-war agenda: "Norma Learns to Can Peaches."
Throughout the 1950s, *Chatelaine* reverted to the relentless
promotion of marriage, femininity, and housewifery. Even when
acknowledging social problems such as desertion, the magazine
upheld popular myths. Welfare workers pointed out that "frequently the wife is far more to blame than the deserting husband
himself." Women were showered with ads and articles about
enhancing their beauty, their charms, their scentless, hairless
underarms; at the same time, such preoccupations were deemed
dangerous. An English vicar, Eric Bailey, was reported to remark,
"What a frightful sight a woman is made to look before retiring for
the night. I can't help thinking this may be the cause of many marriage breakdowns."
The suburbs were championed, in spite of women's uncertain-
ties, as "the best opportunity Canadian women have ever been
handed." Companionship marriages were extolled, where men and
women build a house together and – here's a surprise – the man
shares in the housework. But on the very next page in the June 1955
issue was a piece headlined, "I Quit My Job to Save My Marriage . . .

You Simply Can't Be a Success at Both." Women who attempted to do so (the assumption was that they had a choice) were merely "on a treadmill, to buy frills." The frills were helpfully advertised in *Chatelaine:* matching carpet sweepers for mother and daughter.

In the 1940s and 1950s, single women writers appeared in *Chatelaine* primarily as stern moralists and experts, lecturing women on their behaviour, their hygiene, their responsibilities. Accomplished and well-known never-married women like Charlotte Whitton, Dr. Marion Hilliard, and "salty spinster" Agnes Macphail did not write about their single states, for the most part, but instead championed the virtues of motherhood and community service. As professionals, they stood outside, above the norm, and their private lives, if they were even imagined, did not invite open commentary. The fact that many *Chatelaine* journalists were also single working women, racing around the country collecting stories, was likewise seldom acknowledged.

A wistful 1951 article titled "How Does One Get a Man?" was a rare portrait in *Chatelaine* of an ordinary single woman and her aspirations.

> Take me, at 32. I can cook, hang curtains and fire a furnace . . . I'm not holding out for the dream man of romantic love theory. I'm working on the assumption that one man is as good as another as long as he bathes regularly, drinks moderately and works steadily . . . I have a good job which I enjoy; I am providing for a single old age; and I have a circle of friends, mostly female . . . I have a small but pleasant apartment where I get a bang out of living with my books and radio and records and hobbies and friends. Then why should I butt my head against the barrier that separates me from the eligible men who must live in a city this size? Nature, my dears, nature. Male and

female. Something to warm my feet on a cold night. Sunday morning breakfast in bed. The patter of little feet, and the possibility of one day attaining the rank of grand-mother. (Margaret Crofton, March 1951)

The tone of *Chatelaine* began to change in 1959, when Doris Anderson became editor. In her calm, dry editorial voice, Anderson chose to look rationally at subjects like "female domination" and the tradition of preparing girls for marriage instead of life. Consistently throughout the 1960s, the magazine examined the plight of single mothers, the working poor, and women in public life.

In the '60s and '70s, popular culture was turned on its head by an explosive combination of civil rights activism, aroused feminism, the Vietnam War, the abortion debate, and the heady cocktail of drugs, music, and contraception. *Chatelaine* grappled with issues such as deserted wives, the "privilege" of housework, and "Why Can't We Treat Married Women Like People?" There were articles acknowledging quietly that marriage was not for all women; Margaret Mead suggested in *Chatelaine* in 1965 that only those best suited to marriage should choose it as a vocation; then women such as teachers or nurses or those who chose public service would not feel deprived or pitied or isolated.

By the late '60s, single women were described no longer as spinsters but as career woman. Briefly, perversely, they were role models for married women who had not managed to achieve both marriage and career. In 1968, Jeann Beattie suggested that single women were perplexed and cynical about their shifting status: "I got my lumps as a single woman in the nineteen-fifties when wives . . . were the epitome of femininity, the true woman . . . and so intelligent, beautiful, well-adjusted and fulfilled it set your teeth on edge, especially if you happened not to be a wife and, God help you, you worked. Single, working women . . . were neurotic, bitter, unfulfilled and unfeminine." But suddenly, Beattie declared, singles were "in, in, in . . . gay, adventuresome spirits creating a life of their own."

By 1974, however, this freedom was bleakly described as "The Single-Girl Rip-off," a tawdry succession of smoke-filled bars and lecherous married men, before final morose resignation to a sensibly solitary life, at age 30. In 1977, *Chatelaine* opened a small window "On Being Successfully Single," but the magazine became intensely devoted over the next two decades to the concerns of married women managing homes, husbands, children, and careers: quick recipes, instant redecorating, and financial planning. Single women continued to be a postscript, an afterthought, in the pages of *Chatelaine*.

When we were teenagers, my mother wanted desperately to work but was conscious, in a small mining town, that she did not need to work. Women friends who worked had their own businesses, successful main-street stores like Mary's Ladies Wear and Algar's Jewellery. My mother's skills were not entrepreneurial, they were caregiving. She had hoped to be a pediatrician but became a nurse instead and taught nursing and home economics before she married my father. She was proud of those careers, and towards the end of her life she wistfully imagined having a job again. After she died at 76, I found materials about a teacher's aide course in her desk drawer. They were only a couple of years old.

My mother's unhappiness took the form of a murky combination of secret drinking and what my father called "barbiturates," although he may have been wrong about those; it was impossible for us, the children, to know. It was as if she had two personalities, possibly three: the clever, funny, energetic young woman who could have done anything and happily chose marriage; the stitch-perfect, proud homemaker; and the woman who could not tolerate the loss of the bright promise of the first to the bright emptiness of the second.

My parents were married for more than 40 years, loved each other unconditionally, and died within nine days of each other. I both admired and despaired of their marriage, the role our mother played, and what she did and mostly did not do with her life after marriage. I always thought the adolescent revolution of the 1960s, including my own (although my revolt was desultory), was directed against our parents. But when I looked deeper, I saw that our rebellion was also a protest against what had been done to them, as if the lives our parents lived were not necessarily the lives they would have chosen for themselves.

A half-century later, it is said that the men as well as the women were tricked into roles they did not want. But for the most part, their positions brought them more security and power and choice than the status of homemaker did the women. In the immediate post-war period, women were just as shell-shocked as the men. They submitted willingly to the powerful impulses of a society steadying itself after six years of tumult and uncertainty: to couple and bear children and buy houses and preserve peaches. They could not see choices except those prescribed for them.

The so-called nuclear family is not a modern invention. Whether our ancestors were monogamous or polygamous (or more likely, as people are today, a shifting combination of both), women and men have come together for purposes of procreation and survival, for better or for worse, for life or for the time being. They have shared mats or cots or beds, cohabited, and produced children for whom they provided. It is safe to predict that the majority of males and females will continue to come together for these purposes, will desire one another, will have children, and will raise those children as best they can, according to the social norms of their times.

Coupled with social and cultural structures supporting reproduction are biological imperatives. Both men and women seek bonds with another person, connections that fulfill a complex, fluctuating mix of emotional, intellectual, and purely physical needs. Our bodies and brains thrive on stimulation and exercise. Some forms of stimulation and exercise are intensely private; others require the presence and the mutual engagement of another individual. Sex, too easily seen as a need unto itself, is often the way to resolve a whole range of needs for physical release, for the expression of anger, sorrow, or tenderness, for a response to the pressure exerted by forces as diverse as work or a summer thunderstorm.

Historically, there has been an almost unshakeable connection between sex, marriage, family, and society. Rules governing these institutions are endorsed by every religion and enforced by every state. Premarital sex and extramarital sex: bad. Divorce (once it became the property of church and state): also bad. Virginity before marriage: good. A socially acceptable number of offspring: good. A sustaining family structure, reinforcing responsibility and lineage: also good.

This ordained social order still affects our ideas of sex, marriage, and family at the beginning of the 21st century, even though the reproductive imperative has lapsed. Most sexual interaction has nothing to do with procreation or survival of the species. Couples can agree on how many children they will have and have them successfully, losing neither mother during childbirth nor infants to infection and illness. Many societies are consciously producing fewer, not more, offspring. It is no longer women's duty to keep the numbers up through multiple pregnancies. We can change the rules.

Indeed, over the past 50 years in Canada, our laws, medical practices, economic circumstances, and political priorities have changed significantly. Birth control, artificial insemination, and abortion are legally available to women as choices; child-bearing is thus a decision, not an accident or worse. People are better educated, experience greater technological opportunity, and are exposed to a wider range of cultures and ideas. A growing number of people do not have children, by choice. Many do not formally marry but live in common-law relationships. People choose same-sex relationships and have children within those relationships. Women choose to be single mothers outside of marriage. Both men and women choose to divorce, instead of staying together unto death. After divorce, some form second relationships and have more children.

The reality of modern Canadian society in fact differs wildly from the traditional script: fall in love, have children, live happily ever after. The man will assume financial responsibility; the woman will tend to home and children. But that script, virtually unchanged, is handed out to every generation. It is larded with homilies, preached from pulpits, and extolled by right-wing columnists. There are those who argue it is not a script at all but a pattern so profoundly rooted in biology and cultural history that it is a sacred text.

Sacred or not, it is impossible to escape. It enters a child's consciousness somewhere between the end of breast-feeding and the beginning of school, in the form of nursery rhymes and songs, in innocent play rituals and pervasive television, in the customs of family at table, the yellowed scrapbooks and heavy photo albums, the questions asked again and again, the answers always the same.

For most Canadian women who are single at the turn of a new century, cultural memory extends from the end of the Second World War to the present, a timeframe that embraces the lives and memories of our mothers. It is the period in which they and we came of age, choosing among the paths open to us then and now.

After conversations with many women, single and otherwise, it is possible to sketch a rough chronology of the choices contemporary Canadian women make – different choices at different stages of life – in a changing social context. There are aberrations, of course, alternative routes and times of departure. But there is a recognizable trajectory, a narrative roughly defined by the decades of our lives.

After an exploratory adolescence, in their early 20s, women take one of two paths: into early motherhood, or not. Many feel a profound and sometimes sudden need to have a baby, an urge that thereafter consciously or unconsciously shapes their social and sexual lives. They identify this need as biological and personal; it is not about propagating the species. Most believe they can have a child only within a monogamous relationship and thus begin a systematic search for a mate. Others, fewer in number but equally clear in their beliefs, are prepared or even prefer to raise a child alone.

There are also young women who inadvertently become pregnant and who, by disposition or circumstances, make the decision to keep their children. This choice is relatively recent and has created a new group of single women with children. In the 1950s and early 1960s, unmarried middle-class women who had babies usually gave them up for adoption, carrying the memory of the lost child with them forever. A surprising number of well-adjusted, thoughtful single women in their 50s and 60s whom I interviewed had had this experience. It happened typically at university or at the beginning of careers, when they already saw themselves as autonomous beings who made such decisions on their own. A few, however, were shamed into it by their families. Their working-class counterparts more often kept their babies and either married the father or remained at home with their own parents.

Women who carry babies to term today are more likely to embrace the role of single mother. The stigma attached to single mothers has been transferred from those in the professional and middle classes who work, have nannies or familial support, and are able to articulate their single motherhood as a choice, to those women unfortunate enough to be on welfare. The "welfare mom" is an easy target for those who rage against social assistance, while irresponsible, insouciant fathers slip under the wire and go invisible into the night. The social safety net is hung like a noose around the neck of single mothers on welfare by vigilante critics of Canada's social programs.

In this same group, temperamentally, are women who have babies with men, starting out as a couple, but who separate quickly, becoming single mothers by default or decision. Their situations are likewise financially precarious.

In all cases, single mothers who enjoy emotional and material support from their extended families fare better than those who do not. I interviewed one woman in her early 30s on welfare, with five children of various fathers. Her parents were retired and lived in a trailer on a sloping piece of ground in a village near the Saint John River in New Brunswick. Pattie was renting an old house on the main street, and the owners were counting her rent towards the eventual purchase of the house. When Pattie worked, her children crossed the road and went to their grandparents. In summer they ran barefoot and swam in the river and played endlessly with homemade bows and arrows. The shared commitment of parent and grandparents was remarkable.

Women who do not feel in their 20s the biological imperative to have a child fall into three broad groups. First, there are women who have no interest in bearing children but who want to mate, and do so, sooner or later; for the rest of their reproductive lives, they will be required to answer questions about the absence of children. In most cultures, women without children are considered anomalous, but married women without children bear a different kind of scrutiny. It is still assumed that those of child-bearing years marry primarily for the purposes of procreation.

Second, there are women who don't feel compelled to have children and who choose the single life, a life that may or may not include sexual partners, male or female or both. There can be a lingering desire for a relationship, but these women clearly self-identify as single. Women who made this choice in the 1940s and 1950s (or women who lived in small towns and made a similar choice in the

'60s and '70s) include those who resemble that old-fashioned idea of the single woman as the spinster – looking after aging parents to the point of not leaving home until they were in their 40s, fleeting or unsatisfactory sexual experiences, rich and productive careers. Women who made this choice more recently (who are now in their middle to late 40s) are more likely to have left home and started careers and engaged in robust sexual activity from an early age.

Finally, there are women who did not experience the baby urge in their 20s, who remained happily single for another decade, absorbed in careers, earning good money, enjoying independence and freedom. But they always imagine themselves married and experience varying degrees of anxiety about being left on the shelf. Some are more frenetic than others in seeking both sexual and emotional connections. A small but possibly growing number are, despite cultural hysteria to the contrary, content. They love their work, they are confident and successful, and they tend not to be featured as characters in television sitcoms.

In their late 30s, a bundle of frustrations and impulses assaults some of these women. They want to get married; they want to have a baby. They often do not know which is more important, but they want both and they want resolution sooner rather than later. They want love, romance, maybe even a big, fussy wedding, or at the very least a reproductive mate. At the same time, they refuse to "settle" for someone who does not meet their standards. Some are lonely; they have had a few bad relationships or none at all. Some are financially insecure, wanting a home and a partner and a sense of direction. Or they have financial security (usually in the form of property) but find that a well-paid job does not guarantee fulfillment. They want to date in a conventional way; they do not want casual sex. They have attended too many weddings and no longer accept the invitation to be bridesmaid. They both envy and despise their women friends who are deeply and simultaneously immersed in homemaking, career-building, and child-rearing, the so-called Smug Marrieds.

A few, rare and determined, decide to adopt a child and make a go of it on their own. Thanks to changing international conventions affecting adoption, they are likely to adopt children from other cultures. Although they may have regrets about not bearing a child or finding a partner with whom to parent, they make a deliberate change in their status by choosing single motherhood. Financially and emotionally secure, they usually enjoy the support of their families.

But for many single women in this age group, not being able to make this piece of their lives happen – marriage and motherhood – is a significant and singular failure. In their professional lives they are expert planners, negotiators, and networkers. They are flourishing or at least resilient in the workplace. They look after their bodies, dress well, have busy social lives, live in interesting apartments or condos or houses. There are roses on the coffee table, a queen-sized bed smothered in linen, a cat or a dog, at least one holiday a year, a sensible yet smart little car. But they cannot find a suitable partner. Statistics defeat them; the men in their age group are already looking beyond them at the fresh new crop coming up. Biology defeats them, even though science and technology now support later pregnancies. Society either pities or condemns them for "wanting it all."

For many such women, this decade, with 40 as its zenith, is a painful period of self-examination, often self-loathing, a confusing clash of desperation and acceptance, rationalizing, redefining. Many women acknowledge the biological underpinnings of their confusion, an added anxiety alongside the natural reassessment of priorities that comes as one rounds every decade in life. The collective frustration of single women in this age group expresses itself loudly in the declaration that "there are no men." Women of all ages bewail and believe this. But it affects most acutely those women approaching 40 who are actively seeking men for purposes of reproduction or long-term relationships.

Ironically, married women are often facing similar dilemmas. Although their reassessment occurs more typically between the ages of 40 and 50, they too are questioning their choices and considering the options as the most intense years of child-rearing end. One more child before my system shuts down? Or is this it? Now what? Marriage becomes the theatre in which women – and men – play out their personal and conjoined dramas. They question their roles as partners in marriage, their place in the working world, or their achievements in personal growth. They look at their bank accounts, their bodies, their minds, and their sense of accomplishment or failure. The sexual dynamic changes. The demands of children subside, or at least change, while the needs of aging parents also expand or subside with illness and death. The connection to the larger community alters: for years, schools and the education system have been the paramount concern; in later life, it is hospitals and the health care system.

Around the age of 50, if women divorce or are widowed, their lives begin to look like the lives of those women who have never married. From this point onwards, the pleasures and sorrows, concerns and successes of all categories of single women are very similar. Those with children may become grandparents and will, they hope, have the support of their grown children in illness or old age, but for now this is usually a side issue. Becoming single at this stage in their lives can be a source of excitement and empowerment, even as they deal with significant emotional, financial, and physical challenges.

Despite the dramatic economic, social, and cultural changes of the past 50 years, Canadian single women are not entirely comfortable in their skin. It is still better to have married badly than never to have married at all. Even knowing that for a considerable portion of married or coupled people there is loneliness, boredom, bad sex, disagreement on matters simple and great, bitterness, silence, and lack of fulfillment, all this within a systemic imbalance that favours men over women and conformity over happiness – even knowing this does not release women from the tyranny of a storyline seen and heard from a young age.

The mould of coupledom and marriage is something we dream ourselves into and then struggle in many cases to maintain against all the evidence. We do it for the children, for the parents who would be "devastated," or for an ideal of community and social order that we feel obliged to sustain. Guilt keeps people in marriages that are dysfunctional and plagues them long after they leave, because to fail at marriage brings a stigma. No one says "I am a divorcee" with pride; no one declares "I have never married" in a tone of triumph. There is no positive status attached to being unattached. There are no parades for single women and men, just singles bars, where they try to eradicate, not celebrate, their state.

As a society we are a long way from applauding the courage of single mothers or heralding the resilience of women who have been discarded or have left bad marriages and redefined themselves. We are some distance from accepting the wisdom of women who simply know their own minds well enough to resist the pressures to marry. We are not even sure what to call women who are not "married." Until 1951, separated women were included with married women in census statistics; in 1961, they were shifted to the "other" category, which included widowed and divorced women. Women who live in common-law relationships were invisible, appearing as single until the 1996 census.

Single women themselves are learning to honour one another. Elements of the wider culture are signalling acquiescence if not endorsement. In the areas where women have economic clout and professional status, they are more easily single because their identity resides in what they do, not in who they live with or who they have mothered.

But the tensions linger. They arise from social norms that are so deeply imbedded we don't even clock them. Table for two? Mortgage for you and your husband? You really don't want to have children? So, you've never gotten lucky, eh? Only widows enjoy a mantle of dignity.

There are inner tensions too. Is there something physiological, anatomical, or hormonal that is truly separate from these cultural mores, or are these simply internalized versions of social strictures? Is one human body meant to be in permanent lockstep with another, and that other to be one of the opposite sex, the bits fitting together like good plumbing? Or are our bodies for the most part as anachronistic or atavistic as some of their individual parts, like tailbones and male nipples?

However unanswerable these questions, women are choosing not to marry, not to bear children, to divorce and never marry again, to live alone, to be celibate. They are breaking the rules, and making new ones.

For all single women – those who have chosen, those who are uncertain or in transition, in their 30s or in their 70s – being single is not a rigid, static state. It is a lively, evolving transformation. It is a performance that takes place partly in public, partly in private. It is a dance whose steps are partly one's own, and partly the choreography of family, cultural background, and sexual orientation. The diversity of its rhythms is endless.

Beata

"The biggest problem I have with being single is other people's problems with my being single."

Beata, 36, a television journalist on a disability pension after a plane crash, owns a smart house in Notre-Dame-de-Grâce, Montreal. Cats and dogs, single-malt whisky, good books, music, and photographs surround her. A tall, striking blonde, she wears a back brace and walks with difficulty. Having to deal with disability has brought her maturity and wisdom beyond her years.

"I've made conscious choices about being single. I mean, I bought this place so that I don't need to wait to do things. I'm fully accepting of being single – I could be single for the rest of my life. I certainly want a relationship, but I'm not going to wait for it. I've learned that I can live quite okay and be quite content most of the time.

"My friends got married and now have kids and houses and stuff like that. Their parents would ask me, Oh, so when are you getting married? And that is the only question they can ask me. They can't ask me, How's your life? Are you happy or are you . . . They get embarrassed, they don't want to go further. I don't know if they think, Oh, she's 36, and she's not married. Is she gay? Is she a man hater? Is she having illicit relationships?

"Having loving relationships, having people around me, that's what matters. Whether you care about people, and they care about you. I work in palliative care, I care about people. Why don't those things get top billing? But you have to be defined by your marital status. Even my girlfriends occasionally will say, So, you seeing somebody? And if I say no, it's weird.

"I think the people that are the most perplexed by singlehood are the most afraid of being alone. I know people in couples who have been like that, people who end relationships and are in another one within months. What is that but fear of being alone?"

Judith

"I have a good, liberal mother who said to me when I was quite young, 'My biggest fear is that you will turn into a lesbian.' Not a drug addict or anything . . . but she's been really good since I came out to her. She's single as well. She got her divorce when Trudeau came into power and the laws were changed. She was the first in the community, and we were ostracized as a result."

Judith, 39, is a lesbian performance artist with bright blonde hair and the chic skinny black-clad look of Toronto's Queen Street. She recently moved to Vancouver, where she lives modestly, on the edge politically and intellectually.

"I have been single for seven years, but I didn't identify that strongly with it in Toronto, because it's no big deal in the dyke community in Toronto. I had short-term relationships, I had casual relationships . . . My thing is out-of-town relationships. I move in and out of women's lives. And I had a couple of bad experiences.

"I haven't had a long-term, committed relationship in almost eight years. I'm constantly examining that, especially since I've moved here. Do I want that? Am I willing to compromise? And how much am I willing to compromise? I'm not, because I've had a number of dysfunctional relationships, and I came out late, when I was almost 28.

"Vancouver's very different from Toronto. In Vancouver what I found is the two-girlfriend syndrome. Many friends of mine live with one woman and have a long-term girlfriend as well. There's a lot of that here. And endless negotiation, because the community is much smaller. You can avoid your ex-girlfriend for years in Toronto, whereas here – well, I've just had fuck-buddies here, or just one, really. But the woman I saw for six weeks here, I feel like I can't avoid her.

"Also there's a lot of stay-at-home dykes. There's so much pressure to be a couple or to be in some kind of relationship. The thing about dykes is we didn't get to do this in high school, so we're doing it in our adulthood!

"I've definitely gone through periods when I have so many friends in dysfunctional relationships that I'm just happy to be single. But there is so much stigma around being single here, especially if you're over 30. I know couples who've stayed in horrible long-term relationships because they're so afraid of being single. Which wasn't supposed to happen amongst lesbians."

Parmit

"When I was small, I used to play house with my grandmother. We were neighbouring wives, and we had our husbands at work and we had to look after our children. I bought into the whole role. But as I grew older, I noticed that there was a resistance in me. Something that would not relinquish being alone. It doesn't mean that I can never get married, it just means that there will probably always be a part of me that's only for me and that no one else has access to."

Parmit also lives in Vancouver. She is a Canadian-born Sikh, a film editor, an attractive, poised woman of 40, serene. She lives well in a tranquil, sunny condo hung with rich tapestries, lined with books.

"I was one of the least likely to remain single. In high school, in university, in my social circle, I was considered to be a very eligible young woman, who should have no trouble meeting a man and getting married and having children. My parents were quite progressive. I always knew if they suggested people to me, I would have a chance to meet them and say yea or nay. I've probably been introduced to about 35 nice Sikh boys from the time I was 20 to the last one, when I was 38. A lot of them were nice, and I'm always careful not to find fault with them. I'm a very practical person, and I think that if somebody wants to do my legwork for me and bring me candidates, then I'll be happy to peruse them.

"But there was always something that came along. I had these ideas that I was going to travel the world and have all kinds of adventures, and be a femme fatale. And none of that happened!

"I'm 40 years old. If I'm going to get pregnant, it's got to be within the next year. And I don't like to say that out loud, because it puts a lot of pressure on me. It was never in my mind not to get married and not to have children. Never ever ever. I grew up being quite a traditional girl, but then the feminist ideas around high school began to have an impact on me. Part of that was knowing that I didn't want to be subjugated in any way by a man, just because he was a man. And the other part of it was also a growing sense of what I was capable of, and what I could do with my life, and thinking I'm not ready to relinquish that for domestic life.

"[But] I look at the work I do to make a living and then the work I do because I enjoy it. And they're not me, they're just parts of me. So now I'm far more open to being involved in a long-term, serious, domestic relationship that has children. And now it's down to the wire. The suspense is killing me!

"I feel the need for someone to share my life with, for intimacy that is physical, not necessarily sexual, but which is emotional. I don't have the same illusions that I did as a young girl. I'm not dealing with a princess syndrome here, you know. I met a guy who was very homely, and I was quite interested in him. Which wouldn't have happened 10 years ago.

"Now that I'm 40, my parents' social circle is actually quite cruel to them. People have said things like, Well, all your children are single. There must be something wrong with their karma. Someone must have done black magic on your children. And my mother, even though she's an educated woman, has a weak spot, and these people are finding it. But there's nothing I can do about it. To this day I do not talk about my personal life with colleagues, and I never take anybody home to my parents' place. I'll take a guy home if I know I'm going to marry him, but for a date, I'd never take him home. Because they'd get all excited and start buying him things.

"In Salman Rushdie's book *Midnight's Children*, he talks about this aunt who lives in the basement with this guy she's gotten married to. They don't love each other, but she creates the whole situation. She lovingly places every piece of furniture in the living room, she sets everything.

"So that's something you can do. I think there's a gut-level, intuitive feeling: you know this person is kind. This person is gentle, this person likes me. That's a good enough starting point for me. The rest I can do. It's your mind creating the situation which makes you think that you are falling in love."

Jeanette

"When people think about a long-term relationship, they do want to marry within their own ethnic group. My father would prefer if we would find native men. Native men are closer to God, he tells us girls. So where are they? Tell us. They're either in jail or they're married."

Jeanette is Cree, from a northern Saskatchewan reserve. She's 39, with one daughter and two grandchildren. She works as a social worker in a downtown Calgary community centre. Neat, self-contained, she has a poised appearance and measured speech. She has never married and is currently in a relationship with a Muslim man.

"We have an economic partnership, because it's difficult as a single woman to do it on your own. You've got your boundaries of fidelity and that type of thing, so you are coupled. At the same time it's a strange relationship. Many women come through this centre and say, You can't do it alone. You need to have economic help from somebody else. And if it's a male, you can get other needs met at the same time!

"I chose to be single for selfish reasons. Marriage seemed too restrictive, too confining, and almost abusive. I wanted to be my own boss. The father of my child wanted to marry, but I rejected him. He had alcohol problems and some prior abuse problems. My feelings for him weren't strong enough for me to ignore those warnings, and

I didn't want violence to be part of my child's upbringing. I do believe there should be two parents. I'm old-fashioned in my way of thinking. In hindsight, perhaps I could have tried to make it work. But I think my instincts were right that he was not my life's partner.

"I was 17 when I got pregnant. He was 25. I left my small community and went to Saskatoon, by myself, and boarded with an older couple. I went to my last year of high school there. My parents were extremely supportive. I was living about an hour away from the reserve, so I went home every weekend. We shared her, we co-parented. When she turned kindergarten age, I didn't want her to be so far from me, so I kept her after that.

"I've always surrounded myself with a support system. I was the oldest of six children, so my brothers and sisters came to live with me. I was never really alone. But I've never had live-ins. When I had casual relationships, it was always out of the home. Because what you do in your personal life affects your children in how they conduct their lives. Basically I've had to have my single periods rather than have an asshole around.

"There are a lot of brave women, and I commend them for it. They will stick with somebody because they want to make them change or help them change. Difficult road. A lot of women come here – they're single, they're lonely, they look for a partner. They choose bad partners and the problems just intensify. I try to share my life experiences and say, Well, you don't need that asshole. Best to be alone. They don't have to move in with you. Once they move in, unless he's a great guy, there's a control issue. Because the woman is on welfare usually. She's got economic stability with welfare. The homeless man finds it more difficult to get money, to work.

"I go home to the reserve once a year for the sun dance, for sure. And I go home once a month, by myself or with my daughter and grandchildren. I want them to love the land as much as I do. I have a land base. And that makes me feel stronger. When I grow old, that's where I'm going to go. Same way as my grandmother. Have a little garden, a vegetable garden. I don't want to be alone, but if I have to be alone, I will. I'll make it my house where people can come and stay with me. The same as it always is. That's my dream."

Kate

"I wasn't raised to be not married. That was not in the cards. What I have done has been quite a surprise to everybody, including myself."

Kate, in her 40s, an English professor living in Victoria, is pretty and outgoing and has been involved in a series of monogamous relationships with men. She has experimented with alternatives, however. I wondered whether one of those was a relationship with a woman.

"Yes. In fact, it was that that took me to Oregon. It was very, very powerful. And yet, looking back, it was very transitional. It was the way that I moved out of a dysfunctional heterosexual relationship onto my own ground. That, in a way, is what we did it for. That's a very crass take on it now, because it was a sweeping thing at the time. But whatever [lesbian] tendencies I have, it seemed to be experienced, it flourished, and that was it. Because now I have a very heterosexual focus. It was a transitional thing. It had a place and doesn't have a place any more."

"I have known a couple of women who have done that at the end of a marriage," I told her. "They've gotten out of the marriage, then had a relationship with a woman, and then that chapter somehow just ends. It's a way of getting from one place to the next. I have met a number of young women who are out there as lesbians, but with them it's a way of establishing identity."

"I see students moving through that. They get into these theory courses about gender, etcetera, and it gives them narrative choices they never had."

"And they're safe in an odd way."

"Exactly. And there's a liberation and a comfort. To some extent, I see my own experience as that. I've always seen myself as an extremely receptive person, so wherever there is real life and creativity, I'm going to be attracted. It doesn't matter what the age or what the gender, or whatever, there I am! So there's a volatility, and openness. I wouldn't close off the possibility of either."

From the Diary of a Single Woman

Thanksgiving Monday: I lay in a field today with a woman friend; we had walked, not far, eaten lunch, shared a pear. It was a beautiful day; the sky was blue, the air soft and warm, the leaves unbearably bright, crimson, orange, yellow; people would say you were lying if you described these colours, we said. Catkins were exploding with seeds and then drifting, twisting through the long grasses seeking somewhere to settle, and burrow; they have sharp red tips with which to impregnate the earth.

On the path families walked with dogs, grandmothers with canes, reluctant teenagers in baseball caps and oversized pants. A young couple sat back to back on the hill, murmuring, their hands entwined, eyes closed, soaking up the autumn sun.

We talked, as we often do, about our choices, our circumstances. We are both women who are single after long marriages, engaged in a constant reassessment of our lives. We are at different places in that process: she longing for a new partner; me, much more ambivalent.

We talked about sex. She has a secret relationship; I have none. She wants to end the relationship but wonders, very seriously, how long she could actually go without sex. I said I had woken in the middle of the night from an erotic dream in which my clitoris was as big as a plate. I was rigid with frustration; I turned on the light, found a collection of erotic stories and read to relieve the tension, rubbing as if at a sore muscle, an itch. What an arid, lonely thing to be doing, I said.

She said, Why don't you have an affair with a woman? I said I love women, but I didn't think that was what I wanted. Well, what about a male friend, a married friend? I don't do that any more, I said. I have rules. I don't sleep with married men. I don't do one-night stands because they never work for me, only for the man. And my male friends come to me for conversations and advice about their relationships, but not for sex.

You have too many rules, she said.

Changing the Rules in Toronto

*J*une, a languorous, warm summer evening, after work for the three women who have come to my house in downtown Toronto. These women are good friends: they party together, talk men, sex, and work together; everything is shared. I once saw two of them on the dance floor together. They took up a lot of space. They were good dancers, sexy, laughing, observed openly by all the men and covertly by the women. Their enthusiasm and abandon were infectious.

These women are all at that moment in their late 30s when they feel powerful internal and external pressures to mate and have children. They are the kind of single women who mock *The Rules*, that guide to finding husbands which everyone hates but everyone has read. These women play with the rules, defy them, make up new ones as they go along.

Nancy is a journalist, a bosomy brunette with a warm smile, big personality, sharp restless wit. Karin is a blonde, fit, Scandinavian beauty, an MBA with her own company. Peggy works in social services, a dark, radiant woman, quiet, slim, graceful in her movements and dress. All work hard, long hours in downtown Toronto, live

65

alone in condos or rented apartments, enjoy large circles of friends and acquaintances. They are the *Sex and the City* generation. They are delighted to talk about their lives as single urban women.

MBF: Maybe I can ask you each to tell me a little bit about yourself, how long you've been single, and why you think of yourself as single.

NANCY: I consider myself single because I've never been married. Other than the big high school crush, I have never actually dated a man who I would consider marrying. I'm just 37. I still have hope he's out there, but I haven't met him.

MBF: So you won't be single for the rest of your life, it's just that the right man hasn't come along.

NANCY: I really don't know. I'm not against the institution of marriage. I'm for marriage, I'd be for marriage, for a happy marriage, but it has to be a good one and a happy one.

KARIN: With a guy who's really rich and in a big house, with a really nice car and an extra car for you and a cottage and regular vacations abroad . . .

NANCY: I'm for those as well. I don't want a bad marriage. I don't want it to be ugly. We all know people of whom we say, They settled. They got to a certain age, in their 30s, and they settled. And they're not happy and the passion isn't there. I really do believe that if I'm going to spend every morning getting up and looking at him, I want to like him, be fascinated by him, be challenged by him. Sometimes I'm going to want to kill him, I'm sure he's going to want to kill me too. But I don't want it fairy-tale or anything. It's got to be somebody I like, that's as goofy as I am, and can laugh at me, and sit around and –

PEGGY: Throw a pair of pants on me and I'm yours!

MBF: Peggy, tell me why you're single.

PEGGY: It depends on what day you ask me. Sometimes it's my choice and sometimes it's just cruel. I'm 37, I've never been married.

66

I've lived with a gentleman before – quite disastrous, I must say. Three years altogether, two years living with him, on and off and then on again. Weird. He had his own room. A few years ago, if you had asked me about being single, I would have said it was the most devastating thing I've ever experienced. I was for two years, I'd say, depressed, looking at everyone who had kids, the house, the car . . . There was that TV show called *The Wedding Story*, and it followed couples through their wedding plans. I call it *Salt in the Wound*. I would say, Mum, let's watch *Salt in the Wound*.

I had to figure out some things, like what do I have control over. Marriage and kids is not one of them. I know that there's one person that I'm spending the rest of my life with, and that would be me. So I better get my own act together, and if I get married, terrific, and if I don't, I'll be that crazy aunt from Toronto.

MBF: Karin, tell me who you are and why you're single.

KARIN: My name is Karin, and I am a manoholic. I'm going to be 39 shortly, and I've been single for all of my life but specifically noticed it in the last 20 years. Why am I single? I thought it was because I hadn't met the right man. There are three difficulties. There's meeting the right person, and then there's actually engaging in the dating process successfully, and then graduating successfully to the relationship process. Three different thresholds on which you can fail. And if you fail on the first one, the other two are moot. That seemed to be pretty much my scenario. Though in recent years, I have come to accept the fact that I might be single because of some subconscious thing that I'm doing. My former sister-in-law once said that I was pathologically independent.

NANCY: I would take that as a compliment!

KARIN: I do take it as a compliment. I see what she means: I've been independent and self-sufficient in every way for so long that I don't really see the need for a man in the same way that a lot of women do. I don't see a need for a man for financial support.

PEGGY: I've got my own toolbox.

MBF: Me too.

NANCY: I just hire a guy when I need work done around the house.

KARIN: It really comes down to straight emotional need, and I think a lot of women have trouble looking that one right in the eye: to say, I have an emotional need, to be in love, to be in a relationship. I think it's easier for women to say, I need a father for my children, or I need a partner to help me maintain a home, all these tactical things. I don't need the tactical things. As a matter of fact, I'm so pathologically independent that I wouldn't accept them, because I would assume there was some inference of ownership, which I'm really touchy about. So I haven't given up hope, but as each day goes by, I get more and more pessimistic about the possibilities.

NANCY: Well, some days I'm really glad. I have married friends who say, You don't understand: you bemoan that you're not in a relationship, or you're not married, but you don't appreciate how often *we* think, God, it would be nice to come home and not have to put up with John doing this, and listen to his shit . . .

KARIN: After you've been single for 20 years, you have no tolerance for being in the wrong relationship. You're not willing to put in time for the sake of being in a relationship, because you've already paid that price. You know better. If you're dating a guy and you have him over to your house once for dinner, and he leaves a beer can on the coffee table, you're thinking, Well, there you go. It's a lifetime of picking up his beer cans. So you tend to be hypersensitive to typical male behavioural patterns. And when you aspire to something, you hope for a man who's evolved – put that in quotes and use it gingerly – who understands that women have rights too, and that maintaining a household is an equal responsibility.

NANCY: You look at the statistics, and they show you're still going to do the majority of the housework. I like puttering. I like cooking. Actually, Joe, the newest man, he gets up and he does the dishes and stuff, but still – I've got such a chip on my shoulder about this – I'm going to end up doing the majority of the house-work, the majority of looking after the kids, the majority of the socializing . . .

KARIN: If you're filthy rich, you're going to have a nanny and a housemaid. Don't worry about it.

PEGGY: You two are career women. I don't have a career. I have a job. So I would be quite pleased to stay home and do the cleaning, and cooking . . .

NANCY: I fantasize about spending four years at home with a couple of young kids. Taking four or five years out of the work-force. But I'm also a control freak, and I don't know if I could give up the control that I think bringing in the income gives me.

KARIN: Having seen so many children born to my friends and my sisters and having read a lot about early childhood development, I would not invest the time in having a child if I was not prepared to stay home for the first five years. If you're going to wait 20 years to have a child, if you're going to take the risk of being a so-called high-risk pregnancy, in your late 30s or early 40s, then why not go the extra step and ensure that that child has the maximum poten-tial to grow into a happy, healthy person?

MBF: But is having a baby still something you really want to do?

KARIN: I do, actually, in my heart of hearts.

NANCY: I do.

PEGGY: But I'm not going to do it on my own.

NANCY: This is going to sound really superficial, or maybe I'm Darwinian. I want a husband who can afford me and the kid at home. I'm not saying I have to live in a big house in Rosedale. I actually hate the idea of a big house in Rosedale, but we're not poor. We're not worrying about buying Kraft Dinner. Living in Toronto – God, sometimes I can barely make it on my salary, and I make a good salary. Imagine my salary, with a wife and kids; that would be brutal.

MBF: On one level you appear to be very non-traditional, but that is a very traditional idea.

KARIN: In my mind, a major stopper for getting involved with a man is if he can't even return your phone call, how good is he going to be when you're eight months pregnant, and you're an emotional mess, and you need him to take charge, and be responsible? I very rarely meet a man that I can visualize as being responsible when he's under pressure, with a pregnant wife who doesn't work and who would prefer not to work after the child is born.

NANCY: I want a man who really wants to be a dad. I honestly find myself looking at men these days and thinking, Does he want to be a dad, is he aching to be a dad, is he ready to be a dad?

KARIN: And is he responsible enough to be a dad? There's a difference. A lot of guys want to be a dad, because they're conceited, they want to be immortalized, they want to have their little boy Joey that they can take to the park and pitch a ball with and show him off to all their buddies.

NANCY: It's like my great barbecue analogy. Judy goes to the store, she buys all the groceries, she comes home to the big house, which she looks after, mostly. He does a lot of painting and stuff, he likes to fuss. But she prepares the salads and the garlic bread and lays out the meal and tenderizes the meat, and makes the dessert and invites everybody over for a barbecue, cuts the peppers, the whole bit. Then John stands at this big honking barbecue, a condominium of a barbecue. He flips the steaks and everybody says, Excellent, Jim, fabulous barbecue, that was so great! I could not live with that for 12 seconds, let alone a lifetime.

NANCY: I feel like we're the first generation that is actually deeply offended by inequality. That we actually have this sense of entitlement.

MBF: How do you think that you became that kind of woman? It's very clear that you have standards, very definite ideas about who you are and who you could be with. How did you get there?

NANCY: My parents' marriage. He: domineering. He: engineer. He has all the money. She: stay-at-home wife, very timid and meek, and never argued with him. We're teenagers. He gets killed. She is then the sole parent, falls apart, can't cope, kids become the adults in a way, and we had to become fiercely independent at a very early age. So that's how I became the way I am today. There's no way I want a marriage like my parents', no way.

KARIN: For me, volatile marriage, mother has six children in eight years and subsequently sedates herself for a decade. Valium, drug of choice, late '60s. So she doesn't get out of bed until four in the afternoon. Eventually she left, and I raised her children and took care of my dad and became responsible for a huge household of people at the age of 13, and grew up very quickly and was chained to the kitchen for the next seven years of my life. I remember my 16th birthday, crying to a friend, saying, I feel like I'm turning 35.

Actually, a lot of my early relationships failed because I would be with a guy and I would be able to read his mind. What does he need right now? He needs a cold beer. What does he need right now? He needs to watch TV. I do that really easily, and someone who knows that can take advantage of me. I went out with a guy who had two small children. He was the custodial parent and the mother was mental – a very similar case to my mom. And I felt such incredible sympathy for his children. I felt: I can do this, I can rescue these children, I can fill the gap in this guy's life. And then I just had a moment of screaming awareness: I don't want to!

I don't think men have had a chance to catch up. Women have spent the last 30 years reinventing themselves, redefining their role in society, lobbying for change to laws and social culture, to accommodate their growing role. And all men have had a chance to do is react. Men are genetically built to do battle. You put them in a situation where they have to react, then they're on the defensive. When they're on the defensive, you can't expect stellar behaviour. And I don't think men have had the chance to reinvent themselves in relationship to the new woman, the evolved woman.

NANCY: I think there's a generational difference. Men my age do not want to date me. But you get a guy who's twenty-whatever –

KARIN: And they're adorable.

NANCY: They're just climbing all over you.

PEGGY: And they don't have some of those –

KARIN: The power issues.

PEGGY: I think younger guys like to look at women who are older, because we're much more comfortable in our skin. I think girls in their 20s are too fussy about fashion, and nails. But guys our age are looking for the young, the svelte, whatever.

NANCY: I think they're looking for a power imbalance, a little missus.

KARIN: Men like a good gander and to cop a feel, and that's all. They're too lazy to put in the work. I'm sorry, but this stuns me. Historically, men have ruled countries, men have waged wars, men have built corporations from the ground up, but can they deal with one woman who happens to know her opinions? Nooooo. We're wired differently. I truly believe that. We are two different species.

NANCY: I think your point is that there aren't that many men willing to accept you as who you are. I actually feel pressure to change sometimes.

PEGGY: Oh, God, I was Miss Chameleon. I went out with a rock musician, so I had that whole persona, then I moved on to a preppie. I changed my hair, my clothes, everything. And now I've been single for the last five years, and I dress the way I dress because that's the way I dress. I talk the way I talk. I've finally figured out who I am. That has helped me immensely. I figured out half my battle was with myself.

NANCY: True. I figured out at 35 that I was a slut. I have had a huge number of sexual flings lately, and that was very enjoyable. Very empowering.

MBF: Where do you find men to have sexual flings with?

NANCY: Once I kind of got into this mode, they seemed to have appeared. But they're not relationships.

PEGGY: You have to have sex to get sex.

NANCY: Yes. Once you've got that post-coital glow going . . .

KARIN: You walk into a room and everybody knows it and it comes to you.

NANCY: It's that I'm-getting-laid look.

KARIN: I don't have sex. Maybe once or twice a year, which is sad, being that I'm supposed to be at my sexual prime.

PEGGY: Well, [my connections happen] in bars, because that's generally where we end up going out. No one has ever approached me in a grocery store or a laundromat, or a library.

NANCY: It certainly would take a lot longer. Look at the nice melon, wanna fuck? Whereas in a bar, it's, Nice beer, wanna fuck?

KARIN: I mean, it's pretty clear, if you're drinking and a guy's drinking and you're at a party, or a bar, that if you exchange certain signals, that you'll be going home together.

NANCY: Okay, I'm trying to think of the last six men I've slept with in the last eight months, nine months. Scuba diving, good sport to meet them, scuba diving instructor. In New York, colleague of a friend, sex in Central Park, that was fun. Through friends, in a bar, at a boat show . . .

MBF: Tell me why you do this, what you get out of it.

NANCY: I'm just really into sex at the moment. I went for two years where I didn't have sex at all. There's something to be said for hitting your sexual peak at 37, I swear to God.

MBF: Do you practise safe sex?

NANCY: I could have safer sex. I was never able to take the pill. I could use spermicide with condoms, but I don't, because it's icky. I used to like the sponge. When the sponge went off the market, I was devastated.

PEGGY: I use condoms on occasion. Well, I don't personally use them, but you know what I mean.

73

KARIN: I use condoms as a litmus test. If a guy won't put on a condom, if he doesn't respect my need to respect my body enough to put on a condom . . .

NANCY: But you get to a point after a time in relationships where you think, Oh, we've been together for a long time, we've been screwing –

KARIN: But you've still got to ask the question. One thing that brought this home to me was when I dated a guy who was born and raised in Bermuda. We slept together on the first day we met, but we also had a long-distance relationship for a year after that. He was a rambunctious, sensual, sexual man, and he had travelled a lot. So God knows where the "little man" had been.

KARIN: What really freaks me out is that guys think that I'm clean because I'm a nice white girl. Because I live in a penthouse apartment and I look like I come from nice breeding. But they don't ask any questions about my sexual history. Actually, the last guy I had sex with, I made him use a condom and he had problems working it. I said, Do you use condoms with the other women you sleep with? And he says, No, not really, and I said, Well, don't you think that's a risk? And he says, Well, it's a calculated risk. And I thought, What criteria are you using to calculate the risk? It's all based on what he can see.

NANCY: One guy in Vancouver told me, Well, I'll fuck eight girls out of nine without a condom, and on the ninth one I'll think twice. As far as he's concerned, he's immune to risk, but he's dipping his wick in every candle in town!

KARIN: The one thing the whole AIDS thing has done is make you think twice about who you invite to your bed and under what conditions. I used to engage in sport fucking to a small degree, and a lot of single guys who hang out in bars do it to a large degree. It means there's no emotional attachment. It's a sport, and the sport begins the minute you think you can get it. And what you actually get out of it is minor, compared with the buildup. AIDS makes you think about what that game or entertainment might mean to your life. I don't do it any more, because it's just not worth it . . . [But] I think when you're alone and you're single, there's a certain consolation in having sex, because at least you can say, I got laid. Even if it was an awful experience.

MBF: What is this article you brought, Nancy? Robert Mason Lee, writing about men in the *Globe and Mail* . . .

NANCY: It's about what he calls [in the column] banal sex, meaning anal sex, and how anal sex has become "the greatest unremarked sexual revolution of our time. The equivalent of the postwar mainstreaming of oral sex." I think that's true. Joe and I had this discussion, which actually turned into a fight, about anal sex. I thought, You know, I don't really want to do this. But I asked him, Would you ever want to do it? And he said, Oh, yeah, I would want to do it. And of course my next question was, You've done it, haven't you? And he said, Oh, yeah, I've done it. I didn't want to do it. And he said, Fine, I would never force you. But then he said something like, It's just another expression of love for each other.

PEGGY: It's an expression of his need to find another tight orifice to put his dick in.

NANCY: Yes. Let me just get my vibrator and go after your butt, and we'll just try a little of that banal sex. You have never seen a man pucker his sphincter so fast in his life. It's just another expression of love, honey! Until you're the one who's boned up the butt. [Mason Lee] says guys call him up for advice all the time, that all these hetero men want to know how to get their wives or girlfriends interested.

PEGGY: Well, the next thing is you'll be inviting one of your dogs into the bedroom.

NANCY (reading from the column): "And who are these deviants? For the most part they're younger, decent guys with women and uncomplicated sex lives. But they feel incomplete. I can't stand the thought of dying without having tried it once, one young fellow told me."

KARIN: It's along the lines of sport fucking. Expand the arena. Try out new things.

PEGGY: And once they've mastered that, then it's like, what's next? Here's where we get to fuck the dog and cat. Maybe ear sex?

NANCY: "Men regard it as being a deeper level of connection. When vaginal or oral sex has become as meaningful or exclusive as a handshake, what else remains to make love special?"

KARIN: Well, if he thinks my vagina's a handshake, he can just go home. That's where I draw the line.

MBF: There's this whole business of a sex life and maybe there's a partner out there for me somewhere, but in the meantime, where do you get closeness or intimacy or support?

NANCY: From the girls across the table.

PEGGY: I have boys I hang out with. I love the sound of a man's voice. I love a man's company, so there's a few guys I hang out with on a regular basis. And in my dry spells, that comforts me.

NANCY: I have gay guys in my life. I get a certain male energy from them. And a lot of support and caring from friends and family, a brother.

MBF: Who touches you? If you're not in a relationship, who touches you, or sees you naked?

PEGGY: Just me.

NANCY: And everybody at the gym.

KARIN: Actually that is a fairly sensitive issue. When you're on your own, and every night you get undressed to get in bed and you're looking at your naked body – which I frequently do – I think it's a shame that only I get to see this. There's a lot of sadness associated with not sharing it, not being touched by anyone. Simple things like sitting on the couch, resting your head on someone's shoulder, or someone holding your hand.

PEGGY: I miss finding pubic hairs in the shower. When I was in my big dry spell, I said, What I would do to find someone else's pubic hair in this shower!

KARIN: I read somewhere that a woman who doesn't receive affection is like a plant that is not watered. So twice a year when I'm lucky enough to trip over someone who's actually doable, I picture myself as this plant that's drying up. I have a lot of plants and I'm very sensitive to when plants need to be watered. And I need to be watered! I just wanted to get that out . . . There is a lot of longing. I would say if there's one thing that signified being single for a number of years, aside from everything we've said, it's longing. In spite of all the great female relationships you have, what you long for is a man's touch. It's hard to let go of that, to justify or rationalize that away, to say, Oh, I have friends, and I have self-esteem. Dammit, I want a man's hand on my breast right now!

MBF: How much time do you spend wishing you were with a man?

PEGGY: For a couple of years I was really depressed by [being alone], and it was all-consuming. I went and did my job, but I'd go home and cry. My parents were really concerned. But once I got over that hump, now I don't think I spend too much time on it. I mean, I love talking about boys. We go out and meet guys, there's a certain amount of energy that's put into it. But it's certainly not all-consuming.

NANCY: I have phases. One year it might be a little bit of time, one year it might be a lot.

KARIN: I think a lot of women don't realize when they've sunk to the level of desperation. About 10 years ago, I was racing home on a Friday night after working late, and I got in the elevator in my apartment with this woman. I would be 28, and she was probably close to my age now, 38, 40. And she had a video in one hand and a bag of Kentucky Fried Chicken in the other, and she had the most angry, bitter expression. It wasn't like, Oh great, evening at home, video, food. She was angry, and I could see it in her face. It shocked me. It almost propelled me towards the elevator wall. I thought, I don't ever want to be like that. That is exactly what I don't want to be. When you're starting to slide, you know. All of us, all three of us have our moments where we slide – for a day, a week, a month.

PEGGY: You feel ugly, crummy . . .

KARIN: Then you climb out, or your friends pull you out. For me the test of a relationship is, Does this guy deserve me? You can go through the whole exercise of dating, and at the end of it, you'll think, He wasn't courteous, he wasn't sensitive, he didn't even know who I was. He didn't deserve me.

NANCY: Mine is, Am I having fun? I ask myself that. A couple of times recently, I've thought to myself, This isn't long-term, but it is fun. So I stay.

MBF: Do you think you'll be single 10 years from now? Are you prepared for that? Emotionally, financially?

PEGGY: I'm screwed financially if I'm on my own. I have no savings. I'll be that crazy woman with the shopping cart eating cat food.

KARIN: I might be single. I might have gotten married and divorced . . .

PEGGY: I would never divorce. Even if I married the biggest frigging monster in the world. You get me, you get me for life.

NANCY: I would be heartbroken about divorcing. I have a deep abiding thing for the institution of marriage. I really do. We have friends who have gone into marriage, they've done four years, and when it wasn't quite suiting them, they moved on. I think, God, you seem to be able to do that very lightly.

MBF: What's the worst thing about being single, and what's the best thing?

PEGGY: The best thing about being single is sitting around in your underwear eating the food right out of the pot and letting it dribble down your front and get stuck between your teeth. And nobody cares. That's my favourite thing.

NANCY: Or having the bed to yourself when you're really tired and you want to stretch out and sleep. I really like that double bed to myself.

KARIN: The first day that I moved out of my father's house into my own apartment, I ate peanut butter sandwiches and orange juice in bed while watching TV. I think that's the freedom of choice. We get to do whatever the fuck we please, whenever we want to do it.

NANCY: Yeah. And the worst thing is when you really want to have sex and you want to fuck, you can't.

KARIN: For me, it's when you're having a really lonely moment, and you just want someone to understand that and come and hold your hand. I'm constantly struggling with my business. It would be so much easier if there was someone who came home to me every night and said, Honey, you can do it.

NANCY: I think you tend to be fantasy-prone. In reality, he'd be lying on the couch belching and farting, with the beer can on the coffee table. Hey, honey, what's for dinner? I think you lose grasp of what a day-to-day relationship is. Guys are real. They're not fantasies.

KARIN: Maybe it is true that I have created standards that are way too high for any man to achieve; therefore I will always be alone. That's a hard pill to swallow.

NANCY: Had I married before now, (a) I would have messed it up, and (b) I would have had a severe drinking problem and been seducing the pool boy. I know I would have . . . Twenty years ago I might have married into an unhappy marriage because I might have felt that was my only option. But now I feel like I really have a choice, and unless it's really good and it's what I want, I'm opting not to.

MBF: What made you that way? The family story is obviously part of it, but what else?

PEGGY: Experience.

KARIN: Stubbornness.

NANCY: I think it's a total turn-on. It's an aphrodisiac. It's addictive. The more you see what you can do, the more freedom you have, the more you want.

KARIN: I feel like I am in the first generation of women to be completely free, to benefit from the women before me. I didn't have to fight for freedom. I just had it.

NANCY: Plus, there is confidence, the confidence that if I stay single, not only will I be fine, I'll actually be excellent!

CHAPTER 3

Uncompromising Women

On Prince Edward Island, I stayed in the pretty roadside house of old friends, not far from the shore. From my bedroom window I saw a white gibbous moon rolling in the deep blue summer sky, the moon of Artemis, the hunter, the solitary rider, the lady of wild things, the goddess who stands slightly outside society and makes her own rules.

Single women are oddities on Prince Edward Island, I was told. Leaving a husband, not marrying at all, having a marginally bohemian lifestyle takes courage. The single women of Prince Edward Island move cautiously, discreetly, within a grid of expectations as clear to them as the island's red roads. The term for somebody who thinks she's entitled to be different is "big feeling," as in "She's getting a bit big feeling." Like the goddess Artemis.

There are women who dare to step outside the boundaries and are strong and confident enough to be comfortable there. They are single largely because of choices they have made over the previous 20 years. They have never married, for reasons they have thought about and are able to articulate. They have positioned themselves socially, sometimes politically, as "the non-marrying" type. They would never be mistaken in a crowd for a "wife," but at the same time they would never be considered spinsters.

They have sex and relationships on their terms or not at all. They have recognized the maternal urge and either acknowledged that the moment has passed or are still considering, rationally, the possibility of pregnancy or adoption. But this is not their defining characteristic. These women cast strong shadows. They carry within themselves their own completion code.

A generation ago, they might have been described as "late bloomers" or women who matured late. But I think they matured early. In their 30s and 40s they underwent that process of self-realization that normally comes to women later in life, after throwing themselves onto (or under) the conventional train of expectations and role-playing. These women have created an integrated self. They have gone about building their lives without the pieces deemed necessary for security and happiness. Ironically, they are similar in many ways to women who are in very happy marriages or partnerships: they understand who they are and why they are; they have perspective.

Marcia

"I think I'm good at partnering, I think there is a very strong inclination and desire. But I feel more powerfully that I don't need to make the compromises I see being made all around me. I won't! I can't!"

Marcia teaches history at a university and lives in the Annapolis Valley. At 43 she is small, graceful, alert, articulate, with high mental energy. She has shiny black hair and round glasses. She was once a dancer and musician.

Marcia's father comes from a family of teachers and ministers in Ottawa; she acknowledged several familial academic role models, especially an aunt who never married and was the first woman principal of an Ontario high school. "I would say that she probably influenced me greatly, although I really resisted her. She was assertive to the point of being abrasive. That was how she made her way."

Music brought Marcia's parents together; it was their lifeline and her own first vocation. She was clear about their relationship: "He's a very successful businessman, and my mother, an extremely intuitive woman, very bright. But traditional gender roles. She stopped working as soon as she was married. She knew exactly what she wanted to do: bag my father and have babies. I think she had no regrets whatsoever; that's what she committed to.

"I also think that she tended to live vicariously through me. Then 10 years ago, she started studying cello – absolutely passionately, and she's good! But it took her that length of time and an enormous struggle to be able to put her own needs first. There was no question that I saw this very traditional mother and at some point said to myself, No way! And pretty much kicked against that from a very early age."

Marcia actively imagined having children and just as actively resisted the idea of marriage. "I was very consciously opposed to marriage throughout my 20s and early 30s. Then in my mid-30s, I met a man, and all that went by the wayside. But it just did not work. I'm not giving up my life [for a man]. He can give up his! It's been too many years that I have put in and meandered my way through. There's not enough time left in my life to be meandering. I need to be able to hang on to the solid things. My job here is solid. I see results with my students. So there is something that is promising here.

"What I learned from my most successful relationship is my rhythm of relationship, and what is ideal for me. And that was setting up house with him, where I was upstairs and he was down, and we met for meals or whatever. But that was my space upstairs, and it was just beautiful. It was my floor and that was important. We would have three or four days together out of the week and then he would go away on the weekends. I liked it that way, and I don't think I would ever want it differently."

Marcia said with intensity, "I don't have to put up with the crap that I see everybody taking. It's not interesting to me, and that's the only way I can say it. But it has taken a huge amount of evolution to get there and to get comfortable with it, and I think it'll be a lifelong process."

Marcia was in a long-distance relationship with a man in Chicago and was thinking of trying to become pregnant. Yet she was clearly self-contained, with strategies for how she might make all this work on her own terms.

"Well, this kid thing. If it's going to happen, it had better happen, you know? So I've started planning, and I said to my friend [the man in Chicago], I want to do this, and I will be primarily responsible. I went to the doctor and said, I want you to tell me: Can this body do that? And obviously he wasn't able to say 100 percent yes or no, but he said, Statistically, you've got a year.

"I have my own place. I have my own job. Clearly the most important piece is that it is my life that I have created. For better or worse! I did it, nobody gave it to me." She said suddenly, at one point, "In a way, it's not a [complete] characterization, the singleness."

"You don't think of yourself as single?" I asked, surprised. Most women I met who were in monogamous but not live-in relationships preferred to think of themselves as single, to resist the suggestion that they are coupled.

"I don't," said Marcia. "The single category, the way most people construct that, it just doesn't fit! I have almost always known relationships, just not terribly fulfilling, or what I would like.

"I don't feel 'single' now. I don't know what I am, I don't think there is a word for what I am. I don't think we have a language for what I am right now. I know there's a lot of us out there."

Naomi

"I didn't want to get married. Partly I think because of my parents' marriage. They're still together. But I've had a look at the dynamics, and I thought, In a marriage the woman has the bigger burden. She pays the bigger price. That wasn't going to be me. I wasn't going to be trapped."

Naomi is 46, never married, and has been diagnosed with cancer. When we met, she was in the middle of chemotherapy and had responded to the loss of her hair by shaving her head. She is from a traditional Montreal Jewish family. She does freelance communications work and lives in Ottawa with a young Labrador retriever in a sunny townhouse. She has a beautiful face, huge grey eyes. She greeted me wearing a ballcap.

"Does this cap bother you?" she asked.

"Not at all," I told her, "but feel free to take it off if you'd rather."

"When I'm alone I take my hat off. I went to the door the other day, and I think I scared the person. I always start losing my hair on Friday. They told me to expect it and it wasn't happening, so I thought, Oh gee, maybe it'll only happen in the second cycle. Then it started falling out. I decided to shave my head, so I wouldn't have to go through that. At least it felt like I was being proactive. I wasn't just waiting."

Naomi looked beautiful without her hat, her sculpted silhouette regal and strong against the brilliant painting on the wall behind her. She plunged right into a discussion of who she is while pouring tea for us. "Having a home, and now a dog, is probably the most stable I've ever been. I mean I've always worked, I've always been a good girl, never been in trouble with the law. But I have never quite settled down. Still asking, Who do I want to be when I grow up? Lots of times I like that. And lots of times I don't."

Naomi described her choices through the prism of her upbringing in a traditional, middle-class Jewish family in Montreal. "My parents are of a generation and of a culture where if a woman isn't married, there's something wrong. She's an object of some pity, or questioning; is she good stuff? I know they certainly would have preferred that I had gone the traditional route. Although they also know that I have a nice life and I'm comfortable with it. And I'm aware that there are so many women who make the choice. It's not that they've been passed by, but they have made the choice.

"I wanted to have all my options available. I think now perhaps when you get married there are more options, or women are more vocal and more forceful about getting what they want. Or at least having a say and it being more cooperative. But certainly in traditional Jewish marriages, this is what the man does, this is what the woman does.

"My mother is an extraordinary woman. She went back to school at a time when all of her contemporaries were just joining clubs and doing good works. She went all the way from the CEGEP in Quebec to getting her master's degree. All that was fine with my dad, until she went out to work and earned a paycheque, which in his culture, and his generation, women did only if the man could not provide. And he *could* provide. And here she was having a separate bank account and all that stuff! So in lots of ways she was a great role model, but at the same time she was punished for stepping outside what was allowed."

Naomi remembers herself as someone who was late in coming to relationships. "I just didn't trust men. I felt that I was going to be overpowered. Not physically, in terms of somebody's going to beat up on me. More that I wouldn't have options. That I would be suffocated. Even in university, I didn't want any part of it, until by third year I thought, Hmm! I'm a virgin, this is an embarrassment, let's do the deed. And that's exactly how it was: I did the deed.

"I like men. More for the closeness, because even if sex isn't always satisfying, intimacy is. And sometimes you put up with the sex to have the intimacy and companionship. Do you know what I mean?"

I laughed. "Oh, I think a lot of marriages spring from that kind of trade-off!"

Naomi nodded, smiled. "And I didn't have to make the trade-off that I need a man to support me, because I could always do that. Or I need a man because I can't manage stuff. Because I can, and when I can't, I know where to go for help. But I enjoy their company.

"If I were to characterize [the men I've been with], I think they'd fall into one of two types. Either they were men who I knew subconsciously, or consciously, could never commit, so therefore it was safe for me to love them because I wouldn't have to worry about it. Or the odd commitment type would sneak in there, and I'd think, Oh, my God! He wants something. And I'd end it quickly because I could see this guy was capable and ready and I didn't want it."

I wondered why she thought being single was better than being married.

"Well," said Naomi, "I don't know what it is to be married. But I've seen friends who – well, it's like Chinese water torture. You know: drip, drip, drip. You see slowly, over time, big changes. This is what being close with a man does, this is the influence, and not always for the better, in terms of what she's allowed to think, or friends she's allowed to be with, or her political views. It makes me feel the woman is getting smaller, not bigger. There are some marriages where I've observed that both spirits grow. But that's rare."

Naomi's cancer is ovarian. There was a strong link in her mind between her sexual history, her fertility, and her illness.

"I wanted to have a child. I didn't want the husband, but I wanted the kid, I really wanted to parent. My body conspired against me. I couldn't conceive. I started on the pill, ended up with a cyst, which may or may not have been due to the pill. I had three IUDs and my body rejected them all, I developed horrible infections. So my birth control was somewhat haphazard, and yet I never got pregnant. Not that I was necessarily promiscuous, but I had a variety of partners. And try and find a doctor willing to do fertility testing on just a single person! They always wanted you to bring in the partner, and I said, Look, the one consistent element in all of this is me! So I found a doctor who said, We can do the first step, which is to check you. But if there's nothing conclusive, we would have to have a partner. Maybe it was the times, 1980. So the problem got solved for me. I couldn't have kids.

"There was no need for safe sex, or so we were led to believe. AIDS was a non-issue at that time. Even since then, I have not consistently practised safe sex. When I was in what I thought were monogamous relationships, I could handle it. It turns out a number of those so-called monogamous relationships were anything but. And that scared me, because I did bear the consequences. I got chlamydia. And then I had a virus, and they say one of the ways to bring on that kind of virus is that your partner has many partners.

"We cleared up the virus, okay. But it was more what it did to my head. That sense of betrayal. In some ways, I feel my past catching up to me. Not that the cancer is a result of things that went on as much as the energy of betrayal. Sexual betrayal, emotional betrayal, and where else do you hit but in the womb, the essence of being a woman."

"You connect the cancer with previous partners, choices they made, unbeknownst to you?"

"And choices that I made, in betraying myself. You're rather suspicious [about someone's fidelity] but you say, Okay, I believe you. And you think, I can't possibly believe it, but he says it. You sell yourself down the river. I knew it was unhealthy, and I knew the man was bad news, and I have no idea why I stayed or would go back or allow him back. I now understand abused women a whole lot more.

88

"I'm now in a relationship with someone who is ready to commit, and it's been a struggle for me to be okay with that. What makes it okay is that he lives in Toronto and I live here, and we can only see each other every other weekend. Which is wonderful and terrible. He is the first man that I can imagine living with. In the past, even with men I've really been gaga over, at a certain point, I want to go home. I want to be alone. I like my space. I just like the quiet, being able to do what I want to do when I want to do it. I like not having to interact, I need that. I was so crazed about my place, my way, my thing. I'd be comfortable having my partners in my bed – but not in my kitchen!

"Although I can imagine living with Frank, at the same time we won't be looking at that for some time. He has a teenage daughter, and he's promised he would be in the same city as her until she's 18. I respect that. So this works, although now, especially through this illness, I realize that I do want somebody here all the time. I mean, my mother will be coming next week during the treatment, because he can't. I don't want my mother. I want my partner. And that's interesting for me. Because I've never really felt that, I've been always very independent."

I asked, "The fact that it's happening as a result of the illness, does that make you mistrust the feeling at all? Is that a sign of the strength of the feeling, or a sign of vulnerability?"

Naomi thought for a moment. "Certainly, I'm vulnerable. Friends have said, Why don't you move to Toronto? But do I want to leave my life here? No, I don't. I have community. I have friends, I have things that I enjoy. To move to a new city because of a man, there would be so much riding on him and on the relationship.

"I think ultimately I don't want to be alone, but that's where it starts getting real creative and challenging. How to not be alone, and yet have lots of space, be committed, and be free. I also want that freedom."

Letter from Eve

"I am 41 and have never been married. I have been asked a number of times. I have raised one son (who is 19 and in 1st year college) on my own, with no parenting involvement from his biological father.

"I lived from 16 to 25 exclusively as a heterosexual, almost always involved in committed relationships; from age 26 to 36 exclusively as a lesbian involved serially in committed relationships; and I have spent the last five years dating but not seriously involved with people of both genders. I have cohabited for a total of five years – once with a man and once a woman. Both times I believed I was entering into a lifetime commitment.

"If I were a person who believed in the 'nurture' argument 100 percent, I would say that my avoidance of marriage and/or my homosexual relationships are likely the result of my childhood home life. However, I don't believe that my non-traditional choices were, in fact, made for me by my parents. I think that rejecting traditional values, being open to sex (outside of marriage), and exploring sexuality were in some ways unavoidable for a thinking, liberated woman coming of age in the early '70s. I was surprised that so many young women were following along in their mothers' footsteps when so many other choices were possible. The goal was still to partner, if not partner well. You were still a loser without a partner.

"It has always been important to me that no one control my life. I have made many sacrifices as a parent and feel that I am not a selfish or inflexible person. I simply like living solitary because it allows me the privilege of planning my days, pursuing my dreams, inventing and reinventing myself without consequence to, or interference from another. If you would like to talk to me, please contact me . . ."

Eve lives in Hamilton, in a sparsely furnished condo. We met late on a Sunday afternoon. She was smoking a cigarette, drinking white wine. She is pretty, thin, with big brown eyes, a red mouth, a husky voice. Her son came in and out as we talked. "Don't worry, he knows everything," she said quietly.

"I met these lesbians that a friend knew and found myself extremely attracted to one of them. Then there was about a year when I felt like a lech. I didn't know how to relate to my own friends, that I had this thing in me that was not explained to them, but I wasn't sure how they would feel. I had not been with a woman, I didn't know how to make love as a lesbian, I was stuck. I put my name down for gay counselling; I was in a netherworld. It took a whole year, and then I was told, Well, we can't make up your mind for you, honey. Get out to the gay bars, see what's going on!

"Going to the bars, I did hook briefly with a group of lesbian mothers fighting for custody, but I didn't want to partner with any of them. They had kids. The last thing I wanted to do was blend families. The thought of Betty and Bonnie and their five kids living together – please.

"My coming out? You come out when you meet someone and you fall in love. You think, Oh, I didn't know this was possible. I had never before felt that anyone was critical to my existence, except my son.

"I found the lesbian community . . . fast. They changed partners, they lied. I didn't want to cohabit, I didn't want to partner with someone quickly just because we had some physical response to each other. I wasn't being seen as a person, just a capture. I had three or four relationships of about a year in length and then I would pull the plug. It takes me that long to get past the romance . . .

"I had one relationship, for four years, and if nothing else can be said for it, it was true love. We're friends now, but it was a bad breakup. It laid me lower than I ever imagined. I lost confidence in my ability to read people.

"I was celibate for more than a couple of years, withdrew from the gay community, I didn't want anyone even looking at me. My son was giving me the gears, wanting me to get out and about.

"I ended up meeting men who were interesting. First I thought I would never sleep with them, but I dated three different guys in succession. I was mostly shocked at myself. Is this love, is that love? I wasn't too sure. I didn't think they really knew me, what was going on inside my head. But men don't require that. If their needs are being met, good enough. With women, they know the body language, they know everything.

"All my straight girlfriends, when I came back into the straight world, said, Oh, it would be so good to be with a woman if I could do it, because they would totally understand me. Huh! It's not that simple. It's more engaging, but fraught with all kinds of complications, more than straight life, which I find easy. With men I didn't have to care about what it meant, because as far as they were concerned it didn't matter. They were very much in the moment. Gross assumptions, of course, but that's my experience.

"In the gay community, if you're employed and attractive and semi-articulate, you're in. It's not like that for me. I have a much longer list. I don't want [the same as myself]. You see these lesbian couples, living in the suburbs, wearing identical costumes and looking identical, and I think, No, I need someone very different from me. I don't want to look at a mirror image of myself.

"I had been in correspondence for 14 years with a woman from San Francisco, and six years ago I went and stayed with her and her partner. My God, for eight years I had been writing to this person, and she is wonderful! And she's partnered. Last July, she came up to Toronto, and we now have a romance. She is native American, a writer, very butch, one of those women who could only be what she is. Physically the way she presents herself is almost stereotypical. But butch women are very, very different from men. She is very different from me, and it took me 14 years in the gay world to find out that this is what I want.

"She doesn't want to cohabit and I don't either. Often that is the death of a relationship. I am certainly hesitant about making that kind of commitment. It's a question of how much you have to give, and where. That's what we are exploring at the moment."

Sophia

"I remember reading books by Victorian women, authors who were unmarried, how strange! I'd get this weird creepy feeling, but then I looked at some of the things these women did, and they were the ones who went off to Africa or the women who did all those fabulous drawings of wildflowers . . . The fact was that they chose, or managed to live their lives in a really healthy way. Being single. I found it incredibly attractive."

Sophia is 47, gorgeous, thick black hair, black eyes, slim in jeans, leaping into her SUV as though she were jumping on a horse. She is a small-town, eastern Ontario entrepreneur, with huge energy for renovating houses, running her store, travelling and cooking and friendships. She slipped out of her middle-class Jewish background in Toronto in her early 20s.

"I lived in Quebec for three years, a great time, but also a very difficult time. I was estranged from my family at that point. I lived on a farm. No running water, wood stove, big garden, the animals. My family was just horrified that I would live with a man. I didn't call them very often.

"My mother's 50th birthday happened around then. I never came home for the party. Somehow it just passed over my head that this event was happening. It would have been the last time that we could all have been together as a family. Three months later my brother was killed. I can't, to this day, believe I never showed up.

"I left the man on my birthday; went back to Toronto. Then one day I borrowed my mother's car, and somehow I headed east. The whole time I felt like I was being propelled by something other than me. I knew no one. Absolutely nobody here. But I stayed. I didn't do anything for the first six months except work. I had a bad time with drinking a lot. I was really sad. And then I got involved in the community. I never looked back after that. It was like I was home. I felt safe here. I was 24."

Sophia's path would be familiar to women in her age group who got caught up in the sexual revolution. "I always thought that I would marry late. I never imagined myself marrying before I was 30. And that I would have kids. But that I would have some kind of a career. For a long time I thought I would be a physiotherapist. And for a while I thought I would be a teacher. But then I started smoking dope, and I thought, I'm going to be an artist. And then I was into weaving . . . When I turned 30, I thought, Okay! I wonder if it's going to happen now. Then I was 32, and then I was 35, and you know, you keep hitting these ages. About 38, I was thinking, Oy! I had relationships off and on. But most of them were either inappropriate or totally not interested in having a child.

"And then I did get pregnant. I met this man in Egypt. Came home and was pregnant. It's like, Oh, my God! At the same time, my closest friend was seven months pregnant. It was very exciting. We used to sit on my porch and think about raising our children together in my house. Because she wasn't with the father of her baby either.

"I went to tell my sister, because I was very freaked out about what my parents would say. I thought, Well, it'll be okay. I'll manage and the community will help me do this thing. And I'd work. Because I was making a lot of money then. I went to my sister, and she just slammed me and said there was no way I was going to be able to do this on my own. And she's a doctor, married, with four children. She's very involved in the women's community, but I was like, Why is it okay for other women and it's not okay for me? It was horrifying. Anyway, a week or 10 days after that, I had a miscarriage. So that was the end of that!

"Still, if I think about being in a relationship, I would love to be with a man who does have children. Even if they're grown adult children, I would like to feel that. And be a part of their lives."

Sophia owns a successful small restaurant. She has bought, renovated, and sold houses. She is almost a matriarch in her community. She is active, financially comfortable, and happy with her success. "I really like working for myself. And I know that part of my working too much has been compensation. I wanted to prove myself in a man's world as a successful businesswoman. Because then, in the eyes of my father, I would be successful.

"I don't want to live with someone, I'm really clear about that. I would like to be in a relationship where we can share time. But I want to go home, and I want him to have his own space. I don't want anybody to come into my life that doesn't have a life."

She paused and thought out loud about this business of being "in relationship." "I feel the least true to who I am when I'm in relationship. Because as soon as I start feeling that thing about having somebody in my life, I get obsessive. I get obsessed with where they are, and how come they haven't phoned me, and it's like my mind is always thinking about them, and I'm not 100 percent focused at my work. Right back to being an adolescent! I hate it! Maybe I don't know how to be in relationship. Maybe it's because I've never had a good one. I've never had an equal one, where I'm allowed to be who I am.

"Do you think the choices that you've made, or the way that your life has gone – do you think those were radical choices? Do you feel unusual?"

Sophia nodded vigorously. "Oh, I do. I feel really alone [even though] I know that I'm not alone. But I don't know how to connect to women who are like me. I would love to find a couple of women that would like to travel in the winter together. I have friends who are 65, three of them. And they're off all over the world together, they're great! To me that's the ideal way to do stuff. You live your own life and then it's like, Okay, I'm ready for an adventure, let's go!

"Sometimes I feel completely alienated from normal society. It isn't geared up for people like us. Advertising and what you look at every day, and every single movie you look at, they're not about women like us! I do have really normal desires. I mean, to be around people who love me, and are going to hear my pain when I'm feeling really sad, and are going to allow me to be alone. But I find that we're scary! I don't get invited places because I'm single. I'm a threat! Why? I'm not going to go after somebody's partner or husband. I just want to have a relationship with my friend. But I find that they won't separate themselves.

"I have friends who've met and married men through the personals. I can't do that. I don't want to wade through a whole lot of noodly guys, you know, and make an appointment to meet them at some café wearing a red rose. I can't do that. I don't waste my time. I'd rather be reading a book.

"Maybe I really don't want a relationship enough. Do I want it enough to have to work that hard to go and find somebody? I don't. I think that's why I don't have a man in my life. 'Cause I don't really care. It would be lovely, but I don't really care all that much. It's not going to stop me from living.

"No one has ever asked me to marry them. I won't ever wear that white wedding dress. But I'd love to be that woman for a day. *Ewww!* How can that be? How can I be this woman who is such an individual, and yet there's a part of me that, on occasion, pines to be a princess?"

She was both serious and self-mocking when she said this. I laughed. "Like Barbra Streisand getting married in that huge white dress at whatever age she was . . ."

Sophia said quickly with a sigh, hand on heart, "I know! My first thought was, Well, if it can happen to her, it can happen to me!

And she was 56! Oh God, I just have to wait another 10 years. It's ridiculous. But in the meantime, I am going to live my life. And I'm going to be happy living my life."

From the Diary of a Single Woman

A Friday night in summer: Suzanne and I have a glass of wine in her garden and then walk down College Street to the Italian strip. The streets and patios are teeming with people; it is a hot night that promises no sleep.

It is always interesting to walk down the street with Suzanne, who is taller than I am, six feet at least, and she is blonde, and she wears bright colours and smiles at people. She moves through crowds like a goddess, I think, and then she turns and says something completely ordinary, even goofy, and she is human again.

As we walk, then sit in a courtyard for dinner, then stroll home again, we talk. As always, our conversation – well, many women talk this way – darts back and forth between matters of consequence (we have been working together on a social policy project) and matters of apparently no consequence at all: the best local manicure, the alarming deodorant of the man who has just brushed past us, drag queens at El Convento Rico.

On many evenings like this, or mornings when we meet for brunch after the Y, or while driving together to meetings, we construct for each other our life stories. Like the dollhouses we played with as children. Mine looked just like the house I grew up in, with the same floor plan, and the fabrics in each room the same as those in our real house. We people the rooms, dance the characters up and down the memory staircase, recounting the big and small moments of our childhood, looking for the places where our memories coincide or resemble those of the other. Because we are trying to understand who we are and why we are, and the way that we do that is by looking for mirror images.

Our lives have been quite different, we discover, before this point when we are both single women living in the west end of Toronto, sometimes with children or cats, sometimes with work, always with big ideas and plans and houses that need renovation and cars that are less than reliable.

Her life story – the men, the children, the men again – is operatic in its dimensions. We laugh about our hapless celibacy. Suzanne tells me about a horrible singles dance she has been to recently, somewhere out in Mississauga. I can barely picture this. Suzanne is so singular, so large a persona, so self-contained. Far, I would have thought, from the gritty little indignities of dances with strangers.

But we both have paper dolls and a dollhouse in our memories of childhood, we agree. And a road trip adventure together sometime in the future.

CHAPTER 4

On Mothering

November on Highway 7 in Ontario: black road, blackened trees almost stripped of leaves. There was still a bit of russet and gold in the grasses and in the very few leaves that remained. Every once in a while a lively birch crackled with light against the overall darkness. Passing through towns like Tweed, I hit the unexpected warmth that their main streets emit. They briefly enclose the visitor in some sense of community and then fall away in the rear-view mirror.

This is the time of year when Demeter must send her daughter Persephone back to Hades in the underworld. After the harvest, the earth lies cold and frozen as Demeter suffers four months of separation from her daughter. Demeter is the fierce and unmarried mother figure among the goddesses. When Persephone was stolen by Hades, Demeter roamed the world in mourning, disguised as a crone, suckling the infants of strangers, causing the earth to become infertile. Zeus sent Hermes to the underworld to insist that Hades give up Persephone, but Hades enthralled her with the seeds of a pomegranate, so that she would always return to him. Enraged, Demeter denied the pleas of Zeus to bring the earth back to life again, until Hades agreed to keep Persephone for three months only, and send her back home to her mother every spring.

Demeter stands for the implacable need to mother, to nurture, that some women have. It is an instinct that can be entirely separate from the idea of marriage or long-term commitment to a mate. It is for some women the most important element in their lives.

A significant development for single women in Canada has been the change in attitude towards single motherhood. It has become permissible for women to choose to bear and raise children alone – not necessarily their first choice, but a choice nonetheless. It has become more acceptable for women to raise children after the end of a bad marriage, either in a carefully worked out arrangement with the father or entirely on their own.

The status of single mothers is in itself a reflection of the complex relationship between Canadian families and governments. Single mothers have vexed politicians forever, whether they be widows, women who have been deserted, women who are separated or divorced, women who lived common-law, or – the most harshly judged – simply "unwed mothers." All have received varying degrees of grudging support or pious condemnation and been the subject of cynical scrutiny since governments first considered welfare. Always the debate is a tangle of moral and economic agendas.

Single mothers' support from government has always been pro-vided grudgingly and at rates lower than the family wage deemed appropriate for male heads of families. The Ontario Mother's Allowance, for example, first granted in the 1920s, was given only to widows and women who had been deserted for *seven* years, as a form of "salary" for their service to the country. Eligible recipients were permitted to work part-time, preferably as chars, or to supple-ment their income by taking in boarders or sewing, but there was consistent pressure to lower the rates as an incentive to work, even when there was no work. During the Depression, single mothers (again, only those who had been married) received support on the basis of the husband's failure to provide, either because he was dead or "incapacitated" (ruthlessly interpreted) or because he had deserted. If there was even a distant sighting of a missing husband, the allowance was denied. Single mothers' homes were scrutinized for "cleanliness," inspections designed to detect lapses in morality. As unemployment relief became increasingly necessary, the pension-like status of mother's allowances was eroded and they became just another form of needs-based social assistance. After 1940, mothers who were unmarried, widowed, divorced, or deserted were officially classified as "unemployables."

In 1956, never-married mothers finally became eligible for the Ontario Mother's Allowance, but only after a two-year waiting period, during which they proved their fitness. Adoption of illegitimate children by married couples was considered preferable. In the 1960s, the national "war on poverty" resulted in increased levels of support from federal and provincial governments and an expansion of eligibility criteria. But since the mid-1990s, governments have cut back on support for single mothers. The emphasis has shifted from supporting the needy to encouraging training and employment, and the image of the slothful mother on welfare is used once again to justify restraint and harassment.

It is curious that even the vaunted issue of childcare, which the federal government has alternately trumpeted and choked on for decades, is almost always discussed in terms of the nuclear family. A national childcare policy is resisted on the grounds of a contemporary variant of the male-breadwinner argument. But the family unit for which daycare is often the most urgent problem is the single-parent household, where there is no leeway in the balance of income and childcare costs, unless a kindly relative lives nearby. Curious too are the conflicting views of single mothers with low income or receiving welfare: such women are considered indifferent mothers or just plain greedy if they work and pay for childcare. But they are sneaky and indolent (taking advantage of the system) if they stay home to look after their children and require financial assistance to do so.

Middle-class and professional women can better afford to be single parents, although they experience ongoing concerns about the quality of care. They are increasingly free of moral judgments by society at large, and evolving laws concerning benefits, taxation, and adoption support their decisions to go it alone.

For separated and divorced single mothers, the struggle to achieve adequate financial support for children and a form of shared parenting continues. This struggle has been eased by increasingly liberal divorce and family laws and by decisions in the courts that have addressed fundamental financial and custody issues. As is the case for all single women, the key to comfort is a combination of financial security and emotional support.

Even so, social attitudes remain ambivalent. In my interviews, I found strongly opposing views expressed on the subject of single parenthood, more so than on any other aspect of single life. The role of the father in parenting and the role of the state in providing aid were major issues. Viable single motherhood represents the most profound challenge to the heterosexual-and-married model of the family. I found the most radical options here as well: single women with five or more children; women in their late 30s considering impregnation by strangers in foreign lands; a lesbian couple each bearing a child fathered by a different man; the reassignment of parental roles outside gender-based assumptions.

Critics will condemn these choices as selfish or immoral, evidence of a disintegrating, dissolute society. They could also be viewed as the signs of a healthy society reinventing itself in response to the reality of today's circumstances.

Lyn

"I get tired of the whole stigma that attaches to 'single mother,' this whole concept that I'm either needy or unable to care for myself. There's a whole bunch of things that get attached to it that are quite frustrating."

Lyn is almost 40, a redhead with bright curly hair, a soft, mother's body. She lives in a large, sprawling house beside a lake, a house sprouting additions in all directions. It's not a tidy home: cats, a dog, toys, sewing materials, piles of laundry, bits of lumber, a lived-in domesticity. Lyn's daughter is Joanna, a precocious 11-year-old with a long red braid, at the age where she pirouettes instead of walking.

Lyn has been on her own "always, more or less." She lived with someone for nine months when she was 18. She has never married. Here in rural Ontario, she knows she is considered somewhat of a misfit. "Living rurally as a single woman, it's kind of an odd thing. It's not done a lot. People tend to partner up in one way or another." But she is completely comfortable with her circumstances and lives happily alone with her daughter. Joanna was curious about our conversation but content to disappear to watch a video after taking me on a tour of the house.

After her daughter left, Lyn said, "I haven't found anyone I wanted to commit myself to for the long term. If I knew, going into a relationship, that I didn't think it was going to last, I'd rather avoid the aftermath ahead of time. Friends would say, You're just afraid of getting hurt. And I'd say, No, I know this isn't the person I want to spend the rest of my life with. As I get older, I think maybe I will never meet that person."

Lyn got pregnant when she was 28 and working in the Yukon. She laughed as she told the story. "In the dead of winter a band came to town. I had an affair with one of the band members. He left and I was pregnant. I contacted him later, when I was about nine months pregnant, on the advice of male relatives who said it wasn't fair for me to bear this man's child without giving him the option of participating. He called me back, and he was glad that I had told him. He was surprised, but he wasn't overly surprised."

Neither was Lyn. "I had quit smoking about a year prior to getting pregnant, had not been drinking, and was really living a clean sort of life. So on some instinctual level I certainly was preparing for it. I considered aborting. But I'd reached a point where I decided, I can't wait for my life to happen while I'm waiting for the right person to share it with. And having a child was something I knew I wanted to do. I wasn't going to let that pass."

She has never regretted her decision. She has always been the sole financial support of her daughter, although "I ended up in Vancouver, and – being perfectly honest – not coincidentally, that's where Joanna's dad was. I had hoped that we would get together, but I wasn't admitting that to myself then. He really made an effort at being a dad, but it just wasn't there for him. Joanna was four when we came to Ontario. Part of my coming back here was my mother saying, Wouldn't it be nice if Joanna was closer? It was also bad childcare experiences in Vancouver, and always with someone who was paid to look after her, rather than someone who was really caring for her. Also the proximity of her dad was causing me some emotional issues. I was angry a lot. I just had to wrest control back."

Lyn can scarcely imagine beginning a relationship; her focus is entirely on her daughter. "I do think about it. I came from a some-what dysfunctional family – I mean, didn't we all? And with Joanna being young, I was never prepared to commit to the work of a relationship. I have already made a commitment to her. I believe that a good relationship requires work between the two people. And I don't have that in me right now. I don't have enough time to get my house clean, never mind work on a relationship!" She gestures ruefully to the clutter that surrounds us, but her smile says she is not seriously troubled by it.

Lyn's mother and stepfather live nearby; Lyn is the computer expert in a small-town bank. "I also dabble in alternative healing arts, and that has been my focus, other than computers. If I do go on for any additional education, that'll probably be what it is. That's one of the reasons I bought this house. It is big for two people. I hope to set up a practice here eventually, some kind of alternative health and nutritional counselling perhaps. I'm an ordained minister of the Clairvoyant Church on the West Coast, but I tend not to do aura readings because it's a little too airy-fairy. I tend to be way more left-brain than that. I'm my own worst skeptic!"

"Was it hard to come here as a single parent?" I asked.

"Well, in a smaller area everybody knows each other. So you're an outsider, first of all. I've been accepted, which is very nice. But there is a tendency to want to label, and know who and what everybody is, and I don't fit any particular mould. If you're a single woman, without a man, then you must be looking for one. So you're probably out in the bars, or you don't really want a man, and that brings up a whole other thing.

"When I first came back, I had this conversation with a friend about Joanna wanting to wear shorts to school in November. And the friend said, Well, if my son wants to do that, I just let him wear shorts! And he figures out quickly enough that it's too cold for shorts. And I said, But you are married and a long-time member of the community. If you do it, you're teaching your kid a lesson. If I do it, it's because I was probably out drunk and getting laid last night, and wasn't up to properly dress my kid for school today!"

She laughed at this thought, then said seriously, "I'm constantly being held to a slightly higher standard."

It has taken Lyn years to establish credibility. "When I first came back, I wanted to buy a car, and the bank manager would not lend me money, even with a co-signer, because I was not 'stable.' If I had a husband, it would have been different. Now I can get lots of money, because if my boss trusts me, obviously I'm a good risk."

"Do you have to explain yourself, explain where Joanna's father is?"

Again Lyn smiled easily. "When people ask, Where's your ex-husband, I always like to tell the story for the shock on their faces: Well, I was a barmaid . . . I believe in being honest. I had problems when Joanna was in Grade Three. She had a male teacher, and he obviously felt that she didn't have a male influence in her life and wasn't well disciplined. And he was going to do her the favour of providing that. 'We see this kind of behaviour in bifurcated families,' he said. And I said 50 percent of the kids in schools are being raised in single-parent families, almost all by women.

"I'm tired of everybody assigning blame. Oh well, if you had a man in the house . . . Oh, if it was a more stable environment . . . I know many people in two-parent relationships that are far less stable. Why don't you just deal with the fact that kids are being raised by single parents? Instead of always wishing that those single parents would go out and become non-single parents. It's not going to happen!"

Lyn is smart and capable when it comes to money. "Finances have never been one of my problems. I've always managed to find a good job wherever I go. But I have always lived not hand to mouth but from paycheque to paycheque. I'm a spender, I like to give myself the things I want. I have a strong will, but I have no willpower. So buying the house was a conscious decision, and I pay it down whenever I can to make sure I have some room to play. I'm conscious of wanting to go on into that other life that I intend to have."

In this marginalized part of the country, it is a struggle for single women to beat the odds financially. "They're in a muddle, generally. The single women I see who want to buy a house are on family benefits; they're not working. If you have more than one kid, it's difficult to hold down a job. The bank doesn't want to give them the mortgage. They don't have money for a down payment. It's impossible for them to get ahead, absolutely impossible.

"I spent some time on family benefits when I first came back here. It's such a horrible trap to get into, where you start to feel like you're worthless. You're not out in the community, you're with the kids all day, people look at you like you're a drain on society. And you really start to feel that way. I was only working part-time at first, taking some courses at Queen's and not sure what I was going to do. The social worker said, Oh, keep getting a top-up from social assistance. I said, I make enough money now. I don't need to do that any more. But the social worker told me to take it; the extra money won't hurt. Then three months later I get a letter that says, We want copies of all your pay stubs for the last year. I said, I gave you those every month. Well, we're doing an annual audit now, they said, and you have to get all this together for the auditors. And I said, Fuck off! I'm not doing this!" It was yet another level of bureaucracy demanding evidence, showing its power.

"It's awful. The refusal of people to understand that things are measured in more than dollars. The bottom line is really such a small factor, you know? I don't know how to help children without helping their parents. You can't punish people into living a better life.

"The other assumption is that people have consciously planned their lives. I believe very much that you're a function of what happened in your first eight years. People aren't in touch with that. So even though they think they're making conscious decisions, people sabotage themselves subconsciously. They find themselves in situations and assume that's their lot in life. No one has said to them, You can break down the walls."

I asked Lyn if she is celibate.

"Um, yes, I am. Except for when Joanna's dad visited last year. I haven't had a sexual relationship other than him all this time. That again ties back to my mother. My dad was hospitalized for epilepsy when I was six or seven. My mother went out on dates, but she came home every night, and no men ever slept over at my house. I operate on that basis. Not wanting to expose Joanna.

"The reason I still have sex with Joanna's dad is I suppose I would have a relationship with him if he quit drinking, got his life together. But I don't want to parent him. I don't want a half-baked man. I want one that's all the way done!"

She laughed as she recalled an experience with an Internet dating service. "A guy sent an e-mail, and he told me he was separated, he had two kids, and that he liked to take his older daughter partridge hunting. Now, I'm not a hunter, but I live amongst people who make their life that way. Partridges – I don't know if you know, they are the dumbest birds."

Now I laughed. "I grew up in northern Ontario. I know partridges. You have to stop in the middle of the road not to hit them!"

"Exactly!" said Lyn. "I hit one when I first came back here. I thought it would move, but it didn't. So when this guy sent me the e-mail, I sent him one back. I wrote, Can you *really* call partridge hunting hunting?"

Trudy

"The day I got married, I knew I would not stay married. It sounds so cruel now, but back then, I just thought, Well, I want to have children. That was the priority. The children were much more central to me than the husbands were."

Trudy is tiny, with short, bronzed hair and an open face. She was barefoot, wearing a pretty sarong as a skirt and a mauve tank top. When I arrived she was furiously peeling potatoes from a huge bag on the floor. A very quiet daughter came in and sat for a time. She softly asked her mother to open a package of doughnuts, while gazing at us both with great, round, dark brown eyes.

Trudy has fierce, restless energy. She said cheerfully that her whole family is completely nuts; she has an aunt who thinks she's

Mary Queen of Scots one moment and herself the next. Trudy was living in student housing, in Winnipeg, in turmoil at the time – she apologized profusely – because she was moving to Victoria to do graduate work.

Trudy looks about 30 but she is 38. She launched briskly into her story, spoke in a rush and scarcely stopped for breath for an hour. "Okay, well, I have five children. The oldest is going to be 20 in May, and my older daughter was 18 in December. The daughter you just met is going to be 12 in June. The next is 10, he'll be 11 in September. My youngest, he's six and he'll be seven at the end of November. Only three will come with me. The other two are just recently moved out. They're trying it on their own a little bit. The kids and I have always been together, so it's going to be hard.

"I've been married twice. I was married when I turned 18 and got pregnant not too long after that. I had the two oldest children with him. We divorced . . . oh, I don't even know when it was. The children were still pretty young, not even school age yet. His work in the garage was his life and the children were my life. So it was just differences. He didn't drink, he wasn't abusive, and there wasn't anything on my side, it was just that he would never have changed. I met my second husband about three years after that, here in Winnipeg. I had two children with him.

"I'd had my tubes tied after I had my two children with my first husband because I was allergic to the pill and couldn't take any kind of contraception, and an IUD had broken. So I had to go through the process of getting them undone, and I had two more children, and then we separated. Again it was me that left. He's a very nice man, quite the charmer, it's just that – he lied. Consistently. About the stupidest, silliest, tiniest things. I couldn't trust him. It wasn't even other women. He's with somebody now who suits him just fine. They take the kids every second weekend. Both my exes are exactly the same. They look totally different, but they have the same flaws that for some reason I must have looked for. I just outgrew them.

"I have to say that in both my marriages the children were more important to me than the husbands. I married two husbands who were very self-absorbed, and each just wanted to be mothered all the time, and that was okay up to a point. But I didn't want to be his mum. I was a mum to my children.

"With my last child's father, it was a total accident. I was actually going to have a hysterectomy. They took the test and told me I was pregnant. He was somebody I'd known for a while and it's a long story, but it turned out to be a great delight in the end. My family was like, My God, you have four children, why do you want to have another one? I actually wanted to have eight or ten, but finances did not permit that.

"I always worked part-time during my marriages, running a daycare out of my home, or doing some kind of paper work or computer work, or working in an office, or cleaning. While I've been in university, I've been living on student loans, bursaries, scholarships, and working part-time. Right now I get $200 a month from my second husband. Nothing from the first because the children are older. But it's got to the point where it's not an issue any more. I just don't care.

"You know, they're my children. That's been an issue with my youngest one, because his father is very committed to him and spends a lot of time with him. That's been difficult for me, to let go of that. I mean, I should be so happy! But in the end I always feel that they are my responsibility. They've always been able to depend on me, even though they are very independent. They know this is a safe haven for them.

"I get pissed off when people say to me, It must be really hard without a father figure around. 'I guess you're going to have to go through the drugs, and you're going to be a typical welfare mom.' Well, I wasn't ever a 'welfare mom.' I get so mad at people, at statistics, at everything. Because I'm a single mom does not mean that I can't raise my children the way I think they should be raised, with the values and morals that I think they should have. And the parents who say, Don't smoke, don't drink, don't do drugs, while they are smoking, drinking, doing drugs. You can't teach a child not to do it if you're doing it. You simply can't."

Trudy was preparing to do a master's degree in women's history. She was itching to get into it. It was the next reinvention of herself. "I think if I really had the opportunity to expand my brain, I could go a long way. Three years ago I didn't think I could do anything. It's only this last year that I've been thinking, I can do 'mother' with my hands tied. Now I need to do something I can't do blindfolded!

"[In 10 years' time] I would like to have somebody to share my life with. I would like to go to different parts of the world and teach. I would like somebody to share that with. But I don't want to do their laundry. I want to cook for them only if I feel like it, and I don't want to wash their dirty underwear! I don't want to raise anybody else's children. I would rather have somebody that's younger. That would be nice. I think everybody would like to, don't you?" She laughed giddily.

She was on the move again, darting to the kitchen to put away the doughnuts, straightening the dish towels, picking up a toy. She walked out with me to my car, still talking: all the things she hadn't told me, asking if I've talked to lesbian women. "I've thought about that myself, and – oh, I forgot to tell you, my oldest daughter is in a lesbian relationship, which I am perfectly happy about."

Single mothers differ significantly in at least one sense from single women without children: single mothers must forge connections with society. Their lives are a tangle of legal and financial and emotional wires, no matter where they are on the social scale. Single women without children have much more autonomy; they select or create their communities and connections. Many single mothers have liberated themselves from the tyranny of a bad relationship and the dead weight of a man who is not a good parent, but the price they pay is often considerable. If they are affluent or middle-class, they pay lawyers to fight custody and support battles. If they are poor, they conduct their lives under the relentless scrutiny of bureaucrats and social workers. They must tell, over and over again, the narrative of their mothering.

Bev

"I love my kids a lot; a psychologist told me she has never had a parent stick around like I have. Most of the people I know, child welfare's got their kids, and they want them back just for the cheques. Even when I was on welfare, I fought for them. I didn't sit idle. They call me contentious – a very nice way to say, She's a bitch."

Bev is 45. She works in a downtown Saskatoon community centre as a receptionist and file clerk. She is small and wears glasses; her bright blue eyes don't miss a thing. She has a tough face, a leathery complexion, a husky voice, a very intense presence. I could imagine her being aggressive, making trouble, fighting to stay alive. She is canny and didn't tell me everything at first, waiting to see if she could trust me. Her story came out backwards, the worst things saved to the end. Bev has three children, all boys, 17, 15, and 10, from one unhappy marriage. She is divorced, and her children were all put into foster homes during one especially messy time in her life.

"My ex was extremely abusive. I have a plate in my leg, my eye was kicked out, my jaw has been rebuilt twice. He just started hitting. Anyways, he made excellent money. That's one of the things that keeps [people together], and that's not a cliché. Because on welfare there's so many restrictions, so many things you can't do. Like your kids can't even join a baseball team. Who's got the registration fee? Who can buy the equipment? I don't want to eat wieners. I like to have my barbecued steak, and you can't do that on welfare.

"And housing. You have to take what you can afford, and they underpay you. That's no big secret. So you take a dump because it's bigger, and you can afford it, instead of taking a nice one that's way too small. If you have two kids it's not too bad, because I have done it. But three kids, and all boys, it just doesn't work.

"Fighting child welfare, I ended up with asthma, a stress disease. They said I had mental problems and battered woman syndrome. And over the years I had acquired an alcohol problem. So they say, If you do this, this, and this, we'll give your kids back. So since then I have totally been there every weekend, no complaints. They gave my oldest one back, saying that there have been no incidents, but they wouldn't give me the other two.

"They really hate me at welfare. They give me all the really old workers because the young ones are scared of me. And some of the drivers that pick the kids up from my house? I've had them run out of my house crying. You're a half-hour early, I'd say to them. Go away! I have until this court-ordered time. So get out of my house! I used to do that because it amused me. You people bug me, so it's my job to bug you back. It's my duty.

"They put my youngest on Ritalin, and I really flipped out, because I did all the research and I was afraid. He's been on it since 1996. I have fought it all the way. But when he comes to my house for holidays, like weeks and weeks at a time, I don't give it to him, and he's fine. He sometimes gets a little excited, but he's a little boy. Everything's a syndrome or a disorder now. Is that some kind of environmental thing? That was the start of my problems with child welfare, because I fought the Ritalin. They still put him on it. They are all-powerful.

"I took my ex-husband to court, and now I have a $10,000 bill from legal aid. Even for anyone working, that's a large bill. After I got hired on here, I went off welfare, and I got a bill for almost the same amount that they had given me. That's the new rules. You have to pay a certain amount back. They don't tell you that when you start out. They bought a crib for my youngest one, and that has to be paid back now. Their dad doesn't pay maintenance. I don't know why they don't harass him. He's driving a nice new Camaro. But the unions won't deal with garnisheeing, so I can't even garnishee his wages.

"If my two other kids come home, I'm going to have to go back on a shoestring budget. If I get subsidized by social services, they will take off income tax. So it's a Catch-22. Go to work, but we'll charge you to do that.

"My workers wanted to put me on assured income, because my asthma was so severe. It's not welfare, it's like a disability pension. I refused, I wouldn't take it, but they phoned up [potential employers] and said, This woman has this medical problem or that medical problem and she's not reliable. They didn't want me to work. The employers told me that. They said, What are you doing here? I said, I'm supposed to start work today. They said, Oh, no, your worker phoned and said you're unemployable. I got another job three weeks after that. The same thing. But here, the business manager said, We realize her physical problem and we don't mind. That's how I got this job.

"I refuse to be an idle person. I volunteered here for over two years before I got the job. And I told my worker, Well, if I can do this, why do you guys keep getting in my way? And she says, Because you're very ill. I knew the asthma was a stress disease, eh. I knew if I ever finished fighting child welfare that I would be healthier and I would be able to work instead of sitting at home being dormant, maybe going back to substance abuse. Or just getting depressed, ending up on medication or junk.

"I don't want to live on welfare. I lost my kids over all this. Certainly I've gotten depressed. I'm on anti-depressants and anti-anxiety [medication]. I have to work because it would drive me insane to sit around all day on their assured income or their welfare. I'm not suicidal. But who knows what I might have become?

"I have a criminal record. I just got into a situation I didn't know how to get out of. A lot of single moms get into that. Mostly drugs, alcohol. Possession of narcotics, impaired driving. A lot of things I'm not proud of. Car theft . . . I never did like the drugs that I was doing, but I belonged with those people. I belonged somewhere. I've been clean over four years now. Well, for drugs, longer than that, because there was no more veins. Plus I ran out of money. So I've been about seven years off the drugs, four off alcohol.

"I'll get my kids at the end of the school year. They go to a school now that's too far for travelling. I won't unsettle them, and I've told the child workers that. Like, it's not about me. It's never been about me. It's about families. The kids who are with their parents don't mind being poor. They would just rather be together.

"I'm not venturing out until my kids are home. My full attention is on that. I want that 'unfit mother' stigma off me."

Marlene

"Someday, a frog will come . . ."

Marlene is 49, very attractive, sleek, well-groomed; a teacher, single mother, and grandmother. She lives on a quiet street in Regina, loves her garden and her cheerful, warm house. She exudes resilience, optimism, and determination. She's ready for an adventure. She offered me a glass of wine, and we sat companionably at her kitchen table at the end of the day.

Marlene has spent most of her life in Regina. She got pregnant at 17 and married at 18; the marriage lasted 13 years. She went to university after her first child and became a teacher. "I've been teaching ever since. That's the constant in my life. I have two beautiful daughters. I just became a grandmother at the end of March." She knew this would surprise me; she looks much younger than her age.

"And why did you get divorced?"

"I think because we were pretty young when we got married. I was determined not to be a statistic. I was going to make that marriage work, come hell or high water. It was going to be happy, it was going to be perfect, it was going to be wonderful. But we didn't grow up together well. We did for a while and then we just grew apart. I laugh now. I understand it now. I had this terrific mother thing going on, and I became a teacher and I was doing all this caretaking."

Marlene was one of those mothers who had difficulty sharing the parenting role. She preferred parenting on her own. "It was easier for me. I found parenting in my marriage difficult because there was another force that was pulling, and there was conflict. And he was as demanding as five little children. The kids I can handle; I don't think I do so well with men. We started out with joint custody and that was a schmoz, and then we had examinations for discovery and court things. There was a certain amount of animosity, but to me the kids came first.

"It's only been the last three or four years that I've been moving towards wanting to have a serious relationship. Now I want some commitment in my life. That surprised me, because I guess I was just busy, or I didn't want to. Didn't meet anyone that excited me. I probably went five to seven years just being so blissfully happy at being left alone. Just the kids and I, and it was the first time I'd lived alone, and that was a big part of it too. I'd never had that time."

Marlene has made a number of considered choices about work, money, and the lifestyle of her children. "My friends in Alberta tried so hard when I was first divorced. They said, Get out of Regina. There's nothing there for you. Come here. And I thought, Yeah, for myself personally, Calgary may have attractions, but

Regina's a good place to raise kids. On a teacher's salary I can't afford a house like this in Calgary. And my home is very important to me. Not as important as it used to be, though. I'm finding I'm letting go of a lot of things that I thought were important.

"I only have five years of teaching left. If I had ten, I probably would leave now. But with five, I will stay. Because then I'm financially able to go and do whatever I like with the rest of my life. If you believe in horoscopes, I am the ultimate Cancer. I need security, and I've always taken very good care of that, so I'm not going to have any financial worries. The last few years I've been enjoying life tremendously."

Marlene has been a single mother for almost two decades. For much of this period, she was celibate. "I must admit that in the past I went for a long, long period of time, and I really did forget about it. I think I just died for a while, but now – I think this is a hormonal twinge or something – the older I get, the more I think about it. I've done my bit with the kids, I'm winding down a job. You know, maybe I want a woman life.

"Maybe lack of sex makes you hornier, I don't know. I'm more comfortable with sex now. When I was younger, it was always traumatic because it was expectations and so much baggage and head stuff that went with it. Now I'm a big girl and I can do whatever I like. When I went to Italy – I don't know what is in the air there, but something happened to me, and I've never been the same. That was three years ago. I went by myself, I was totally free, I had a wonderful time. And everyone said, Oh, watch out, Italian men are going to be all over you, they're just disgusting . . . They were fabulous. I never felt so female. They just admire you with their eyes. I never once felt leered at or ogled or any of those ugly sorts of things. I loved Italy. Even the women. I loved it.

"I went to Hawaii at Christmas and I met a fellow. Actually, this was an ego trip. I got picked up on the beach. At 48, that's the first time in my life, right?"

"What about married men? Do you have affairs with married men?"

"I did, and I just felt ugly about it. Now if I find out they're married, I think, Get your life in order. Particularly now; what would I want with a married man? How can he and I enhance each other's lives in any way? I believe in monogamy. And I don't think there is a married man on earth that's going to leave his wife. No, I don't want them. They have nothing to offer me.

"There were times, nights when I would cry and think, Why is life so empty? What's wrong with me? But you come to terms with that. I'm a firm believer that we are not in total control of what's going on here, but we have a big part to play, and we can be happy or we can be sad. I don't sit around and mope, but I tell you I've walked around that lake a few times. Normally it takes about 45 minutes from here, around and back, but I've done it in 25. So you know, the feet are pounding . . .

"But life's like that. All these women my age are talking about facelifts and getting all anxious, and I don't buy that. I'm so happy now. I think all the stress of life is over. Now come the good times."

From the Diary of a Single Woman

There is a large green bowl on my kitchen table. In late November, it is filled with oranges, pears, and pomegranates. My daughter loves pomegranates and I buy them every autumn, even though she is living on the other side of the country now. I think of her as a child, cutting into the rough red skin, like cheeks roughened by cold, spurting red juice and seeds all over herself as she bites into the heart of the fruit. I send her an e-mail about the season of pomegranates, and she writes back asking what is the story about pomegranates anyway, and I write back to her the myth of Demeter and Persephone, knowing, as I write it, that I am telling her how much I love her.

"But before Hades sends Persephone home, he offers her the famous pomegranate, the seeds of which she eats, and she is thus bound to him (not sure if it is love or memory or just one more great forbidden fruit). When Demeter learns this (which awful fairy-tale rule did Persephone break?), she makes the deal that Persephone will spend most of each year with her, and – you guessed it – winter with Hades. Happy pomegranate eating, dear daughter! See you soon . . ."

Winnipeg: Someday, My Prince Will Come

The end of April, a muggy grey day in Winnipeg, early evening at a big old house in a quiet neighbourhood near the city centre. Wine, cheese, crackers, brownies; four women including me in an intimate dining room off the kitchen. This house feels like a serene place; it is both home and work space. The three women here know one another well. I feel that I am joining a conversation, or series of conversations, with a deep history.

The linchpin is Lydia, whose house this is. She is 37, a warm woman who speaks with confidence. She has shiny dark hair, brown eyes, a lively, open face. Formerly a lawyer, she is now self-employed as a consultant. She is very pregnant. Gail is also 37, a very attractive blonde, the most reserved of the three women, with a quiet, straightforward charm and a clear, pure prairie note in her voice. Her first career was as an emergency room nurse, and she now works in public relations. Marie-Claire is tall, 46, a strong personality, strikingly dressed in bright colours, intense, articulate, restless; she slips away a couple of times for a cigarette. She has been a lawyer, broadcaster, translator, and teacher.

GAIL: I was raised on the farm, I guess a middle-class family, with traditional values, some of which I hold, some I don't. Certainly [I had] a rather progressive mom, even though she was a mom who worked at home when she started having children. She had a nursing degree and went to college and also raised three daughters to believe that they could do anything.

In my family, independence was encouraged. You didn't have to marry financial security or marry prosperity; you could do that on your own. And you could look after yourself. You could learn to drive, travel to places on your own, basically make your own decisions.

I'm not sure what to say about why am I still single. I do not have children and have not been married. At some points, I'd have to admit, I've felt pressure, but just gentle pressure. People wondering, What *is* wrong with you, why *aren't* you married?

And it's not that I'm against it – I'm not this radical feminist that doesn't believe in marriage as an institution. I just think it should be the right choice. At the risk of sounding egotistical, I always tell people that I've never had anybody make me a proposition who was not only up to the task but worthy of the reward.

LYDIA: I was married between the ages of 22 and 29. I have a seven-year tolerance for anything. It's the seventh year on my own – I'm now 37, and so here I am, pregnant. Actually these two women were witnesses to my first real in-love, excited, dating relationship in those seven years. It lasted from May to September. It was a fellow who was a tennis player here from Brazil . . . I had a premonition I would get pregnant. I didn't plan it and he didn't certainly plan it. I went into an aboriginal sweat [lodge] and had an emotional and spiritual transition from youth to motherhood. I moved into a different emotional and spiritual place, and then three days later I conceived. In three weeks, I'll have the baby, and so I'm going to be a single parent, a single woman with a child. I really like my solitude, so for me the biggest challenge will come from not having this wonderful place to myself any more.

I come from the same community that Gail does, a more working-class family; my parents are first-generation Canadians from an eastern European background. Very hard-working. My parents were fairly strict, we were well disciplined. I excelled in school. I went on to get a law degree and worked in the legal profession for seven years, and then I started my own business as a consultant. Now I'm faced with some difficult decisions about whether to stay freelancing, or to try to make my life balance financially.

I still don't know if [the baby's father] is going to be involved with me. But I'm from a very strong matriarchal line. For me, I have my child, and it doesn't matter if there's money coming or not. I'm certainly not going to fight for it and beat somebody over the head to realize his responsibilities. I'm not prepared to do that.
MARIE-CLAIRE: I was born in 1953 in New York, of French-Canadian parents. My mum had decided, in a bold move, to get out of the stereotypical mould and get a job in New York while my father was in France studying medicine. And finally my father had finished his studies, they met again and got married and had me, and that's why I am the only American of my very French-Canadian family. Immediately after my birth we moved back to Quebec City, where I grew up.

It was probably the sole autonomous act of my mother, because she is, contrary to what you are describing in your families, a very typical homemaker, traditional wife to a traditional man who is in a traditional profession. And she never instilled in me a sense of being autonomous or able to move on my own. The only reason I became independent and studied law was because my father thought I was fat and ugly when I was young. I could not participate in the female stereotypical role, so the only way I could try to please my father was to become very good in school, which I did.

But I paid dearly for that, because for a long time I had very poor self-image. When I passed 30, the panic button started to ring; and I guess out of a sense of fulfilling the role, even though I didn't feel very apt at it, I got engaged to a man who was literally a lunatic. He zoomed in on me because I was vulnerable and recovering from a love affair that didn't go well. After meeting him in February, I moved here in June, engaged to be married, and after two weeks I realized he was really crazy. I think this is the reason why I am still single. I felt that if I was stupid enough to make such a mistake, I can't rely on my own judgment, and I would be very careful about committing to somebody [again]. After that followed a string of various lovers who were unavailable, so I wouldn't have to make the choice. I am still in a relationship with somebody who is totally unweddable, and in a way I feel safe because of it.

So my single state is not a true choice. It's rather an avoidance state, but it gave me the opportunity to become independent and to do what I wanted to do, and to also feel like a man, entitled like a man, to deal with my own life. I've done a lot of soul-searching and spiritual development and have a very good network of friends, and I feel that I am powerful in my own life in my own way, and that I don't need to be married to give myself credence or status of any kind.

I live alone, in a condominium that I bought in the good old days when I had a job, and I'm getting ready to sell it because I've decided to go for the dream. I want to dance. I'm going to do some studies so I can, before I am walking with a cane, explore things that I've always wanted to explore.

I believe for women, the right to explore is not there. A man who explores is adventurous, a woman who explores is hysterical. I challenge that, and I want to be able to go wherever I want to go and, when I have enough, to be able to leave. But I feel the stigma of being 46 years old with no fixed career, and no specific interests except things that are very flimsy and very out to lunch.

MBF: Do you feel that you are making radical choices in the way that you're living your lives?

LYDIA: I never ever thought that I would consciously choose to be a single parent. Although I never appeared to be concerned about the clock ticking, it was there on some level. I don't think it's as radical as it used to be for a woman to raise a child on her own.

It was radical for me to leave the legal profession. I felt more pressured by that decision than by the decision to leave my husband or to have the child. So I think I've made radical choices about not being the frightened woman who grabs at the first opportunity for a man, or who grabs at the first job that comes along, or who sits around biting her fingernails worrying about money, or in this case worrying about labour and delivery or worrying about how I'm going to care for things.

MBF: It's quite radical for women to set aside something that everybody else values and that you have been taught to value and say, No, that's not for me, and to step out of the box.

LYDIA: I'm extremely fortunate not to have manipulative or conditional-love parents. If I didn't have that, I don't know that I'd be so brave and courageous as I think I am.

GAIL: I don't consider myself radical in choosing the way I live. My independence is important to me, always was as a kid, always will be. I made my own choices for my own reasons, though. I don't know that I was avoiding anything, at least not consciously, or thinking my parents would want me to do this, or society would want me to do this. I became a nurse because I enjoyed people, wanted to travel. My mum said, Well, why don't you be a doctor, not because it was more prestigious, but I had the brains. I had scholarships, and she knew I would tell the other doctors what to do and get them organized. Which I did anyway as a nurse, so it didn't matter! I did reach a ceiling in terms of advancement, and also it was exhausting, mentally and physically. I thought, I don't want to do this for the rest of my life, I want to do something else. So I did.

I don't do anything that's all that extraordinary, but if you looked at my high school friends – honestly, I don't have a lot in common with them. Many of them married the guys they were seeing at 21 or who they went to grad with for that matter. I'm not saying that in judgment, I'm saying that in observation. My world is bigger. I lived in Australia, I travelled in southeast Asia. I did my own thing, I always have.

MBF: So you've never been married or in a long-term relationship?

GAIL: Not really long-term; one-year, two-year, three-year long-distance relationships, which my friends also analyze and say, Maybe that says something. Why do they always live somewhere else? Because it's easier? Maybe unconsciously I choose them because they're not here, in my face, in my world every day. And so it is easier. I've had lots of men who were interested in me and casually would say, I'd marry you if you were interested. But I didn't feel the same way about them, and I never felt I had to marry somebody to be somebody. No one makes me feel inadequate, at least directly, like a leper or anything. I guess that means I'm irresponsible, I'm the free spirit in the family. I really am.

MARIE-CLAIRE: That's part of my makeup as well. It took me a while to acknowledge this in myself, but I really thrive on change. It was not easy to find out that I felt trapped in any kind of job. There's this feeling that my life had to be something else, it had to be bigger, I had to be able to travel, I had to be free. Freedom was more important than money for me, for most of my life.

I feel if I were a man, this capacity to explore and try things and fail and switch from one thing to another would be so masculine and so cool. But because I'm a woman, something is wrong with me. I'm not a good woman, I'm not a good mother, I can't stick to anything. What do you mean, you want to wander off in the woods? You're supposed to stay home and watch the wheat grow, woman.

MBF: Do you have any kind of yearning at all to have a child or to be in a relationship?

GAIL: Yes, to both. I'm not anti-relationships or anti-marriage, not at all, and the same with children. If it happened – like Lydia, if I found myself pregnant tomorrow, I would have that child as a single mom, but I'm not consciously looking to make that choice. If a kid showed up in my life, in my uterus tomorrow, great, I'd have him. As I say, this may sound crass, but I haven't found a sperm donor I can live with.

To say that you're not complete without a child is the same as saying you're not complete without a partner. If you have to actually bear a child to feel that you've met your biological instincts or your biological destiny, what does that say about women who are unable to conceive, or adoptive parents? Or what does that say about men, what does that say about half the population?

LYDIA: I always considered I would be a mother, I thought I would have a child in my marriage. Then I realized that would be disastrous, once it was evident that the relationship was abusive, and I didn't want to subject a child to that. I guess my bottom line is that I have the rest of my life to have a partner and I don't have the rest of my life to have a child. I don't know that that was necessarily connected to any vision of what represents true womanhood or the fulfillment of my role or destiny as a woman. It was maybe a feeling that I have a lot to give a child, or that I would be a good model for a child, and that I could raise a human being with love and support so that they could realize their potential.

My parents and I have discussed the irony that if I had chosen to have this child within the marriage, what a disaster that would have been, and how this situation is actually far preferable all around. I don't want to sound constantly negative about what it is to be in a partnership, but I have yet to be in a truly supportive, fulfilling partnership, without that person simply abdicating to me. I feel I'm capable – with the support of my loving friends and my family – of doing this. I think this child is actually going to be the community's child, as in a lot of cultures of the world.

GAIL: It takes a village to raise a child . . .

LYDIA: I think that's even a healthier approach, surrendering in some ways . . . my ownership of it and the ultimate absolute responsibility for how this child relates in the world. You know, maybe Auntie Gail has something to contribute to this child's development, and maybe Tante Marie-Claire will influence the child. If you're two people as a partnership, the world assumes you're complete, you're whole, you're self-reliant, and you can do this job they call parenting.

MARIE-CLAIRE: This is a very difficult subject for me. Because I do regret not having a child, and now it is too late. I'm 46 and I'm not in a situation where I would have a proper home for a child, and I don't have any means to have a child. I never really saw myself as a mum, ever, even when I was a little girl, even though I had dolls and played with them. When I was thinking of my life and my future, it was always in terms of travelling, writing, being on my own, having a house by the sea, being free, being adventurous, being in love, being with a man, but not necessarily having children around me.

I was once pregnant and I had an abortion, a terrible experience for me. I got the abortion because my boyfriend at the time was married and suffering from a heart condition which was hereditary. He couldn't stand the idea of fathering another child, and I was left with the moral debate on my own, feeling that I was not ready to give birth and to really be on my own having a child. I was 28. I told my mum that I was pregnant. My family was ready to support me, they are very Christian. So when I got the abortion, I had to pretend that it was a miscarriage, just to be accepted in the family again. But somehow, they knew the truth. I remember when I took the train home after the abortion, my father let me, for the first time, walk from the station alone in the rain with my luggage. When he opened the door, he said to me, I don't ever want to discuss this.

I feel I made the right decision, I don't have any moral problem about abortion per se, and that was a situation where I didn't have much choice. But to this day I feel that possibly I've missed out, and possibly just because it was the wrong timing. It was not necessarily the wrong thing to have been a mother, and if I had been, my life today would be very different, I would have had an experience of womanhood that now I won't have a chance to have ever again. And so I have pain about this even though I don't regret. I have pain.

LYDIA: It seems from my narrow experience that a lot of women have been faced with similar choices. A lot of women have had to abort children, many of them for circumstantial reasons, lack of support, the feeling of being alone. A friend of mine who's married aborted a child recently. She's as good as alone in that marriage. Even the decision itself she made without that person's full input, because he refused to participate in that decision. To me that's a huge tragedy.

In a sense I feel sorry for men, because they're removed, they're removing themselves from what has the potential for tremendous fulfillment and closeness. I sometimes look at my friends, beautiful, talented, giving, loving women, and I feel we are wasting our potential. I mean, we're active, we're busy, we're doing all these things, but in terms of human relationships, what the fuck are we doing?

It's like being in a zoo. You're on this side of the cage, they're on that side of the cage, a couple of them are smart enough to unlock the key and walk out, but most of them – I mean, they're Neanderthals, and you're sitting there going, This is hopeless. And the ones who seem to have some potential, for me, are bisexual, or they're gay.

The possibility of having a fulfilling relationship seems to be getting more and more remote. And yet, I retain this optimism that there are people out there that I could be a partner with. I've said so many times – you know, facetiously, and sometimes not so facetiously – God, just to be a lesbian, for heaven's sake. If physically that would do it for me, I'm there, you know, I'm there.

MBF: Most women have said that at some point.

LYDIA: We're doing something fundamentally wrong in this society. We are really socializing men and women too disparately: they are miles apart. I don't buy this "men are from Mars, women are from Venus" crap, and yet I'm saying to myself, What's creating and what's perpetuating these differences? Women have to look in the mirror and say, What have I just done in this relationship? When have I not been honest and straightforward with this man? When have I not been myself?

MBF: Wait a second, what do you mean by not being ourselves? That we are responsible?

LYDIA: Oh, totally. We frequently spare their feelings and couch things in gentler terms. We don't come right up front and say how we feel, because we're worried about jeopardizing the harmony and stuff. What it requires is the courage to walk away when something isn't working and instead we bang our head against the wall.

It's surprising the number of women who have suggested to me about the pregnancy, Maybe this will work out in the long run. Or they ask, Have you heard from him? I have a few friends who are real romantics and I just want to say, Girls, get real. If I'm surprised one day and this person matures and comes back and wants to be a parent, great, but let's get a grip on his alcohol problems, and let's get a grip on the irresponsibility. I can see, from what little he's told me, what's contributed to where he is today, and I can see what he is avoiding, and I can see where he needs to go. He's the last one to know, you know what I mean? And so are most of the men in my life, they're the last ones to figure it out. I have a brother who's extremely developed, extremely self-aware, and that's the standard that I have. I'm not willing to put up with a Neanderthal any more.

MARIE-CLAIRE: But for me, it's not a matter of "men are from Mars, women are from Venus." I acknowledge the difference you're talking about. It's almost a natural path, given the way society is now, to treat men as Neanderthals. It's not working well.

For me, the reason is a lack of spirituality, a lack of development and integration of the feminine face of God, in this very patriarchal society. It creates monsters on both sides. We live in ego-boosting, narcissistic little units, each one creating its own life. We can't communicate, and it becomes easier to live apart. And you have these poor souls, male without female and female without male, living sorry, isolated, self-aggrandizing lives. In reality, we are a gregarious bunch of humans, having to grow into humanhood, never mind malehood and femalehood.

LYDIA: I don't disagree with anything you're saying. However, I guess I still hold some kind of ideal, and I don't want to look forward to relationships in the future as being a constant struggle, or making allowances or making excuses. With the right people, things can work easily. So while I accept what you're saying, how long are we going to wait until women really change how they're doing things and men really change how they're doing things?

GAIL: I think Marie-Claire is looking at the ideal. Wouldn't we all like to be spiritually evolved and both developing –

MARIE-CLAIRE: It's not holding up an ideal, it's recognizing that something sick is happening in this society. And it touches too the whole idea of living alone. Why is it that you and you and you are living alone? We are in a society where individuality is exaggerated to the point of breaking up the gregarious nature of man.

MBF: Many cultures do not have this degree of individuation, this number of single people in their society. The family and the community are much stronger forces. Something about our society has created a breed of single people.

LYDIA: And statistically, is it women who are mostly spending their time alone? Because it's my theory that men just go right back into relationships.

MBF: This is what we experience, this is what we see. We're supposed to be more or less the same in numbers; perhaps there are a few more women than men. But the reality is that everyone knows a lot more single women than they do single men.

LYDIA: Well, the men can choose the 20-year-olds if they want to.

MARIE-CLAIRE: My choice is limited. I'm bored with old guys, I only like young men, and young men only like young women. If you are a woman between 35 and 50, your scope is so limited compared to a man's. A man between 35 and 70 has the whole age range.

LYDIA: My experience in the last seven years has been that I could be with someone aged anywhere from 28 to 52. I know a lot of women in their 50s who are getting younger mates, and it has a lot to do with their belief in what's possible.

MARIE-CLAIRE: Whatever you believe is very nice, but go on a cruise and who are you going to be with? It's the old geezer who thinks that now at 70 he can get me – a 45-year-old girl.

LYDIA: Look, the guys my own age are not on the same wavelength, but what's going to make a friggin' 60-year-old of interest to me? I guess they're still harbouring this weird belief that we all want security and we all need a rich old guy.

MARIE-CLAIRE: My boyfriend is four years younger than me. And he's the oldest I've ever dated. The difference is in the mentality. Men who are a few years younger, or men who date older women, do not have the same attitude, and this is what I'm looking for. [But with] a typical 40- or 50-year-old now, you're cast into the role of the bimbo, playing Let's Entertain Mister. I get so angry, I can't make love, I can't kiss them, I can't do anything. I'm turned off.

I have a very definite difference in my mind between love and lust. I can feel lust and be attracted to a man without feeling love, I can have sex without being in love, and I can be in love without having sex. I hope to get both. But you meet women who seem unable to dissociate sexuality from love. It's like they have to be in love to allow themselves to feel sexual. I have been sexual as long as I can remember, I have always felt I own my sexuality, I always felt I was entitled to pleasure, I don't need to be romanced to feel sexual. I like sex for sex, and I can be turned on by a good-looking man. I know other women who will be sexually aroused if the guy has money and says the right thing. For me, if I'm not turned on by the body and by the smell, I'm not going to bed. And if I kiss, I kiss because I want to have sex, almost like a man. I won't tease, I won't be into the fluffy romantic mode and play with you and leave you hanging. I want it just as much.

LYDIA: I'm turned on by the interaction, and to me what they look like and what their body looks like is secondary. Which explains why I haven't gone out with lots of really gorgeous men or whatever, but –

MARIE-CLAIRE: I don't mean they have to be gorgeous. They just have to please me.

LYDIA: For me it's all about the interaction with the person. If I'm entertained by them and I'm humoured by them, it's all the theatre of sex. It's a fluid thing . . .

MARIE-CLAIRE: Well, for me it's almost instinctive. I see a man, I smell him, and I know.

GAIL: I'm with Lydia. I like the interaction, the flirting, when you know it's mutual. I have to be attracted to him, whether it's looks, whether it's intellect, whether it's wit.

MARIE-CLAIRE: Let's say you have this man in front of you. You realize – whoa, there's something really fascinating here. You like the way he thinks or the way he speaks, even if he's not relating to you. Don't you think that no matter what he says, you would interpret it as being part of the romantic dance? And if he is remotely sexual, he picks up the vibe that you're sending.

LYDIA: I need more directness. I've got the kind of personality, or maybe I've got really deep insecurities, that they have to be acknowledging me, acknowledging particular things about me. I guess too I found a lot of men to be visually fixating on the obvious and I

want them to notice the colour of my eyes, I want them to notice –
MARIE-CLAIRE: Wait until you're 46, honey, you're so happy not to be invisible, never mind the fancy little subtleties there!
LYDIA: What about the book *The Rules*, which says you do everything as deceptively as you can, be as manipulative as you can, then get the ring on your finger and get married. That is the end goal. And then what? What do you honestly think marriage superimposes? Like, if it's shit to start with and you put a plastic bag over it . . .
GAIL: It's shit in a bag!
LYDIA: Do you harbour a dream or an expectation that there's a Mr. Right out there for you?
GAIL: I guess I do, or at least Mr. Close-to-Right. I'm not looking for perfection. I certainly don't think I'm perfect. But I'm not willing to settle, and when it comes to Mr. Right, I want someone who loves me as deeply as I love them.
MARIE-CLAIRE: There is not a single Mr. Right. There are people I can relate to, and it's up to me and him to create the relationship. I haven't fallen in love with my current boyfriend. I am happy to be in the relationship, I'm happy to have a man in my life. He's not the man for me, though. I just don't think any more that I'm the marrying kind, or that I can actually live with somebody, or that it's in my destiny to be in partnership with a single man. So maybe my path is to have a succession of lovers who will be more or less important depending on who they are and how they relate to me. I feel very nourished by various relationships in my life – either with women or men – who are friends, who are sustaining me, allowing me to feel connected.

I certainly do not think any more that there is a Prince Charming with that set of attributes and qualities that will come and sweep me off my feet on his white horse. We all dream of that somewhat perfect fusion where you remain yourself but you are really connected with somebody. But I'm not expecting it, I don't necessarily believe in it, and it's not really important for me.

LYDIA: Well, I'm a huge optimist, despite being cynical, and I feel that with my own personal development over the last several years, the relationships I've had have gotten successively better and deeper and more meaningful, and I feel that I am on my way to meeting somebody where there will be a massive click and a massive devotion to each other. Maybe I'm deluded, but I truly believe that will happen. For me [what happened last summer] attested to that whole notion that I have the ability to bring into my life something out of nothing. So I feel I am very close, it's just a few steps away. Despite everything I've said, maybe I do sound like one of those schoolgirls . . . "Someday, my prince . . ."

We all join in, singing, laughing, overlapping harmonies: "Someday, my prince will come, someday, my prince will come . . ."

CHAPTER 5

Out of Wedlock: Divorce by Choice

I still keep a wedding picture on my dresser. I look at it with curiosity and affection, not animosity. I sometimes wonder why this photograph remains in my bedroom, but I would never take it down or turn it to the wall. Nothing can replace that moment in my life, or the 20 years that followed from that moment. If I had another partner, would I do differently? Feel different? I doubt that such photos are displayed in the house of my former husband, who has happily remarried.

The picture is of a younger version of me. I recognize that person, but I am no longer her. She is the person – not yet a woman, I would say – who at 24 became a wife, took the name of a man from another country, and moved to that country, where she almost immediately began to struggle against the assigned role of Wife. (In New Zealand in the early 1970s, I was not allowed even my own first name; I was Mrs. John Fraser.)

I have another photo on the bookcase beside my desk, a photo I love, of my daughter and her father. They sit on a low stone wall, in the warm autumn sun of Corsica; she is nine or ten. Her hair is cut short and she is wearing his yellow sweater and my yellow scarf, leaning back against him. Their hands and mouths are identical; their gaze is directed towards the road that we are driving along, not at the camera. Photographed with her father, she looks like him; photographed with me, she looks like her mother.

The picture makes tangible the closeness of their relationship, our triad relationship, and the life that we shared. It is a photo, like those of her and me, that also references the person taking the picture, almost as clearly as a shadow in the frame. The third person, the photographer, is the other parent. When I look through the albums of a 20-year marriage, it seems that after our daughter was born there were hardly any pictures of the two of us, man and woman, husband and wife, together. The story of our marriage became the story of our parenthood. The marriage lasted 20 years; the parenthood continues.

In many ways, we had a good marriage; we lived well together, we were good friends, and we loved our daughter. But the marriage itself became hollow. It looked better from the outside than it felt from the inside. True intimacy subsided. I can tell only my side of the story, but I felt increasingly trapped inside the box we had constructed together. After 20 years, I could not see how the next 20 would be any different, unless we stepped outside the box to see if it could be put together any differently.

From a Diary at the End of Marriage

The domestic me is not the real me. It partly is, but there is a restlessness, a dissonance. Domesticity is also a trap in which there are many ways to procrastinate. Security, comfort, and familiarity are powerful temptations, yoked to sympathy, affection, and reluctance to hurt. I often think of what our friend S. said, the first time he met me; I was in the throes of moving, deep in domestic, organizing, wife mode. He said, "You are a ballplayer out of uniform."

We are housed in the shell of marriage. I hear a discussion about marriage on CBC Radio's *Ideas*, and I instantly recognize the feelings being described and articulated and resolved as I cannot seem to do, the business of struggling to escape from the paradigm. At some level I know what is wrong, but I cannot work through either the emotions or the principles, the ideas of value and self-worth. Being a good mother and wife; being true to myself. Authenticity. Responsibility. Seeking wholeness within, not just in conjunction with a man. Why do so many women I talk to about this crave solitude and independence?

I am on a beach with great waves crashing over me, and I cannot get to my feet; I am on the floor, curled up, under a blanket, wanting to become invisible.

Men don't leave. Or so says my sister, unless they have somewhere to go. Men rarely leave a marriage unless they are involved in a new relationship. Marriage is said to suit men better than women; statistically, married men are happier and healthier than any other group of adults. This is not a hard and fast rule, but it speaks to the experience of a significant number of Canadian women who came of age in or since the 1960s. Some of these women were actively involved in the movements for change that exploded – there is no other word for it – in Canada in the '60s, '70s, and '80s: the peace movement, campaigns for birth control and against violence, for abortion rights, pay equity, and constitutional rights. They came and went as participants in the Royal Commission on the Status of Women, the Fédération des femmes du Québec, the National Action Committee on the Status of Women, and a range of provincial and local radical or socialist feminist groups. They went to rallies with babies slung on their backs. They threw away the progression of life stages that had governed the lives of women in decades previous: school, work, marriage, child-bearing, child-rearing, retirement.

They did everything at once, or tried to, and in addition engaged in multiple forms of political and social activism. In this context, the institution of marriage and the reality of married life came under close public scrutiny and merciless personal re-evaluation.

June

"So if I'm gonna be a wild woman, I might as well be one. But I think you've got to take care of yourself too. There's ways of doing that without getting yourself hurt."

June, a retired psychiatric nurse, lives in an apartment at the back of a small, old-fashioned house in a subdivision of St. John's. She is short, wiry, with curly salt-and-pepper hair, glasses, and a hearing aid. In her mid-60s, a recovering alcoholic, she spoke freely about her well-disguised dance with drink. June is lively; she has a light that comes from within. She radiates fortitude and energy, even though we sat without moving for two hours.

"We were married 27 years when I just left the house. I knew I had to get out. I had left twice before, and he kept chasing me and begging me to come back. He just couldn't give me the space, you know? Friends would come and try to talk me into leaving, and my daughter said, Mom, you don't want to go back there, Dad is not going to change. I went back, but I didn't stay. I just didn't feel safe.

"One morning, I went out to the country house and sat there for six hours and listened to my inner spirit, my inner wisdom. I went home that day and I just told him. I said, I can't do this any more. I'd like you to go. But I went.

"He was really devastated and really angry and really broken up. But I could remember about eight years before, he had been on a binge, drinking and whatever, out with the boys. And I said to him then, Jim, someday you're gonna be sorry for this. I'm not gonna be able to live like this the rest of my life. And he said,

Well, I don't know where you'd find anything better out there.

"When you're in it, I don't think you even know how bad it is. You do the things you're supposed to do. You got children, you got laundry, you got meals, you got homework and groceries. I did all of that and stuffed away a lot of feelings. Then I drank to cope with it.

"But you know why I really left? He wasn't able to acknowledge my suffering. He was always sorry and he tried to make amends, and he would buy me things, and he would do nice things around the house, but he didn't want to talk about the past. He never got honest with me. I found out that he has a daughter walking around St. John's who would have been born 13 years before we split up. No wonder I didn't feel safe. And he spent a lot of time accusing me of having affairs. Every time I went on a trip for work, he'd say when I came back, Who did you screw today? It was just sick, and I was sick to be there.

"We managed to have an amiable divorce. We didn't have to go to court, and we split up our belongings. I wanted out so bad that I didn't fight for anything. I felt like I had been let out of prison. I was ready to fly. I was just ecstatic at having my own place, and my own space and whatever. But it took me about five years to unhook from Jim. My life was good, I loved AA, I was getting sober. I was doing theatre and I stage-managed plays, and I took art courses and painted. But what I found most difficult was: How do you become single again, after 27 years of marriage? What *is* single? I didn't know. I didn't know how to do it. What do you do, how do you date, how do you relate to men?

"I took a freedom trip, a year and a half after we separated. I went off to Mexico. I was 50 that year. My friend went out shopping with me. Now, she said, June, you're going to have a great holiday, you're going to pick up men, and you're going to have a grand time. And she made me buy this gorgeous, bright yellow, 100 percent cotton blazer. I've still got it, and I still wear it. I call it my freedom jacket.

"I packed a bag and went off. First time ever on my own. I was terrified. I did have a friend there, so I made her place my head-quarters in Mexico City. What an awakening! I was just so excited. And I didn't get lost, and I didn't get robbed, and I didn't get kid-napped, and I got picked up by a gigolo. He was only 25, and I was 50. He chased me around the whole day; I couldn't get rid of him. We went through the anthropology museum, and he took off his jacket and put it around my shoulder. Oh, my God, what's going on here? I said, You go now, I'm going to have lunch. Oh, I will buy you lunch, he said. No, you won't buy me lunch. Go. He wanted to come to my hotel room and I said, No, no, we can't do that, and I wouldn't tell him where the hotel room was. He had a girlfriend, but I was his love for the day.

"For two years after I separated from my husband, I focused on getting well, I just wasn't interested. Then I met a really beautiful man in AA who had seven years of sobriety. He was divorced, and I had a relationship with him, on and off, for about three years. He taught me how to be honest. I loved him dearly, and I know that he loved me. It wasn't so much a sexual relationship as a really inti-mate friendship. We went on a holiday together, and that's where we realized our differences. We ran on two different speeds! I'd be up in the morning with my foot out the door, ready to go, and he'd be on his third cup of coffee and third cigarette.

"I really believe that he was in my life at that time to nurture me and take care of me and help me to see reality and not be so impul-sive. Well, they say of alcoholics, and my Type A personality, that if they come to a frozen pond, they will run right out into the middle of it, and probably fall in. That's been the story of my life – head-long into anything and everything, and not a whole lot of caution.

"There was a guy in Belize. That's got to be the most sensuous place I've ever been. He was younger than me, a wildlife guide, and he owned a resort and he was just charming! And very sexual. They are, the men down there. And it threw me off for a while; I had never been approached like that in my life before. You know, let's not fool around! So we had a great time, except I ended up feeling guilty, which was stupid. It's that old Roman Catholicism: sin and suffering, poor woman at the well, either a virgin or a whore. And sometimes I felt like a whore.

"When I met him, he told me he was married but separated. I happened to go up to his resort for a weekend and a swim, and of course, he was my tour guide. It was just like a Crocodile Dundee adventure! Of course we didn't have a whole lot in common to talk about, but boy, he could find every bird in Belize and tell you what it was. So we did a few trips together in the bush and went down south to the jaguar preserve. The second year he was back with his wife and I should have left it, but he was on my doorstep. Finally I went on a last trip with him. I said, Shag it, might as well be hung for a sheep as for a lamb. So we went out for three or four days, and it was the most magnificent time I've ever had.

"I don't look [for a man] any more, it's not an issue in my life right now. But I tell you what I do find about being single is that I miss the couples' world, the social life. Jim and I had a wide circle of friends, most of them were mine, and we had dinner parties, and we'd go visit their country places and they'd come to ours. There was always something going on. I don't have that any more. And I also miss male energy. I don't have to get married. I don't want to look after, I will *never* look after another man as long as I live. A soulmate is what I would want, but – I mean, don't we all? You read about it in books, right? I have lots of male friends, 'cause I'm in AA, and I do have male company when I need it. But I miss the intimacy, and I miss having a buddy.

"And yes, I miss sex. I've always been a very physical kind of person, I touch a lot. I like hugs, and yeah, I do miss sex. So I do it myself. When I get desperate! I used to have fantasies, a fantasy that Sidney Poitier . . . my God, I had him around for a couple of years. But I don't do that any more. I usually try to love my body and treat it well.

"[After my divorce] one of the profound griefs I had was: Where is the family home to be? Where will my children bring their grandchildren? I felt I was destroying this centre, this family communion place, the hearth. I think that's why I really work so hard at being a good grandmother. I take the kids out looking for bugs, and I take them berry-picking, and we do all kinds of marvellous things together. My children are very supportive; they said, Mom, you did the right thing. It worked out fine. Fine! We don't need an eternal home for the grandchildren. Everybody comes here!

"They get a kick out of my adventures now. I guess part of my soul was always adventurous and wanted to see the world. I was up in Labrador for a month in March with my son and his wife and three children. Did a lot of cross-country skiing, and we went dogsledding. My daughter-in-law, she said, Well, I can't ever imagine my mother doing that. She wouldn't even go near those dogs. And I guess that's who I am. I tried to be a lady, and to do the 'right things.' And it just doesn't fit, it's not me."

From a Diary at the End of Marriage

This day seems yet another point of passage, when again I cry and cry. I prepare the list of how we might divide our things and am overcome by sadness. These things are the bits and pieces out of which our nest was made; they are in themselves not much, just things, but it hurts to tear them apart, to put them in separate piles. They are truly greater as a whole than the sum of their parts.

He says how difficult it is to begin again after 20 years, how I am so much part of everything in his life, how he will miss being part of my life. I say I will miss him too. He is often the first person

I think of. He says he thought that we were forever. I say that maybe as a result we took each other for granted.

For a very long time I have thought that we do not bring out the best in one another. I think we are both capable of more, and I do not see that more coming out of our relationship. I can see only the comfortable, familiar ruts of our relationship in the road behind us, and see those ruts asserting themselves forever, and I know that would make neither of us happy.

I have been in one man's boat, a good, solid boat, only occasionally wobbly, for 20 years. I need to get out and be on the island in the middle of the river for a while. I am not ready to get into another man's boat. I also don't understand why I see the boat as his, more than it was ours, or my own.

Louise

"Right now, I'm 'closed for repairs.' When I think of a man, I think there's lots of things I'd like. But then I think – the big word – responsibility. Are you okay? How do you feel? And am I doing this wrong or that wrong? And that's part of the freedom I feel right now. Not having to be responsible for anyone else's happiness."

Louise lives in Kingston, in the front part of a duplex, not far from the lake in one of Kingston's historic neighbourhoods. She is a beautiful, serene woman of 56, with a delicate British Caribbean accent. Once a career diplomat, now a science writer, she was married for 28 years to a Caribbean East Indian. They have two grown children.

It was Louise who first broached the idea of separation. "I went away to do a master's degree in Toronto. I had gone back to school twice, once to do law in my 30s. That was meant to be a launch pad to get me out of the civil service, because I was getting frustrated with the bureaucracy. Then I got this job in a consulting firm. I worked there for 12 years, got fed up with them, and so I decided to go back to school again. I thought, Well, here's the crunch. I now see that we were both in the process of making room in our minds to have a trial period of living without each other and seeing what it felt like.

"I found that two years living away from him was a huge relief in many ways. I mean, I love him to death but . . . And I think he found two years without me was a huge relief too. For some reason we had become a weight on each other. I think that he also experienced a great sense of liberation, not having to worry about me, not having to think about me, and not having to monitor what I was doing. And so when we came back together, it was quite difficult. My children are now 28 and 26. They'd already left home. I came back and was restless and agitated and unsettled, and we just didn't seem to be able to resettle into our old way."

Louise proposed a permanent separation.

"You know, it was a very shocking thing to come to that realization. And especially with no particular reason. I know a lot of people in our circle couldn't understand. And still don't. One friend who knows us quite well said, The two of you are veritable poster children for the institution of marriage. If you don't make it, no one will! Because we are good friends, and I think we wouldn't have been good friends if we had stayed on together. I think we were getting to the stage where we couldn't salvage what was good about it. If we hadn't had the guts to say, This isn't working, we would end up hating one another, because in a sense we were in each other's way.

"I remember my husband was very concerned about what other people would think, and I said, Look. Who cares what they think! It's our recipe to make what we can of it. And I think that's what we've done so far. It's still all quite new ground. Of course the problem comes when someone else steps in between, and it becomes a threesome, and we have experienced that a little bit. Because he's been sort of dipping around with women. So we've been talking about it. His stance is that if they can't swallow me, then they have to go. And I say, I don't think that's realistic, frankly.

"I still think about this a lot, because life is not events or outcomes, it's all process. We're still on very good terms. There was no bitterness or anger. It was just a kind of acceptance that we had grown apart. That we were, at root, quite different. Not racially, but just in our ways of being and our interests. We had come together for a while to do a job, which was raise the kids, and have a life, which we did. It's just that to do the kind of growing that you need to do, you need to separate, otherwise you're thwarting some kind of growth that has been retarded in the other person. I think that worked for both sides.

"I said, I'll go. It wasn't hard, fortunately. And that was the way it worked. We haven't sorted money out or anything. I just can't stomach the money part. People say to me, Oh, you should make him sell the house – because I've been a bit short of money – or, Oh, you should do this, you should do that. And I think, Well, why would I? The investment is being protected. He's looking after it. Actually, he's done some alterations. I think that was him putting his mark on it. And if he sold it, I might go and spend my half. Which frightens me too. But again, if he gets involved with someone else . . . then it gets messy. But we haven't got there yet."

I asked her if she felt guilty about ending the marriage.

"Guilty? No. I should, because I came from a guilty kind of family. My mother's family were all priests in the Caribbean, all Anglican priests, and I was brought up by grandparents who were very into guilt. I've had to fight guilt a lot in my life. I've got really interested in Buddhism in the last couple of years. Guilt does not exist in Buddhism. It's a matter of skill and acting in ways that are skilful, and ways that work well and have the right result instead of ways that are bad. I don't feel guilt now because we both agreed on it. Neither of us would have it any other way. I feel sad that it didn't work out. Because my own parents were separated when I was very young, I had always sworn to myself that this would not happen to me. I would have one of these marriages that would go forever and I really wanted that. And wanted security and stability."

"So what is it you think you want more than security and stability?"

Louise said slowly, "I want to be the person that I'm capable of being. In some ways, marriage, any major partnership, means dwarfing or thwarting some really important parts of yourself. And you can do that for quite a long time, but I think that those parts fight to come through. We had some major differences. I'm a rather reclusive and quiet person, and love to be on my own. I don't like a lot of socializing, which in the Caribbean is an unusual thing. My husband is extremely gregarious and loves company. He was a wonderful companion. He had a lot of good humour, was a wonderful father. Great around the house, a good househusband. He certainly looked after me, I often felt, more than my own family ever did. I sometimes think maybe I was just ready to leave home. It was as if he had fathered me in some ways, and I suddenly felt I could do this on my own."

"What about your sexual connection?"

"It was pretty good, but it had kind of petered out. We found it difficult to re-establish when I came back. By that time I had begun to think separation. But it had not been a bad connection, you know, throughout our life. I think, to be truthful, it was more important to him than it was to me. I don't know how common that is, but it's pretty common among my friends. I think if he had had a choice, he would have had it more often."

"What do you like best about being on your own?"

She smiled, looked around her little room. "Not being beholden to anyone. Just feeling that I can leave the light on all night, read all night, go at my own pace. My husband was a very monitoring kind of person. If I'd drawn the curtains, he'd pull them. If I just put my shoes there, he'd come . . ." She mimes the realignment of shoes.

"No matter how you did it, there was always a better way. And now I can do it according to my own. He's also a very hurry-hurry person. One of my resolutions for myself in my new life is that I do everything slowly, according to my speed. If that means earning less money, so be it."

I said, "The choice you're making is unusual. It's not one that society expects or wants women to make. Do you feel that what you're doing is radical in some way?"

Louise was thoughtful. "I think of it as being something that's allowed by the times we live in. That you can grow together for a while, and when the need for you to be together is not there any more, it's a choice that we can make as human beings. People talk about promises, and I'm a very promise-oriented person, I'm a person who keeps my word. You start to think, Yeah, but you promised that you'd stay with this other person. And I did! And I meant it at the time. But what we also promise is to love, and if love has gone out, that kind of love that keeps you together, then you're not doing it anyway. So I think it's more honest. It's a more honest way to live.

"I look back over my life, and I realize that I was telling myself some lies. I think I knew deep down that we were on different wavelengths or tracks. And that we would, in the end, never be able to be truly ourselves if we stayed together. But I didn't want to know that at certain stages, so I worked incredibly hard to keep it going. I felt we had a successful marriage, actually. I think if one of us had died two years ago, people would have said that was a wonderful marriage. And it was. And I still think I would be the chief mourner at my husband's grave if he died tomorrow. But we were feeling smothered by each other in some strange way. And it would have been dishonest to stay together.

"I was also a workaholic, and I now see that workaholism was related to escape. That's the only way the marriage was probably tolerable – it was for me to forge my identity outside of it, so that the time we spent together was quite limited. I only see these things now, I didn't see them at all then. For example, we often went on separate holidays.

"I think the art of a good marriage is to really put spaces – I always think of typesetting. A page with a lot of print on it is no good. You need white spaces. And I think of the space as white space to set off what's there. There has to be enough white space on the page. And I think that we did that very well. But I drove myself into the ground with the work. And I realize that in fact, that was not . . ." She paused.

I said, "Productive white space."

"Yes. I got rewards, I got recognition, but I knew all the time that that wasn't what I wanted either. I'm not an ambitious person. I'm a very interior sort of person."

"But," I said, "the end of a marriage forces confrontation. Society says, Stay together. Something's wrong with you if you end a marriage. You're supposed to ride into the sunset together. That's the track people get on in marriage. Do you think it takes courage to get off?"

Louise replied, "No. Every time anyone says the word 'courage' – well, my idea of courage is feeling really frightened, and being really brave. It's not courage. It would be courage to stay in it. To stay and suffocate yourself, which would take a lot more energy and effort in the long run. To live a front for other people's sake.

"He had a major operation this July, and I was the one who was around. I know that if I got really ill, he'd probably do something similar. But the relationship has been considerably enriched by being away: we're not cross with each other any more. So we can really talk."

I thought about the marriages of other friends, and women I have met across the country. "A lot of people cannot imagine that," I said. "They cannot get to that point. Some couples try to create a more flexible relationship, for example, through unconventional living arrangements. He lives upstairs and she lives downstairs. Some way of saying, Can we do it differently? People can't imagine how to do it differently. So the only route is divorce."

Louise said, "It's very experimental. I mean, I feel that we have saved a lot. We have salvaged the best parts of our marriage in many ways. Our ability to talk and converse, our shared family, we've saved all that stuff. But we don't have to live in the house with one another. And it's still an open book – I mean, whether he will get involved in another relationship or I will. He said to me the other night, You know, no one will ever know you as well as I know you. And no one will ever know me as well as you know me. No matter how long we live. We've moved countries together, we've had kids, we've been different places, we've known a wash of friends, and we've shared just such a lot. Just to throw all that out – I don't know how people can do it!"

She paused for a moment. "I'm making this sound easy, but it was hard as hell. Not that I had any misgivings about it, I knew it was right. But trying to start a new business, and trying to start a new life, and gain a new perception of myself. I didn't have a home, I didn't have a job, I didn't have a marriage. I was very depressed, and I had a very difficult time. I'd just come off two years of doing a degree which exercised all my brain cells to the ultimate. So I was highly primed. And yet, it was all too much. I couldn't launch a business and get through the untangling of this relationship at the same time. I knew it was right, but it was really difficult."

"I'm glad you said that, because even though you can make the decision, it takes a very long time to work itself through your system. And to feel –"

Louise finished, "Whole again. I'm just beginning to feel that now. It's been two years. You know you're making yourself over. You're finding who you are. You don't have any idea. You just have a sense that whatever it was, it wasn't right. I'm articulating it better than I was able to do at the time because I've had time to think it through."

Louise sat very still, spoke quietly, without rancour or edge, expressing complex emotions with gratifying clarity. I felt as if I were gazing into a mirror.

From a Letter Two Years After Separation

I am going tomorrow to the lawyer's office to "be served" with the petition for our divorce. I feel like a criminal; the person who called me could not even bring herself to say the word "divorce" on the phone, so why should I feel easy?

I am afraid to go; I don't want to go and in fact have already cancelled one appointment. When I got off the phone, I went straight home and cried and cried. It was exactly the same kind of crying I did just over two years ago when we began our separation. All of these things are fresh and bright and hard in my memory, it seems.

When I think over the past two years about my moments of emotional intensity, they are always to do with our marriage. The times when I crash into crying are all about you. Against these feelings I put the actions of both of us – choosing and settling into very different houses and getting on with separate lives and relationships and careers.

I see our marriage as a big old wooden house that has been emptied of furniture. It is still a place where the rooms shine with light in spinning trails of dust and there are echoes of voices and of music. (Have you heard Callas singing in *Philadelphia*? I could not help but think of you then.)

Some days I feel like a widow; I know that's silly but that somehow describes my emotional state and lack of interest in anyone. And the mourning that seems to go on and on.

CHAPTER 6

Crosshanded: Women Alone Through Desertion or Death

At midsummer, I was tucked into a cabin on Middle Battery Road in St. John's, with a view of the harbour through a chain-link fence and a wild cat for company. Higgledy-piggledy wooden box houses, some brightly painted, are stacked on the hillside. I took a glorious walk up to Signal Hill, through clover and roses and blue-berries, past dark birds nesting in crevices, offering glimpses of pounding water on rocks and distant capes. I was immediately at home, reluctant to stir for a week.

I went to a folk festival in the park to hear Anita Best: big woman, big voice, lots of toe-tapping white-haired people, more plain folk than hippies. Best's a cappella CD is titled *crosshanded*, which is a fishing term for working alone, literally managing nets and lines single-handed, without a mate.

I asked her if this might be the Newfoundland equivalent of "solitaire," and she, part of a long tradition in Newfoundland com-munities of stalwart, free-spirited single women, agreed amicably to this interpretation.

Not all women choose to be single. Not all women who divorce do so with a sense of purpose – and death makes widows out of wives. For some women, desertion, divorce, or widowhood brings with it freedom, release, and the chance to remake themselves. For others, the transformation is a terrible and unexpected shock.

The immediate aftermath of divorce is almost always bitter and painful, even when both parties intend otherwise. In legal terms, divorces are "no-fault"; in personal terms, blame is irresistible, and the woman still bears the burden of guilt when marriage ends, even when she is abandoned for another woman. It is not helpful to hear "You'll be better off without him," however true, if you believe in the institution of marriage. Every divorced woman I know regrets the failure of her marriage for a very long time and can name, in admiration more than envy, the two or three couples whose relationship she regards as ideal.

The older a woman is when she becomes single, the less likely she is to remarry. As time passes, many women come to prefer their independence and their solitude and find it increasingly difficult to cohabit, especially if they can afford to do otherwise. They still desire companionship and intimacy but, unless there are obvious advantages, they hesitate before combining households, bank accounts, and retirement savings. In cases of sudden rupture and divorce, some women say they have merely arrived sooner at the state of widowhood than their contemporaries.

Leah

"I was so devastated that the only thing I could do to cope was just to stay alone – and use the house as the excuse. My mortgage payments are too high, I can't afford to go out. I just secluded myself for a number of years."

Leah is 47, blonde, and thin. She wears her hair in a braid and sports large-framed red glasses. She works with children with

AIDS in Halifax, a competent and confident professional. Her sorrow is not visible.

"I am single, not by choice. I was with a man for 15 years. We started living together when I was 25. I made a decision not to have children of my own. I made that decision and had it taken care of physically, without consulting him. That was my choice. I had a pretty deprived childhood, and I wasn't sufficiently together in my head to be a good parent. My partner and I agreed we could look at adoption as an alternative, if we so thought, as the years went by. But it became apparent to me that that wasn't going to be an option either.

"We were both all over the place. My partner was a physician and I'm a registered nurse. I went over to West Africa for two years with CUSO as a midwife and ran a clinic there with just nurses. Fabulous job. I got the feeling there was a little bit of this itch happening, that Josh wanted to have his own family. So when I went to England and to Africa, I said, If you find someone else, that's fine. Both times it seemed that the decision [was] to stay together. So that's what we did.

"We [took a trip] around the world. And it was really a fabulous trip, at least I thought it was. Maybe his opinion was different. We came home and we bought a house in the spring of 1990, and in late summer 1991, he said to me that he was going to leave.

"I was pretty blown away . . . I was left with the house and 15 years of memories. I thought we were going to live into our old age together. He subsequently got married, and now he has two children. Yeah, he moved pretty fast. And I'm pretty bitter, to say the least. I'm just living alone with this house, which I didn't want to leave. I handle the mortgage on my own, which is hard as a single woman. I didn't want to have anyone else living in the house for a while, because I wanted to wallow on my own."

"During the time you were together, were you building your life as a couple, as a partnership?"

Leah said slowly, "We were together, but we had our own lives. I had my friends, and I went out on my own, as he did. We were always going out on our own, and then coming back together.

"We also had a few relationships outside of our coupledom, particularly when I went to England and Africa, because that was the whole point of it. And Josh, being the kind of man that he was, had women falling all over him. But when we were together we were very together. It was what I considered – at the time – a very healthy, interesting, growing relationship." A rueful smile.

"It sounds like the kind of relationship a lot of women would consider ideal. And yet it didn't last."

"No. I felt totally abandoned. I felt that it was completely unfair, after 15 years and allowing him opportunities to make that choice. And then after one year of settling in, him saying, This is it. We turned 40, and – what? Did he hit a mid-life crisis? Going to be doing *this* for the rest of my life? Or, *I* want some babies!" Her voice was mocking and tremulous.

I commented, "It's interesting that you're just now dealing with this. That you've carried this for eight years. I know these things take a long time . . ."

She shook her head. "It's really hard to say what I have done. I found it very hard to be in social situations. You just can't go out as a single woman by yourself. It's not done, it's not safe, and it is also very difficult. Just to go to a bar downtown, or to go to a movie. Check out things at the museum, interesting little walks, or go hiking or go camping – you can't do those things alone. Maybe it's just me. To arrive alone, for me, had this incredible stigma attached. Especially in Halifax, which is a small place. It wasn't that people would be saying, Oh, there's Leah, oh, she's alone – but that's what I was thinking and feeling.

"At first everybody was pretty supportive, but that support only went so far. Then I was told, Enough is enough. It's time for you to shut up gabbing and move on with your life. But when you're grieving and going through that sense of loss . . . Maybe it was everything in my childhood that I was grieving for, not just the loss of Josh.

"But you've got to take the time you've got to take. And friends are either going to deal with that or they're not. Most of the time they can't deal with it, because it just gets tiresome. I had to put on such a facade. Such a facade. I would keep those meetings and connections down to a bare minimum.

"I go home every night and I have chips and wine. Chips and wine and Oprah, chips and wine and Rosie, or chips and wine and a book."

Bonnie

"I'm sure I can manage without."

Bonnie is a square-looking woman, tall, in an absurdly pink sweatshirt, with white hair, glasses, an iron jaw and broad shoulders. She is 75, very proud, a service wife. She and her husband, Ted, came to this northern prairie farm to retire in 1983. A son owns the property. Open yard, no fewer than six kids' bikes, a wagon, and a great big old collie dog. A screened-in porch fronts a very simple house, a bungalow with a television aerial. It looks out on a gravel road, a garage with MTV, an aging Impala, and bits of crapped-out machinery. Bleak. And lonely, I would say, staring out that window. It was hard for me to look at that place and see a farm. A sign out by the road says "The Tucker Ranch." There were no signs of a man, no signs of prosperity.

Bonnie has a clipped, brusque way of speaking, economical with words and emotions. "My son? Oh, he's here at the house right now. He's sleeping in the basement. He's home right now, but he's hoping to get back to the oil fields in the next few weeks." Her voice dropped to a whisper, and she told me her son is an alcoholic. He quit his job. He's spoiled. His daughter also lives there most of the time, pretty much cared for by Bonnie.

Her husband left in 1996. "He was leaving more than me. He went to the other kids for a while, then took off for southern Alberta."

"So he just left," I said.

"Yeah," said Bonnie. "Maybe because of my son's drinking too often. It had to be something, but he won't say what. I can't do much on that. I think he's living in a home with a couple. That's the impression I get from my one son that keeps in touch with him. I don't know if there's another woman or not, don't ask me! There were, over the years." She laughed abruptly, more of a bark. "But that's the way life is. He did a lot of time away from home. That was all quite understandable where I'm concerned, because when you're away for six and seven months at a time, you aren't always as faithful as you're supposed to be. I don't care what anyone says.

"But he was a good husband and a good father when he was around. He was good to the kids and never beat them, never beat me – or I'd beat him back. When the kids were small and he was away so much, that was hard. Now that the kids are grown up and I'm on my own, I'm sure I can manage. I've been used to managing."

"Are you quite happy here, by yourself?"

"Oh, yes, it doesn't bother me to live in the country, but I'm not going to stay here. I think next summer will be the last, and then I'm going to move to Fort St. John, where most of the grandchildren are. So I can be with them for a few years. I have 15. I have five children, all boys. And we have four great-grandchildren. All girls."

I wondered if she had ever imagined being alone at this point in her life.

"No, I didn't. But that's something that happens. And where I'm concerned, in life the good Lord never gives you more than he thinks you can handle. I can manage. I've always been very independent. My mother was the same, a very independent person. She lived for years after my dad passed away, finished bringing us kids up in the Dirty Thirties.

"I was in the military for two years. I was a cook in the navy. I quite enjoyed it. I was in Winnipeg, Sydney, Nova Scotia, and Halifax. I liked Ontario. I would like to have settled in around Gananoque and those places. But my husband wanted to come back west because all his family was this way.

"I kind of had a hunch when we came to Alberta that our marriage wouldn't continue. I just had that feeling. I think retirement was hard on him, I really do. He was so used to having everyone do things his way; any place he went, he mostly got to be boss of whatever it was they were doing. He was so used to having people jump when he spoke. And, of course, you get into civilian life and that isn't how things go at all. He's 70 this year, so . . ." She sat very still, almost rigid.

"I think he enjoyed his years in the service, and I thought he was going to enjoy his years out here. Our son had this land and he said to his dad, Well, you always wanted a hobby farm. So my son bought more land and more cows, and we did cows for 10 years. But he took on too many, and I said, That's an awful lot of cows that are going to calve this spring. And it wasn't a good year for calving.

"That sort of finished my husband right there. He didn't want to handle any more dead animals. And then his sister lost a son, and he had a nephew that was really ill in Lethbridge. One thing led to another, and the next thing I knew he had filed for divorce. I heard through the grapevine that he had. And he said in his papers that there was no hope of reconciliation. I said, Fine, if this is how you want it." She sat tall, looked out the window.

"Had he ever discussed reconciliation with you?" I asked.

She laughed again. "He had never discussed divorce! So it was kind of a shock when I found out he'd done it. But as I always said to him, If you want out, say so. Don't try and stay in a relationship that isn't working. Because I wouldn't have stayed myself if I didn't feel happy. I would have picked up my kids and gone. I'm not saying it was all honey and roses, because it wasn't. But it was a good relationship as far as I was concerned. Things went well, the boys did well – until our oldest one started drinking, and I think the problem there was my husband trying to force him to quit. There was just so much animosity between the two of them. And then when his father left, he really went to pieces and really drank for about two years. He's just now straightening around a bit.

"When my husband left, we were quite a bit in debt so I said, I'm staying. I won't move. I can't sign my name to something and not see it through. This is not how I was brought up. You take on a job, you do it. I said to him, Do you intend to come back? And he said, Only time will tell. And I said, Time had better tell pretty soon.

"He took his personal belongings. When somebody who's just going for the winter takes all their personal belongings, you can put two and two together. At least I can. He did come home the first Christmas, but he came on the 24th and left on the 26th, and that told me he didn't intend to come back. He came out in September for about two hours, and nothing done around the place was right to him, so I said, Maybe you'd better go back to Lethbridge. And so he did. And that was the last . . . I saw him last fall in Fort St. John, but he didn't speak, not even hello."

"Do you miss him?" I ask.

"I did at first, but I was so used to him being away. Really and truly, I can't say that I've been too terribly lonesome. There's always been somebody around. There's times I think, Oh, if he was here, I could tell him this and that, but you know, you can't tell him this and that. The last time I talked to him on the phone he talked for two seconds and said goodbye. Maybe he's having a hard time dealing with what he's done, but I can't help that. I didn't apply for a divorce, he did."

"Are you mad at him?"

"No. I don't know why I should be mad at him. He never did anything for me to be mad at him, except to walk out, and he could have discussed it before he did it. When the kids knew that their father had applied for a divorce, they said to me, Did he talk it over with you? And why didn't you tell us? I think they felt a bit resentful, because they thought I was keeping something from them, and they were supposedly grown-up people. And I said, Well, he didn't discuss it with me, so I didn't discuss it with you. And it's going to be over and done with, so stop worrying.

"My parents were both strong people, the type that if you said you were going to do something, you stuck to it. I never would have walked out on the marriage. I don't believe in that. Things mightn't have been great, but they could have been a heck of a lot worse. I was really disgusted with my kids when their marriages broke up, but it wasn't the boys that walked out, it was the girls. If it had been the boys, I would have sent them back. Back there where you're supposed to be."

We both looked out the window. The road was dry and dusty for this time of year. No cars passed. There was silence, inside and out.

Most of the time Bonnie is alone in the house. She cleans up, listens to the radio, cooks for her granddaughter, visits a neighbour, drives into town for a bit of shopping, looks out the window.

Bonnie said she was in good health, except for arthritis. She told her kids she would live until she turned 97. "That's the date I chose. And I'm quite sure the good Lord will let me have it."

"Where do you think you'll be buried?" I asked.

"Here," said Bonnie. "We've got plots in the cemetery, so might as well use them. He's already got his funeral paid for here, and his ashes will be returned and buried in the local cemetery. And that's where I planned to be buried.

"But as I said to the kids, should we be living elsewhere in this country, I don't want my ashes returned here. Bury me where you're close and don't play around. I don't believe in this business of carrying ashes for millions of miles. Although I've always told my kids I want my ashes walked to Manitoba. And I've been told to pray for a west wind so it won't take long to walk there." She laughed again, a short harsh sound.

Helen

"On the weekend I'll be visiting some friends, and one woman will be there who I haven't seen for two years. She was widowed last fall. So I was thinking about what I wanted to say to her. If she needs anything, wants to talk . . . Because when it happened to me there was no one available, no one who had lived through it."

It was a hot simmering summer day in Halifax; I was in the kitchen of a cheerful family house with Helen, an attractive, athletic woman with shiny straight black hair, bangs, and easy, efficient movements. She was widowed at 34; she is now 46, a French teacher at an elementary school. Her husband was killed in a farm accident in the Eastern Townships. One child, a sweet-faced son, drifted around the edges of our conversation.

I asked her, "How old was your son when your husband died? He must have been just born."

"He wasn't even born. The day of the funeral, I remember saying to my brother – he and I are very close – I said, There is something going on. Don't be surprised if . . . And I was right. I'm not a religious person, but I thought, This is something I have to recognize. We had tried for years and years to have a child. And I had decided it wasn't meant to be. And he said, No, we're not accepting that. If my husband could give me any gift . . . Why not before? Why then?" She was crying a little, suddenly, unexpectedly.

"Those feelings don't go away," I commented.

"No, they don't."

"So you came here immediately after your husband died?"

"No, a year or so later. I remember my brother and me talking to Mum, saying it's good to wait for a year. I thought, Logically, yes, I should wait a year and let things settle, and then I'll know where I want to go. Yet at the back of my mind, I knew I would come home. I tried to teach one year in Quebec. I didn't last the year, I hated it. But when I came home I thought, What am I going to do now? Here I am, single, I've got to bring this child up. I knew the most practical career would be teaching, so I said, Okay, here we go again!"

"Have you made a choice to stay single?"

"No. I don't want to be single! Good men are hard to find. Actually my son is saying lately, So Mum, when are you going to find a husband, Mum? Well, David, you just can't go out and find one. David says, Well, why not?"

"How long have you been thinking about it?"

"There was the grieving period when I wouldn't. And then I don't know when I started thinking, All right, here, I'm ready. In winter '92, I started to [take notice]: Oh, there's an individual who looks kind of interesting."

"Have you had any relationships . . ."

"No. None. My friends have sent me on blind dates a couple of times. One was *yech*, and the other one was fine, it's just there was no chemistry there. And then the friend says, Well, there doesn't have to be. Wouldn't you just like a new friend? But I don't want to lead the person on. At the same time, I don't want to stay home all the time."

"Where would you meet men in Halifax?"

"I don't know. Someone says in the yacht club. You have to join, all that business. I need my money . . . Of course, the nightclub stuff, but you have to pay for the sitters. Ah, the career – been through that. Through friends of friends . . . I looked around, and nothing.

"I was married to a French Canadian. Quite honestly, when you're used to a certain flair, and a certain appreciation . . . I mean, I believe in equal rights and all the rest, but having been treated specially by a French man, perhaps I'm spoiled. Someone said to me, If you want to meet really good men, go to Montreal, or Quebec!"

"Do you think you'll stay here?"

"Yes. I'm comfortable. I was born and brought up here. I know how the city works, and I know the support system is out there. My brother and his wife are very supportive. My mum will do anything for me. We'll be here for a few years. But if it weren't for David, I wouldn't be here. I would love to travel. But this is the way of grounding."

"Do you have a feeling, apart from your own needs, about his need for a father? Do you feel that?"

"Definitely, very much so."

"Does he think he needs a father?"

"He would like to have one, yes. He says that. He says he misses his father, and I say, Well, this may seem cold comfort, but you can't miss something you've never seen or tasted. Are you telling me that you would like to have a father? Yes. Okay then."

"Are you unusual here, or do you have friends who are in a similar situation to you? Widowed or . . ."

"Single parents, there are a few around; actually, there are quite a few. But 99 percent of the time, it's a divorce situation. I remember when I became widowed, thinking, Who am I going to talk to?

There is nobody my age. They're all elderlies. We don't see eye to eye on a lot of topics."

"Do you get lonely?"

"Oh, yes! Oh, definitely. Enough's enough. I feel like I've put in time – no, not put in time, I love my son dearly. But I don't know if I have the strength to go another 10 years as a single parent." She scratched at the tabletop, blinking back the tears. "I want, I need somebody to share life with. It's too lonely. I hear myself talk, I hear myself talk to the kids at school, and I'm not a happy camper. Also, maybe it's age or something, looking back and thinking, I've climbed mountains, I've done this, I've done that, enough! I want to enjoy life, but not alone.

"I'm 46 now, and when I'm 50, I'm going down south. I don't care who is coming with me! I'm going! So in that sense, I guess I'm looking into the future. But deep down, I don't want to see into the future."

Elaine

"My first thought was, I don't care if he's an invalid or vegetable, don't let him die. But I knew that really, he'd never want to do that, to live like that."

Elaine is tall, striking, classy; she is 80, English born and bred, elegantly dressed, with thick white hair, beautiful skin, and masses of energy and wit. She has weathered two marriages, one child, a whirlwind, make-do life as a governess for badly behaved children, and several tumultuous love affairs with wealthy men.

This is a portion of her life story, beginning about 30 years ago.

"So I haven't got a job – what am I going to do? I'm back to square one. I phoned my cousin in Bermuda and got a job there in a hotel. It was a nightmare of a job, but it was interesting. I was in

charge of the housekeeping. I was supposed to count all these
sheets and pillowcases, and I used to go, One, two three four, two
hundred. Five, six, eight, one thousand. Most of the day, I was
rushing around cleaning up rooms.

"I'd been there only about nine months when they told me that
I was no longer needed. It was a terrible shock. I had nothing to
come home to. I had no money, very little money. But before I left,
the hostess at the hotel did my cards. And a card flipped over, and
she went white. She said, That's a death. You're going to be travelling overseas, over water. You're going to get married again. And
she said, You'll never have to worry about money. Of course that
was a joke.

"So I came back to Canada with absolutely nothing. I didn't
know where to go. Somebody put me up in Toronto. Her husband
arranged for me to have an interview at the Park Plaza, and it was
totally useless. It was November and I had no boots, though I did
have a really good coat and a hat. I was walking down Bloor Street,
and I looked up, and there I saw the agency I'd used when I'd been
looking after children. So up I went.

"It was one of these narrow stairs with linoleum on the floor,
and you got to the top and it was rather gloomy, with a lot of for-
eigners filling out forms. I was helping somebody fill out a form,
and finally this woman came along and asked, What can I do for
you? I said, I'm looking for a job. I have to have somewhere to
sleep, so I was thinking of the Y, or matron in a school. I said, I
don't want to look after other people's children ever again. She
said, I do have something, to look after an elderly gentleman who
has had a fall; he's staying with his sister and wants to go back to
his flat. And I said, God, no, I'm not serving at table or doing anything like that. So she said, No, I don't think it's like that. This is a
family I've known for a long time. Go and see if you can get the
job, and it'll get you over Christmas.

"The following day I arrived at this building and there was a black man at the door. Very nice. He said, Come this way. He took me upstairs, double doors, lovely big apartment. One of the doors opened and there was a nurse. My first thought was, I've got to cook for the nurse.

"Then in the background was this really gorgeous-looking man. He welcomed me and took my coat. The drawing room was huge. I said, I really don't know how to start this interview. Perhaps you'd like to ask me something. He had a clipboard, and he said, My children have got lists of things for me to ask you.

"He said, Are you sure you won't be lonely here? And I said, No, I don't think so. I started there and it was great. His wife had died eight years before. I just looked after him . . .

"He did have a tendency to drink too much. Sometimes I would put a rug over him and leave him sleeping it off, and go to bed. And then it was a question of going to Barbados for the winter, because he had a very bad heart condition. He said, I've got to have somebody with me, you're coming with me. And it was a day when there was a strike and a snowstorm. We had to take a bus to Buffalo and get on this little Barbadian plane in first class, and he drank his way across, and by the time we got over, I had to have help getting him off. And I was cross. I said, This is not good enough, Mr. D., I'm here to help you look after yourself, not to get so drunk. He'd been to the resort before, so they knew him and loved him dearly. A sugarcane place; Princess Margaret used to go there. The staff were all there to greet him. We had cabins alongside each other.

"After lunch he always had a rest, so I used to go back and sit in his cabin, reading, while he rested. We played cribbage every night. I loved him as a person, because he grew on you. I was sitting there one afternoon, reading my book. And he said, Elaine, will you marry me? And I said, Oh, my goodness. I can't marry you, what would the family say? He said, I'm not marrying the family, I want to marry you. I said, Well, let's think about it. And so the relationship changed a bit. I used to go in and have a cuddle with him. I was very nervous, because he had this very bad aneurysm.

"And so we were there for about a month, and when we came home, we both looked fabulous. The following day we had dinner with the sisters, and the eldest sister said, I've got something to show you upstairs. So off I go upstairs into her bedroom. She said, Michael says he wants to marry you. We'd be very proud to have you as a sister-in-law. I do wish you'd marry him. I said, I'll never, never leave him, I promise you. Anyway, then I said yes. We had this lovely marriage and we were very happy.

"But he was always needing to be rushed into hospital. In the summer of '74, he'd just come out of hospital, and we were sitting here, having lunch. And he looked at me and he said, You know, you're a very beautiful woman. I said to him, You're prejudiced. We had a pepper mill that was giving problems. He said, I'm fed up with this. I'm going to get my tools and deal with this. So he went out the door, and the next thing I heard was this terrible crash. I looked up and he was on the floor. And he died. Very quickly.

"We were married two years, two months, and three weeks. I thought, What am I going to do, what am I going to do? He had a little diary, which he'd written in every day when he went to war, in the First World War. So I typed the whole thing so that his sons could look at it and see what a wonderful father they had.

"Then I met this man George. He's five years older than I am. I still see him once or twice a year. But he married somebody else. Absolute swine of a man. He had too many women anyway, but I didn't know that. As a lover, he is the worst, I think, of anyone I've ever known. He is *so* deadly! I don't know how men can be so deadly with all that's written about sex.

"So I have been alone for 25 years. It's dreadful. I don't like it. It's lovely to wake up and know somebody else is breathing in the house. I'd love to have a friend. I'd even like to have a woman friend.

"Which reminds me, I did have a proposition by a friend of mine once, years ago. She said, Why don't we go to bed together? I said, You're joking. She said, No, I'm not. I've never tried it, have you? So I said, No, I haven't. I don't think I really want to. She said, Why not? Anyway, I never did.

"But I'd really love to have a friend to go places with, to do things with. I'm no good on my own, I come much more alive with people. I have had some wonderful affairs in my life. Men that I really remember. Men I wish to forget. And I've treated men badly too. Very badly. I had a rip-roaring affair on the ship going to Pakistan, with the wireless operator. That was quite fun . . ."

I have watched Elaine run a dinner party with what seems a carefree dottiness but is in fact precision and perfection. She draws friends of all ages and is herself ageless. A brush with breast cancer barely slowed her pace one summer. When she walks into a room she commands attention. She creates a home for whoever visits and draws other people into her rituals of care and generosity. She is quite simply one of the funniest, smartest, and most beautiful women I have known.

Grace

One of the most contented single women I met lives a short walk from the shore on the northeastern coast of Newfoundland. Grace is tiny, barely five feet tall. Very short, dark red hair. She is spry and quick moving. At 55 she lives with two grown sons, two dogs, and six cats. She was wearing blue rubber boots and a turquoise shirt, and she darted about with amazing energy for someone who says she's lazy. She loves to bird-watch and would garden constantly if she could. "I loves to fish too," she said. "Spring comes and I gets myself a pole, puts on my boots, and down I go in the car to the pond behind the house."

Grace played in a bar band for 10 years, "me and six guys."
She reads everything and anything, borrows books, never buys
them. The only writer she can't abide is John Updike.

Grace has lived in this village most of her life, and her family
has been there since the early 1800s. "I was born 200 feet down the
road in the house that my mother lives in. I went to school here,
graduated from high school. Then I went into nursing, which I
didn't like. Left after six months. Then I bummed around, working
in restaurants, working in a hotel making beds, washing dishes.
Then I went to secretarial school. I worked again in a hospital for
nine years, and during that course of time I had a son, Jonathon.

"I wasn't married. I kept him myself until he was a year old. I
don't think it was that unusual around here. I don't know of any
babies that were ever given up for adoption. There was lots of us in
my generation, right? But I had my job, and I had an apartment,
and I had my own car, and I was playing on the road, in the band.
So I could afford to keep him.

"But I didn't want a child growing up in Gander, which was
your typical suburbia. Houses stuck together and just a babysitter
looking after him. So a job came open here, and I took it. It wasn't
as much money, but we moved back home with Ma, and she
looked after him while I was working. It worked out fine.

"When Jon was seven, I met my husband. I was on the beach
one day, a bunch of us, suntanning, and this gorgeous person
walked down the beach. I turned to one of the girls and I said, See
the boy coming down the beach here? Well, I'm going to marry
him. Go on, she said, you fool. And I did! He'd been working in
Montreal, got burned out, came home with a guitar and a knap-
sack. He wrote poetry, he wrote songs, he sang, he played. Read a
lot. Loved music. I moved in with him two weeks to the day after.
So it was real quick.

"We told Jon we were all going to see a movie. We picked up
two friends, and when we got to Gander, we told them we were

getting married. We rented one room at the Holiday Inn for all of us. The next morning we got married, and came back and told people we got married, and I went home and cooked supper. And that was it. We were married for five years, and then he died. And I never bothered with anybody else."

Grace's husband was killed in an accident at sea in the 1980s. Their son, Alex, was five at the time. She has been "single and celibate for 17 years." She laughed and lit a cigarette. "By choice?" I asked. "By choice," she said firmly and then, thinking about it, added, "I don't know why. Maybe I don't want to get involved in a relationship that fits, that's that close. That intimate. I got my male friends. They're dear, and the life to me, but I would never think of sleeping with them, or they with me. But other than that, I think it's just the bother, the hassle of an intimate relationship. I'm quite fine on me own, right? I enjoy being alone."

Grace used insurance money to build her own house, a bright, neat bungalow with generous decks, surrounded by expansive, colourful gardens. She took me for a ceremonial stroll around her garden, which hugs the house and sprawls back into the woods. "I have an annuity. So I've never had to work, though if I wanted more money I suppose I could, but I'm too lazy for that. I'd rather make do with what I got."

"What do you do with your days?" I asked.

"First thing, if it's warm enough, I got to walk around the garden. Check everything. Then I'll come in and I'll feed all my animals. My six cats and two dogs. I get them all organized. And I takes about a half-hour to whisk through the housework. And then my day is mine. 'Cause I don't have to cook any more. I got no time to cook. Plums and bananas and grapes and yogourt is my main diet. I spend the rest of the time visiting with friends, or reading, or listening to music. Or playing music or berry-picking or walking the dogs in the wintertime. When the ponds are all frozen, there's a trail that goes down behind the house, and I can go for miles and miles in the woods. Pack a lunch, Thermos of hot coffee, have lunch, come home again. In the evening I takes them for a walk on the beach. It's a gorgeous beach.

"Other than that, I see my mom every day, twice, three times a day. She's an old-fashioned type, got to cook a meal every day. She says she can't cook for one person, so it works out grand for me. And Jane cooks for me, and Andy and Rosie cooks for me. They got a meal on, and they got enough to spare, and they'll call and say, Come on in, we've got some fish chowder for supper. So I don't have to dress sharply, and I just drop me garden rake and go on, and that's it."

"Are you unusual? Are there lots of women here like you?" I asked.

She laughed. "There's lots of single women, but I don't think they're like me. I got friends from 15 to 50, I can relate to anybody, from 12 years on. Babies and small youngsters I'm not all that great at, eh? No, when I look at some of the girls that are married around here, that I went to school with, I can't believe that I'm even the same generation. In my mind, I'm not a day over 25. Fifty-five is just a number to me. It means I've got less days left, but other than that, it don't mean a thing. No.

"I like my own company. But if I get lonely, it's usually for my family. I wish my boys were home, because it's so quiet. There's no music blaring and there's no doors slamming, and people coming and going. They comes home every weekend. And the basement door is going, and the top door's going, and the driveway is full of cars. I love that. The louder the damn music, the better I likes it, and it don't matter what they listen to."

"What did you imagine for yourself? When you were a girl?"

"Well," said Grace, "I always wanted to play in a band, and I did. I always wanted to marry a guy that I really loved, and I did. Because I saw a lot of girls around here getting pregnant and getting married just because they were pregnant. Or from force of habit from going out with somebody for 12 years. I never imagined that I would have my own house, which was probably what I would have really liked, but thought that I never would have. Now I have my own house and as many animals as I wanted. I never thought that I'd have kids. I was footloose and fancy free! I found it a bit hard to be married, but once I got the knack of it, it was easy."

"Do you still miss him?"

"No. That's another life. Somebody else's memories, almost like it didn't happen to me. I don't remember much about it. I probably was in shock, and trying to raise youngsters and everything else, right? I remember knowing with certainty that he was dead. They never did find his body. And his family were all around me, and my family and everybody came to visit every day for months. And they wouldn't let me sit still.

"But our friends were all couples. And for a while I used to feel really strange, because I'd go somewhere and I'd be the only one without a companion. But when I moved here I started out in my own manner, doing my own entertainment. I invited singles, and couples and aunts and uncles and grandparents and youngsters, whoever felt like coming, and we had a party. And now I'd say my closest friends are married couples. But they are like me. They're still young. They can still party all night long."

"Is there anything you would have done differently in your life?"

She slowly ground out her cigarette. "Oh, my. I probably shouldn't have got married. I'd say I should have kept on being single. Now I had a happy marriage, but I found that I'm happier single than I was married. I'm too independent. I don't want to compromise. I'm very outspoken. I sometimes think I want something else, but it's not a man. No, definitely not a man. I'd like to travel with a companion, a male, but somebody

I'm comfortable with. That I don't have to sleep with, or make excuses for not sleeping with, right? That sort of thing."

"And you're happy sleeping alone every night?"

Grace smiled, glancing out to the porch where her two big bulldogs were watching our every move. "Oh, yes. Two dogs. One on either side of me. Oh, yes."

The Condo Queens of Edmonton

The month is April; it is cool and raining. Spring has yet to penetrate the city. It is evening, after an early dinner. Five women friends and I sit around a coffee table, drinking wine. Like those of many single women, their friendships cross generations and circumstances. Two have never been married, two are divorced, one is widowed, and several have children.

All the women but one live in this condominium complex. It is a low-rise, rambling development similar to those that have erupted like rashes on the fringes of almost all prairie cities. When this complex came on the market five years ago, the model suite was decorated with an eye to the male purchaser, all black leather furniture and dark striped sheets in hearty colours like navy and burgundy. But most of the condo owners in this building are single women. The price and the timing were right for them.

The colours in this unit are pink and green. The guest bathroom is madly feminine, overflowing with fragrant piles of soaps and matching towels. The living room has deep flowered chairs and sofas, ruffled curtains, piles of books. The cat, Lulu, has pride of place in the household. Her demands have become more imperious and eccentric with age, and her owner dotes, unabashedly. The main bedroom is regal, rich dark red and green with matching wallpaper, curtains, and bedspread, ornate bronze candle holders, and a large walk-in closet and dressing room. This is the living space of Connie, an emphatically, exuberantly single professional woman.

The women are connected through her. They have travelled together and enjoy affectionate and supportive friendships. There are minor rivalries; these are people who have become friends in mid-life, and they bring with them very different histories. They don't know all of one another's secrets.

Ann is in her early 50s and speaks with a Québécois accent. She is vivacious, sharp-witted, with a smoky, sexy laugh. She works for a menswear designer.

ANN: Why am I single? I'm single because I chose to be. I had a very happy marriage, but things turned around. I couldn't live in a marriage where you can't trust and you can't respect and you aren't secure with the other person. That's not a marriage. I have a good relationship with him now, because of our youngest daughter, who's handicapped. We have to communicate. We were married for 29 years. It's about six years that we've been separated. It's really hard to go on your own. The biggest thing when you're divorced is that it's not like a death; there's no closure. He's still there, still very much part of the family, with the children. So like it or not, you have to be in touch. He even attends the same church. A lot of times we sit in the same pew at either end, or in front or behind each other. It's rough, it's really hard. I've had him for Christmas and Easter, and the kids love it. They think this is just wonderful. [If] I get into another relationship, I'll change it, because I know they could never be in the same room together, just like I would never want to be in the same room with his new partner.

DEBORAH: My situation is different. I was married for 29 years, and my husband passed away, so I didn't choose to be single. We had a very good relationship, and a very good marriage. A good family life, and then I found myself on my own.

Deborah is discreet about her age; she is around 60. Tall with elegant posture, hair well coiffed, graceful even when seated. She speaks in a soft, low voice, measured tones, dresses tastefully, probably never completely casually. She is an accounts payroll receptionist.

DEBORAH: I've been alone six years. I have two children and three grandchildren. My husband died of a heart attack. It was a big shock after being married for close to 30 years and doing things together. Not that we were together all the time because he was away . . . I was a grass widow half the time, you know, sales and business. But we travelled together, and what I find now is that it's hard travelling. Not that I don't have fun now when I go with my girlfriends, but it's just not the same.

MBF: Do you think you're single forever?

DEBORAH: No, I don't think so. It took me a while, but I've been going out, I meet different people. But I think I'm very fussy. I don't like to be by myself all the time, so I can't see myself living on my own, but who knows? As the years go on, I might not want anybody in my life . . . I went back to work and I like my independence, because I can do what I want, and I can say no, yes, or close the door and be quiet, have no one over . . .

MBF: Are you still living in the same house, in the same situation?

DEBORAH: No, I moved out. That's one thing I did that was good. About a year after, I sold the house, had a garage sale, and went to work. I think that was the best thing I could have done, because I've seen other women in the same situation, and they really get into a rut. I have gone out and met new friends, even the girls that are here, they're all new people. A few of my old friends will invite me, but the wives will treat me as a threat. Because the guys, my husband's friends, they're very good to me, and you can just see their wives . . .

MBF: Do you think they're actively interested in you, the husbands?

DEBORAH: You don't know. I don't think so.

Connie is 45, full of zest and warmth. Not tall, but abundant, large-bosomed – "zaftig" is the word that comes to mind. She is a lawyer in a downtown firm. Very bright, big personality, and a small, sweet voice.

CONNIE: Sometimes I think I'm single by choice, and sometimes I think it's what fate has dealt me. I've met probably three guys over the last 25 years with whom I would have liked a long-term relationship. Unfortunately, two of them were gay! And the third one – I was very young, early 20s, and it just didn't happen.

I see a lot of women in relationships where they're very controlled, and I have a big fear of that, someone telling me what to do, having to be accountable for my time, my energy, my money, my self.

I have a good life, I have good friends, I'm busy, I don't want for very much. I date, so I certainly have men in my life, and sometimes I think, Gee, it would be really nice, if I want to go to a show, or if there's an event coming up, that I had someone to go with. Like on the weekend: I went to a house party and I was the only single person there. I felt odd, not that I wanted any of the guys that were there – that was really scary! But it was – the extra chair, because I'm the fifth wheel. That was the first time in a long time that I felt that way. I make a point of not staying late at events, so there's never any idea I'm staying to pick up a man.

I don't think I will ever get married. I don't feel that I've got this void in my life that needs to be filled. Even as a little kid, I knew I never wanted kids, so that has never been an issue for me.

The Condo Queens of Edmonton

From the time I was 18 until I was 29, I worked, just keeping body and soul together. My 30s were spent at university. A big chunk of my life was concentrated on that, so now I've got a good job, I've got an income, I've been able to purchase this condo. Now I'm really starting to live. But, gosh, I'm 45 now, not 25 or even 30. There's a big difference. And I'm pretty set in my ways as to what I expect. Like, I will *not* be with a man for the sake of being with a man. I'd rather be alone than do that. That was something I saw on the weekend with one couple. She had met him a few months ago, and she was lonely so she married him, and everyone is – *Ewww*, recoiling in horror. And I don't ever want to be seen like that.

Maggie is the youngest woman in the group at 39, a freelance designer, slim, quiet-spoken, lots of curly red hair and granny glasses, a crocheted hat, bohemian style, contained, reflective.

MAGGIE: I don't know that I would say I was single by choice, or that it's just the way things have worked out. I remember very clearly when I was about 16, promising myself I would not get married until I had established myself in some kind of career. Really from my teens and into my early 20s and even into my 30s, I was very focused on building my life, making it something that stands alone, as opposed to just half of a couple. I dated all through my 20s but never lived with anybody. I've been in a relationship about a year now that has, I guess, the potential to become serious. Whether that will evolve into a marriage, or into a living-together scenario . . . I've always really liked the idea of partnership. Homosexual couples refer to someone as their partner. I think ideally that's what it should be; it should be a partnership.
MBF: You haven't felt the hormonal drive for children at any point?
MAGGIE: No, not really. If the man I'm involved with were to say tomorrow, I really think we should have some kids, I'd probably do

it. You know, he has two cats . . . We treat them like our children.
So it's there, but it's deflected. I have three nieces, and I adore them,
and enjoy spending time with them, but if it doesn't happen, I think
there are other things that would fill the gap. Work is a very big
part of my life, and probably in this relationship the biggest thing
I've had to compromise is the amount of time I spend at work.

Barb is petite, comfortable-looking, dark-haired, thoughtful, probably mid-50s. More reserved than her friends at first, she gradually
warms to the discussion. She is a postal worker.

BARB: I was married for 18 years, and there were some real good
years which I look back at, and I'm really happy that I did have some
married life there. But sometimes there's circumstances that . . .
people just don't discuss why they split up. I have a daughter who is
mentally handicapped, and we were having a hard time with that.
Right now we're good friends, we handle her illness really well.

The breakup was hard, but as time went on, [my situation] got
easier. Then I got to like it, and actually I've gotten to like it a lot.
I like my independence. I'm not saying that if the right fellow
came along, that maybe one day it wouldn't happen again. I've
had one relationship [since my marriage ended]. But maybe not,
and I'm certainly not going to sit back and worry about it. I'm
really quite happy.

ANN: The relationship I had was with an Italian, and oh, my God,
they're nice. It was through a personal ad thing. We hit it off right
away. We were together for three and a half years. We never lived
together, but we were always together. But it came to a dead end.
He thought I was spending too much time with my kids, and he
didn't want to share. I had to choose between him and my kids,
and that's not fair. But I miss him. God in heaven, if he appeared at
my door I'd let him in, I really would!

Connie brings out a mammoth cake on a glass platter, a dark, sweet cake smothered in a thick white icing, along with pretty china plates, silver dessert forks, and cloth napkins. She cuts and serves.

ANN: Oh, my God, and I'm trying to lose weight.
CONNIE: You know something? This cake has no fat in it. The icing does but the cake itself doesn't, because it's made with crushed pineapple. It calls for *no* fat at all.
ANN: And no butter?
CONNIE: No butter, no fat, no nothing in the cake part. That's why I made it for you girls.
MBF: How do men come into your lives? How do you meet men to date?
ANN: I joined telepersonals, and I think it's great. I don't like going to bars. I don't like going to dance places; to me, that's a meat market. Sure, a lot of people say they go there to dance, but the men go there for other reasons. I never want to meet a person in a situation like that.

With telepersonals you are in control. You put your own ad in. The men have to activate it. They have to pay to get access. I've gotten a lot of calls. And just by talking on the phone, you can tell if you want to meet them or not.
CONNIE: Well, *I* can tell if you want to meet them.
ANN: I have Connie come over, honest to God, and she listens to the messages. I would say 99 percent of the time she's right. She says, He's an alcoholic, he's American, he's this, he's that. I usually meet them at a coffee shop or for a glass of wine in my area. I'm in my neighbourhood, I feel secure. I can honestly say I've met 50 or 60 men, and maybe there were two complete duds, idiots.
MBF: Over what time period, 50 or 60 men?
ANN: I would say in less than two years.
MBF: This sounds like a full-time job!

ANN: Yes, it is. Sometimes I'm meeting three or four a week. One day I had two in one day. At lunch, and the other was supper and a show; I couldn't believe it!

MBF: Have any of these developed into something other than one meeting?

ANN: There was one guy. I was taking golf lessons from him. Not bad, very successful. But it just wasn't there.

MBF: In those situations, how long would it be before you would consider going to bed with somebody?

ANN: It depends. Everybody says you have to have at least 36 hours of conversation before you go to bed with somebody.

MBF: Standing up – 36 hours of conversation standing up! Where does that rule come from?

ANN: Connie made it up.

CONNIE: I didn't make it up. I got it out of that book, *The Rules*. It was on *Oprah* or something. I thought it was a fairly decent rule.

ANN: But it depends. If you're on holidays and you've got four hours dancing – hey, that's okay too. I can't honestly say I never went to bed the first time or the second with a telepersonals guy.

MBF: Connie, do you do the telepersonals?

CONNIE: No, I don't. Not because I think it's not a good idea. Ann's been successful at it, and Cheryl, another friend of ours, too. Part of it is being a lawyer. When you tell someone that's what you are, men can become very intimidated. There's a lot of assumptions about female lawyers, like you're going to bust his balls, or you must make a lot of money.

For me, there's men I've met through friends, through politics, although I have to admit that my political party has the largest number of ineffectual males on the face of the earth. I have met some men through work and some at the college. I used to go to the aquafitness classes there. I can't say I have trouble meeting men, but I have trouble keeping men.

ANN: She can talk to anybody and everybody.

CONNIE: Sometimes I think men are intimidated by women who are very self-confident. I'd like to think the reason I'm single is because I'm so bright. But there's a lot of bright women out there who are in good relationships.

ANN: Most men just like stupidity and big tits, and that's it.

CONNIE: Well, I've got the big tits part, but you're right. A very good friend of mine finished high school at 16, went to university, majored in languages, won a silver medal for sciences. Yet when I would see her with her husband, I didn't recognize her. Who was this clinging, dopey, eye-batting, silly girl? I refuse to do that. Maggie, you must run into that, because you're bright.

MAGGIE: I'm just trying to think – how bright am I? I think men have difficulty with the combination of bright and assertive. I sometimes wonder if opposites do attract. I think bright women tend to attract men that are control-oriented because it's a big challenge. You know, I'll wrestle this one to the ground, I'll break her spirit.

ANN: We listen to CBC, and that scares people.

MBF: It scares men that you listen to CBC?

ANN: I put that on my profile. I thought, I'll weed you suckers out right off the bat. You wouldn't believe how many comments I get.

MBF: When you put an ad in the telepersonals, do you give your age?

ANN: Nope. I always say early 50s.

MBF: And what age are the men who respond?

ANN: I've had some in their 40s that want older women.

CONNIE: 'Cause we're the best lovers!

MBF: What about celibacy?

CONNIE: As an option?

MBF: Or as a choice. I've been reading a book about celibacy. The author says that she has now chosen celibacy, and she's very comfortable with that.

CONNIE: So obviously she's not dating. When I hear that someone has "chosen" celibacy, I have to wonder . . .

MBF: But if you're not in a long-term relationship, what do you do about sex?

CONNIE: Well, I've always got my old friend Edward there in the background . . .

ANN: You're so bad.

MAGGIE: For women it's different than it is for men. We can make that choice and live with it. Whereas I don't know how guys do . . .

CONNIE: They don't, they masturbate in the shower.

DEBORAH: Thank you for sharing!

ANN: For women, once you're not having sex, it becomes less of a need . . .

MBF: A friend in the book business told me that most of the people who buy erotic fiction through the Internet are single women.

CONNIE: That's because they're actually reading. Guys just want to look at the pictures; men are very visual. For women I think sex is more of an intellectual venture; there's a lot more involved than just the physical aspect. "Geez, he's got a nice ass" comes into play as well, but there's more involved than just that physical component.

MAGGIE: It's easier to have imaginary erotic sex out of a book than to actually deal with the reality. To make relationships work takes time and energy.

CONNIE: A lot of time and energy. And you can have a relationship with somebody, it can be very equal, but once sex enters into it, it becomes a whole different ball game. All of a sudden all that self-confidence and security in yourself is gone. It's like, Can I phone him now? Will he think I want to have sex with him now?

MBF: So, unlike in the '60s, when casual sex was something every-body did, would you have casual sex now?

BARB: No, I wouldn't.

MAGGIE: No.

MBF: One-night stands?

DEBORAH: I wouldn't.

ANN: Except when we're on holiday!

CONNIE: I think one reason is health. Now I'm a lot more picky, or fussy. It's not a matter of urges.

MAGGIE: If you've been in a long-term relationship, and had a healthy and good sex life, generally speaking, the first time with anybody is usually not great. The 14th or 15th time, you're starting to get there. So you know, going into a one-night thing, that it's –

BARB: Good for him but definitely not for you.

MAGGIE: I met someone one night when I was out with friends and went back to his place for a drink, and things got pretty friendly. I didn't sleep with him because I wanted to see him again.

CONNIE: If I met somebody and I didn't want to see them again, I probably would have sex with them and not think twice about it!

ANN: When you're on holidays, you know damn well you're not going to see him again.

CONNIE: You can use any name you want, it doesn't matter.

MBF: So tell me about the holidays.

ANN: You're in a different mode, you're not in work mode – you're not in Edmonton mode!

CONNIE: It was my first time away on holidays with a bunch of women. We were in a hot place, and it was a foreign country, and everybody was topless, or wearing really tiny Speedos. Sex was everywhere. In the air. Like a summer edition of a magazine, like *Elle*, where you're looking at all these sheer beach cover-up things. And you think, Where the hell would I wear that? But on holidays, that's all we wore. You become a lot more comfortable with your body. We found that most of the men we ran into liked larger women.

ANN: They did. Five guys from Austria – oh, my God. They loved you!

CONNIE: It was nice to have that kind of attention, which I don't get at home. Cuban men and European men, they loved it that I was big, that I had big boobs, a big ass. For them that was very sexual, very sensual.

MBF: So, would you go to bed with these guys?

CONNIE: I would have done a couple of those Austrians . . . It was interesting. But what was really interesting was that the Europeans had come for the black hookers. And they made no bones about that. That's what they were there for: for 10 bucks they could get a whore.

MBF: What about practising safe sex?

ANN: Well, it's very important. But when men get older, unless they're on Viagra, it's pretty hard for them to use contraceptives. It is, because they're just not as erect as they used to be.

MBF: But would you insist on having safe sex?

ANN: I did. Once. Well, it all happens too quickly!

CONNIE: I know we talk about safe sex, like, It's really important, you need a condom. But I also think that if I'm choosing to have sex with somebody I know, as opposed to a one-night stand . . . AIDS crosses every economic and social group, it's not a poor person's disease. But I think, as we get older, and maybe it is a false sense of security, but . . .

BARB: You think, For sure, I'm going to insist on safe sex. But when it comes right down to the nitty-gritty, in the throes of passion, are you going to?

ANN: You think it's the last time you're going to be getting it for a hell of a long time!

CONNIE: And if you're wanting to be in a relationship and the guy's going to say no to condoms, what does that leave you with? Do I want to keep the guy, or am I going to have an issue about the condom? I'll keep the guy. I'm not going to worry about the condom.

MAGGIE: When I got tested, I asked the doctor, What age spans do you see? And she said, Women in their 20s, I see them almost too much. They're always getting tested. But women in their 30s and women your age, I don't see near often enough. And you're the ones who are catching it, [women who] maybe had unsafe sex in the late '8os when AIDS was still a gay disease. Maybe you've been carrying this around for five, seven years. That was enough to scare me into thinking I'm going to be more careful. But I know from my friends, it's a tough one to bring up.

CONNIE: There are some men out there who are responsible and who will talk about it, but if you've met someone you like, you're thinking, What are they going to be thinking if you bring up the subject? Boy, what kind of a wing nut is she, how many guys is she sleeping with if she's this concerned about it?

MAGGIE: Now why are female condoms so offensive?

CONNIE: Well, have you ever seen them?

MAGGIE: I've used them!

ANN: What's it like? I've never seen one.

CONNIE: I'll get you one.

Connie goes into her bedroom, comes back with a package of female condoms, opens it, shakes one out. It is clear plastic, a loose tube with a ring at either end, almost as large as a hotel shower cap. Everyone talks at once.

ANN: So do you put the damn thing in before?

CONNIE: Yes. It took me half an hour the first time.

BARB: How does it work? Like a diaphragm?

CONNIE: Kinda like a diaphragm, but it's very technical, and it's stupid-looking.

DEBORAH: Like a very large condom.

MAGGIE: Like a Baggie, almost. Oh, my God, it's mushy.

CONNIE: This part goes inside, past the pubic bone. This part fits over the outside. It's got spermicide in it. It makes a hell of a noise!

ANN: Why is it so frigging big? Most men aren't that big!

MAGGIE: How does the man feel when you're wearing this? Would he rather you wore this than he wore a condom?

BARB: I've never met a man that didn't complain about condoms.

ANN: So what if they want to do cunnilingus?
CONNIE: You can't with that.
DEBORAH: It seems like a lot of work to me!
MAGGIE: I wouldn't call it a first-date thing.
CONNIE: It does hang out, no question about it.
ANN: They'd look at that and run . . .
DEBORAH: And is it a one-time thing?
CONNIE: Yup. And it's expensive. Three of them were $10 at London Drugs.
BARB: What are they called?
CONNIE: "Reality."
ANN: *This* is Reality?

CHAPTER 7

Sex, Celibacy, and Secrets

From the Diary of a Single Woman

*I*t is 15 months since I have had sex. I go for days, weeks, not even aware of this hollow in my life. I think of my hormones as dust motes lying around in the corners of my body. Then suddenly desire and irritation and heavy erotic dreams. I awaken one morning soaked in sweat, the mirage of a sexual encounter fading even as I grope for it with my eyes shut. I will stop at the sex shop tomorrow and get a vibrator. Or a dildo – there, I've said it.

I walk in after work and peruse the stock, picking up a magenta battery-driven "G-spot" number in silicone, $27 with a hooked lump at the end of it. No, I think, in no way does this remotely interest me. I cannot imagine wanting to shove this large, lifeless thing up inside me.

There is a chart on the wall: cordless versus "remote control," the pros and cons. The display includes big black ones and tiny cream-coloured ones, with what looks like a shell at the base. Some are, to my eye, enormous, tall (standing on their testicle bases like kitchen appliances), and thick. They come in a range of colours.

Others are rigid, expressionless tubes or simply goofy; one looks like a smirking porpoise. Still others are designed for two-way penetration; one of these looks alarmingly like a scorpion attached to a chastity belt. There are prim, rigid poles that don't look like cocks at all; they seem as artificial and detached as – what, zucchini? Carrots? I look at these objects and feel bone dry and very, very alone. It would be as sexy as flossing. I would rather read about dildos than use one.

But several months later on a Sunday afternoon on Queen Street, with purpose, I buy a vibrator, a clear red ribbed thing that looks like a sculpture in raspberry Jell-O. It wobbles, on its own, and vibrates at varying speeds. It runs off two AA batteries housed in a white plastic box attached by a cord to the bottom end. The accompanying instructions warn against using the cord to pull out the vibrator. They suggest using a condom on the vibrator if "it moves" from vagina to anus. It cost $36; the instructions also suggest that the life span of a battery-operated vibrator may be less than that of a plugged-in one, maybe as short as two weeks. In constant use?

The vibrator is more or less life-sized, in my experience. It is only vaguely anatomically correct, unlike others that are perfectly moulded, surely from life, down to circumcised foreskins and squishy, bulbous testicles. I have bought it because, although I have not had sex for 18 months, maybe I will soon, and I worry about closing up, being too tight, the born-again-virgin effect I have experienced before and would prefer not to go through again. I buy apricot kernel massage oil and some books, one a collection of Susie Bright erotic stories and the others somewhat more academic, about celibacy and spiritual sex.

My first encounter with this device is disappointing. I lie down with the books and the oil and some music. The vibrator hums pleasantly on my skin; it lolls, it has a certain weight if a somewhat disconcerting, gummi-baby texture, which the oil helps to obscure. I move it up and down, up and down. It is tepid, not warm; it has no capacity to change shape, to either squeeze its way past the opening or expand to fill the space. The orgasmic sensations induced by the vibrator are insistent, but shallow and mechanical. I feel not that I am making love to my body but that I am conducting an experiment. My imagination is not engaged. It's too much like vacuuming.

People do not talk easily about their solo erotic experiences; this is the stuff of journals and diaries, or covert visits to women's bookstores, or, increasingly, the thrillingly private purchase of erotic literature on the Internet. It is easier to speak of anal sex than of masturbation. There remains some shame to masturbation. It is no longer a sin, but it is a sign of aloneness. To make a study of masturbation, to take it seriously, is to recognize the reality of one's celibacy.

Don't think of it as sex, or lack of sex, one woman said to me (in her late 60s, celibate for 10 years). Think of it as getting pleasure from your own body – no, *with* your own body. The connection between two people having sex and solitary "pleasuring" – as we learn to say – is all in the head, where, for many women, most forms of sexual pleasure happen in any case. But despite the delirious openness now about dildos and cunts, butt-fucking magazines in the village convenience store, and cheerleading sex therapists all over television and radio, women who are alone do not find their sexuality especially well served. Well-written collections of erotic bedtime stories are hard to find. How much fun can it be to get into bed on a Friday night with a banana and a badly produced pornographic video (at the women's bookstore in my neighbourhood, they now come with a wetness rating) unabashedly made for men?

> The sex drive of the normal woman is capable of giving
> her great radiance. It's the force that makes her gentle
> with children; it's a power that can knock the cover off a
> golf ball and take her down an almost perpendicular ski

> trail; it's part of the passion she feels when an animal is
> mistreated; it's in the understanding she can give another
> human being who is desperately lonely . . . Female
> biology can illuminate or desolate – but it can never be
> underestimated. ("Dr. Marion Hilliard Talks to Single
> Women," *Chatelaine*, February 1956)

If the sustaining myth of 1950s popular culture was a *Chatelaine* or *Good Housekeeping* happily-ever-after marriage, the refrain of the first decade of the new century is "There are no men, and women are desperate."

The hit TV show *Ally McBeal* is about a thin, neurotic thirty-something lawyer who pines for Mr. Right. She and her roommate go on dating binges, but the search turns up only dull losers (prime time is hard on earnestness) and sleazebags. When Ally's ruthless, pragmatic colleague Ling rounds up a crowd of hunks off the street and invites her to choose one, Ally is unnerved. Ally is always unnerved, but, surrounded by the sweet smell of upmarket testosterone, she falters and spurns them all. How could I love someone who responds to a cattle call, she asks. Why these men (curious, adventuresome, lighthearted, and really cute) are less eligible than those she marks while trolling at the discos is not clear.

How seriously do single women take *Ally McBeal*? Much of the appeal lies in the fact that this is a trans-genre show, insouciant in its kleptomaniac approach to television. The setting is a farcical law firm with a unisex washroom (like the couch set in most sitcoms) where key dramatic moments take place. The court cases are extended riffs on the obsessions of the characters: sexual harassment, jealousy, revenge, sex, and love, love, love.

People admit to watching *Ally McBeal* for the washroom scenes (often brilliant physical comedy), the courtroom scenes (clever musical comedy), and the bar scenes. They don't talk about the cosy home-alone scenes, two cute girls in their jammies feeding each other ice cream because – sigh – there are no good men. Where are they? asks Ally in her baby voice. At home with their wives, replies her wise sidekick. Many of the shows end with everyone paired with a lover, kissing in a doorway, or dancing chest to chest, except Ally. Hair swinging in the light, she is a fragile, transparent silhouette, walking home alone (no exuberant cap-throwing) to a plangent, lonely-hearts music track, dreaming of perfect men and unicorns.

A part of every young and maybe not-so-young woman watches Ally for the primal yearning for true love that McBeal acts out over and over again. Why is this search for men so compelling, so awful, and yet so irresistible? The good news might be that the thinnest girl on TV can't find a man; the bad news is that everybody tunes in to watch this while secretly, silently hoping that she will.

The other television program purporting to be in tune with youngish single women is *Sex and the City*, starring Sarah Jessica Parker, a frizzy-curled bone-rack blonde with spoiled, pouty lips and a deadpan glance. She smokes, talks to herself, is neurotic, and seems very nervous for an upscale professional on the Upper West Side. The show consists of a series of vignettes of lousy dates, men and women behaving badly, and fast, noisy sex. Lots of women in teary, shrieking, low-cut huddles clutching wineglasses. Lots of conversations about oral sex, anal sex, and dildos.

Curiously, the sexual revolution at the turn of this century is not much different from that of the 1960s and 1970s. Through sacred (we thought then) texts like *The Joy of Sex* by Alex Comfort and Masters and Johnston's *Human Sexual Response*, women learned to enjoy intercourse and have "real" – meaning vaginal – orgasms, to heartily swallow semen, and to help men with their ejaculation problems. Initially, the interests of feminism and the sexual revolution seemed joined, although a rereading of some of this material reveals a disconcertingly male-centred agenda. The voracious, predatory sexuality of the women in *Sex and the City* is strikingly reminiscent of that in Helen Gurley Brown's *Sex and the Single Girl*. *Ally McBeal*'s sandbox is filled with women in short tight skirts and male cads; *plus ça change* . . .

And what is Viagra but a male fantasy cocktail for aging Alex Comforts? Forget everything you have learned or taught about creative, consensual sex, about the rewards of other forms of intimacy, and get your man hard again. The coupling of Viagra with some of the more frenzied experiments in hormonally prolonged sexuality and plastic surgery may mean we are headed for a very, very long millennium.

Single, sexually alive women at the turn of the new century are less hampered by ignorance and convention than they were in the 1950s, although probably under greater stress to be sexually active. Then, single women were advised to submerge their sexual longings in a whacking good game of golf and a hot bath. Many single women probably still do. But now we are expected to play another game as well, for much longer. Liberated ideas about sexuality and sexual activity focus on opportunities and gadgets and stimulants for more sex. They rarely entertain the possibility of deliberate, contented celibacy. Women who go months without a sexual thought or flicker of desire are made to feel like underachievers. Women have always masturbated, but now there are cheery stores promoting masturbation workshops and selling exuberantly explicit erotica and "know thyself" videos and appliances that will make the housework – forgive me, the handwork – so, so much easier.

Celibacy: Choice or Default?

"It was an aching, really strong, it pervaded everything. It's like a force, a feeling that takes over and you can't pay attention to anything else. I spent half of my life in a state of longing for that connection with somebody that would transcend everything. But I lost the feeling. I can't remember when I lost it, but I woke up one morning and it wasn't there any more. I felt quite free. I don't close the door but I've lost the longing." (Anna, mid-50s)

What happens to your needs for sex, intimacy, physical contact when you are single? Are they channelled elsewhere or sublimated, and how healthy is this? Most single women express a desire for something other than lifelong solitude and celibacy. Not marriage, necessarily, nor even a live-in partner. The implications – sharing the same bed every night or, even worse, sharing a bathroom – are, for many women, unacceptable. But while they cherish and revel in their freedom, they are almost always conscious of an absence, something lacking.

Women often believe that they can survive without an active sex life. They emphatically prefer no sex to bad, indifferent, or obligatory sex. They readily admit to masturbating, but not on a daily basis. They are less likely than men to seek out one-night stands or sex with strangers, especially as they grow older. Women are more self-conscious about their bodies and more reluctant to undress before strangers. Women may not experience the sexual gratification of an orgasm during a first sexual encounter with a man. And many women are unnerved by the thought of the safe-sex conversation with a stranger. All in all, going without is the simplest solution.

Many of the single women I spoke to see themselves, with varying degrees of optimism and self-awareness, as between relationships. In some cases, the "betweens" are of far greater duration than the relationships. But sooner or later they expect to find another partner. They are celibate as a matter of circumstance, not as a result of choice. They are making a conscious decision to be temporarily celibate, in the sense that they are not interested in casual sex or in relationships that begin with sex. They are more likely to be cruising the Internet than the bars, actively seeking candidates for relationships. Others are intentionally shut down for a while, renovating, as one woman described herself, not paying attention to either internal or external sexual signals, going for weeks and months feeling neither frustration nor lust. But this rarely means that their sexual imaginations are utterly dormant. Celibacy is a state most women are reluctant to embrace permanently. It suggests an asexuality that they do not feel. (In French, the term *célibataire* does not suggest anything specifically sexual; it merely means single, not sexually inactive.)

But it is interesting that several of the purest celibates I met were of exceptional intelligence. They stated clearly or "accepted" that they had a low sex drive. They had made conscious, incisive choices, and were almost nunlike in their dedication to a celibate lifestyle. None recalled or admitted to sexual trauma as children. As one Montreal woman said to me, in an earlier age many would have become nuns, because in the convent they could realize their intellectual ambitions, free of the expectations of the outside world.

Paula

A powerhouse of a woman in her late 50s, Paula has a strong, solid body and hands, a big voice, and a big laugh. Thick bushy hair sticks out over the top of her head in a ponytail. Her fabulous cat is the largest I've ever seen. Paula is powerful in a daunting way. It's hard to imagine the person she says she once was, the passive half of the relationship. She owns a bed and breakfast in the Gulf Islands.

"The most important relationship of my life ended 12 years ago, and I have not had any relationships, no romances, no dates, no nothing in that time. That relationship was the big time for me. That was like, *Wooo!* Knock your socks off. I had no idea, even having been married three times previously, that it was possible to feel like that. An astounding experience. When he left, I was devastated. And then I decided that the most important things in my life were my career and my youngest child, who was still at home with me. Men were out of the picture. It was a total about-face. My life had always been wrapped around my relationships. I never went more than a couple of months when I wasn't in some kind of a relationship."

"And do you miss that?" I asked her.

"I would say maybe in the last two years it seems like more of a possibility again. But in the 10 years before that, no. I didn't allow myself to think about it. I never considered I might be with a man again, so it was best not to let it surface in any way. I didn't feel attractive or attracted to men. I was just doing my own little number, being the general, and calling my own shots, and that's just how it was. Men didn't play a role. Except I've had very good male friends, so getting to hang out with men allowed me to dissipate a lot of that energy."

"So, completely celibate."

"Totally celibate, totally, totally celibate. [Physically] I always felt fine. In the mindset of it, I'd think, Oh, my God, am I just setting myself up to be celibate for ever? Am I never going to feel sexually interested in another man? The thought of it seems weird to me. But on a day-to-day basis, it feels totally all right."

"Do you imagine being in a couple again?"

"I can't really imagine, except in very old age, being coupled in the traditional sense. Mostly because I believe there aren't too many men around that could handle me, that could handle how bull-headed I am, and cranky, and how I want everything my way. I suppose if a person seemed to be able to handle that, I could imagine being coupled. But I don't really believe it's possible. It feels like I'm going to have to mellow a lot, and I'm not ready to do that.

"For one thing, if I'm screwing a man, I figure he owes me. What he owes me is to stay sweet-tempered. If he gets sullen or sulky or disagreeable and he doesn't let me fix it, even if it's not my fault, it pisses me off. It's up to them to stay vibrant and cheerful. I could see some kind of long-distance relationship, getting together four or five times a year with somebody, but keeping our own spaces. I've still got to be the boss. And I never ever want to be in an unhealthy relationship again. I just don't have the time.

"I feel real powerful now. The most important thing for me is to decide what I want, because I feel like I'm capable of getting anything that I want."

Marta

After three marriages and two children, Marta, a large, sanguine woman in her middle 60s, lives in a southern Ontario farmhouse.

"Since your marriage ended 10 years ago, have you been with anybody? Have you been celibate?"

"Almost completely. Twice I've broken celibacy in 10 years, that's all. I've had opportunities, and I backed away from them. Because the marriage was extremely harmful, extremely damaging. And I wasn't prepared to put myself in that position of being rejected again. I was celibate in the marriage for the last nine years of the 13. After climbing walls in those years and crying myself to sleep every night, I finally threw up my hands and said, Oh, well. So much for that.

"I had one one-night stand with a man, and a relationship of several months with a woman. That was a real breakthrough for me, because it told me I was still sexual, I was still attractive. Once I realized it was still possible, I could walk away from it, and it wasn't as painful.

"I'm not hung up on women, but that was a tremendously positive, affirming thing. She was half my age, very attractive, brilliant writer. It was just fabulous that I could feel that way, and that I could make somebody else feel that way. I think that was what brought me to terms with who I am, and that I can, but I don't have to. Now I'm alone and happy to be so."

The Hunt

My friend insists I try Matchmakers on the Net. I am not keen. Everyone does it, she says; no telling what will happen. She has corresponded with several men, each time getting a little closer to revealing her identity; this is the frightening part for women.

I sign on for the trial period. I don't know how much to say in the "essay" section, so I put down everything. Only when I discover that these details are immediately available to thousands of people, that my profile is being hunted down and browsed through, that I am a person with "open mail slots" – something akin to uncrossed legs – do I go back and edit vigorously, cursing my naïveté.

I do not immediately understand what I am doing, or what to do. I click on "Who's On," thinking this is a file of likely matches for me. There are 89 names, listed in order of sex (male first), sexual preference, and age groupings. I then realize that I am one of 89 warm, breathing bodies who at that moment are checking out one another's profiles. It is like being at a dance but not seeing anyone. We are all cruising, browsing, matching, searching, mailing, updating our profiles, marking one another with stickers, "hot" or "funny" or "peachy," squelching people in chatrooms, blacklisting one another from our mailboxes.

Oh – and four invisibles; who are they? I too want to be invisible, when I grasp what that means: to cruise silently, overhead like an angel, above the action but not exposed. If you're in "Who's On," does this mean you want to chat, leave voice mail, immediately make a connection? This is too scary, too fast. I become invisible.

Within two minutes of my profile's debut, there is a flashing indicator next to my mailbox. Someone already wants me! Well, wants me to want him: Johnycanuk367. He has read my profile, his letter says. He sends a second letter two minutes later. After 18 months of celibacy, I am being hunted fast and furious! Check out my photos, he invites; whaddaya think? I delete the letters. I am not ready for this.

Next day, I haul the first letter out of the garbage ("Read Deleted Mail") and answer ("Reply," 12:40), gingerly, ambivalently, with a fake name and extreme caution. I then do a "Search" by putting together a broad range of criteria. Some 2,000 men are apparently considered in five seconds, and only one survives the inspection: David654. I scan his profile. He lives in Montreal. He is sarcastic. I send a careful note telling him this. How can he possibly be flattered?

I check "Who's On": 77 warm bodies. Johnycanuk is there, he is actually sending. I check his profile; letter from me has been read. Back to "Who's On" – he's gone; back to main page – mailbox flashing. Be still, my beating heart. He is allergic to cats, says no point in continuing if I have them. He reminds me of the male-to-female ratio for "our age group" (he is at least 10 years older than I), implying that I shouldn't lose any time. He makes a mildly risqué joke (with bearded smiley face, he is in dangerous too-cute waters) about sex in a canoe . . . Hmmm. He also gives me his real name, his phone number, practically the directions to his house. My friend has told me that the men will be really aggressive. They want to get down to business, not fool around with lengthy correspondence. I decide to wait and reply tomorrow.

Day Three of Manhunt. There is an unbidden adrenalin surge when you log on. It's only nine in the morning, and you are out hunting in your nightgown. The clock is ticking; this is a trial membership, and there are 12 days to go. I have sent two letters of the 100 allowed. I have been browsed 23 times. I send a careful reply to Johnycanuk. No, I don't have cats; no, I am not ready to phone; how long have you been widowed (subtext: Don't rush me!)? There is nothing in my mailbox. I swing over to David654. I learn that he read my letter five minutes ago. Back to "Who's On" – he is not

Sex, Celibacy, and Secrets

there. Like me, he has chosen to be invisible. I see from his profile
that he has been on this system for almost 18 months and has
"been browsed" 752 times but answers only 16 percent of his
letters. I have already been dumped.

I do "Match," which gives me 50 profiles to scan. The profiles
are listed in descending order of "Match You" percentages. This
is completely arbitrary, indicating only that these people have
responded to some of the questions (income: none of your business; car: European/sports; neatness: at least I *have* a sock drawer)
in the same way that I did. As if what is sought is a mirror image of
oneself in the opposite sex.

But the profile is the only ground for interest or rejection, and
already I am ruthless. Bad picture (moustache, Birkenstocks) – pass.
Travel history: "Been to the US, does that count?" No. Music preference: pop/top 40; shudder. Short? Forget it. Any essay with
spelling or grammatical errors: zap. Essay declaring desire for
young, gorgeous blondes: zap and swear; consider sending con-
temptuous put-down. Dragonfly222 has been browsed 2,414 times.
Centre-ice looks like a crazy redneck. Bozo486 sounds exactly that,
and he smokes. By the time I log off, still no letters in my mailbox.
Johnycanuk has read mine and not replied. Dumped again.

Matchmaker.com is a reality check. It makes you understand
a little better your own priorities and prejudices. People tell me a
widower would be perfect, no baggage. Johnycanuk is a widower;
he looked after his wife through serious illnesses. He is apparently
financially comfortable; he has led a diverse and interesting life; he
can portage a canoe single-handed. He wrote about "bringing you
coffee in bed, or in the sunroom overlooking the lake if you prefer."
He sounds cuddly, romantic, and thoughtful. He wants to drive up
the Alaska Highway in an RV. He has a perfectly nice house but is
willing to relocate. One of his photos shows him in black tie. (It was
the one showing him portaging a canoe that got my attention.) But
he has made me feel anxious, as if there is no time to lose, and from

his perspective there *is* less time to lose. I am not facing the same way, yet, as Johnycanuk. We are in slightly different phases of our lives. Timing is everything.

Daniele

A lush redhead with a voluptuous body, Daniele, 29, is in communications work for a government department. She owns a house she has renovated herself. An avid gardener and glass-blower, she lives in Winnipeg.

"Are you actively looking for relationships?" I asked her.

"Yes, I am. I just recently joined a dating service, which is not something that I've told my family and friends, because there is a certain stigma to that.

"I would be most interested in meeting someone my age, 28 to 35. I didn't give them much of a physical description to work with. Not because I don't care, but because it's one of those things that I think you determine in person – you know, do I care if he has blue eyes? Not really. I would insist that they're clean and well-groomed, that kind of thing."

"You hope that's the only kind of people they get through the dating service."

"One would hope, although you can never be too sure. What else am I looking for? Somebody who has a stable personality, somebody who has a sense of humour, someone who is intelligent, someone who has a good work ethic.

"Again, I'm not especially concerned about what profession, I'm not looking necessarily for a doctor or a lawyer, but I would expect someone who has got an education and someone who is committed to working for a living. Someone who is sensitive. Non-smoker was another important one. Not previously married and no children."

"That's pretty clear."

"Which is also probably why I'm still single! When you're younger and you're dating, you make allowances that you wouldn't make later. I've dated people who were not going to school, not employed, not especially interested in being employed. I've dated people who have kids; I wouldn't do that again. So the more time passes, there are more things that I'm not willing to do. It would be a waste of my time and his."

"Do you think there's any connection between the struggle you have had with your weight and some of the choices that you've made? Or do you see weight as a detriment to establishing a relationship?"

"Oh, I certainly have thought that. When I was sitting with the person from the dating agency, she asked me what my size and weight was. I wasn't crazy about that question, but I knew why she asked it. It's because she will be asking the men, Is there a size preference? I asked her, Will this be a barrier to your matching me up with someone? And she said, I hate to be so blunt about it, but yes, it will.

"Well, great! This is what you're judging me on? As a potential mate and life partner, you're judging me on my dress size? It's incredibly offensive. But people do it. She told me that it's particularly younger men, in the 20-to-30 range, who are looking for Barbie. So that's probably not an issue for me, given that I'm older. If somebody at 35 thinks I'm physically attractive, he's probably at the same life stage that I am anyway. But yeah, it certainly has affected my dating life."

"Do you think it's harder for smart women to find men?"

"Yes, I do. That's another thing the woman said, that women with less education who don't have broad experience of the world, with not very high standards, are incredibly easy to match. And if you want to meet somebody who is above average intelligence, has a good sense of humour, and is a professional, it's going to be harder. I've dated a couple of guys like that, and it hasn't gone anywhere, for a variety of reasons. Sometimes they are genuinely interested in smart women, and sometimes it scares the bejesus out of them."

Alice

Alice is a fit, self-assured blonde, 49, a librarian and teacher, a single mother. She has lived in Regina "forever."

"How do you meet men here?"

"I gave up after years and years. Your friends don't introduce you, because all your friends are single and we all say, Forget it: if it's alive and male, he's mine! So I tried the local computer dating service. I just decided to do it one day, and I phoned and said, Are you open? And she said, Yes. I said, Can I come right now? Because if I don't come right now, I will find a million reasons to talk myself out of it. I looked at it as sort of a research project. I decided to meet as many men as I could and find out what they're like. I've had some amazing experiences. Some of them have been crazy. But nothing bad, you know."

"How many men have you dated through this source?"

"Probably 25, 30. And they're all really nice men, but they're not for me. I have certain requirements, and I won't settle for less. I don't need to. I need someone with energy and life and someone who wants to travel and someone who will not try to possess me. Some of them take you out for dinner twice and they try and get in your skin with you, they're just clingy. I find men are very needy. Women are not the weaker sex; men are. They're little boys, and particularly the men whose wives have left them for another man. They're just shattered."

"Did any of these result in any kind of relationship?"

"A couple, for a while."

"In those circumstances, do you practise safe sex?"

"Oh, God, yes. I'm absolutely adamant about that. Men find it difficult, they don't like it. And I just say, I want to live to be a really old lady."

"But some have agreed to do it."

"Yes. But then they moan, complain, and whine. Too bad! I had one ask me, You're not fertile, are you? I said a couple of very unladylike words. The last two men I've met have both been impotent, and that really surprised me. Early 50s! I wasn't ready to deal with that."

"It's enough to make you start thinking about younger men."

"We all think about them, we talk about them, we joke about them, but . . . My girlfriends think that's the ultimate answer. And I just say, I've got a 33-year-old son-in-law and somehow, younger men are like my kids. I don't want that. I want a truly grown-up man. One who has his life together. That's what I am searching for."

Night out in Vancouver. First stop was the Shark Club on Georgia, a tacky sports bar. The room is overwhelmed by outsize statues; Wayne Gretzky looks 10 times his normal size in his L.A. Kings uniform, a sinister white shark hangs from the ceiling. The expansive dance floor was empty.

All the men working in the bar looked like proto-boxers with bulked-up bodies, tiny heads, and short hair. All the bar girls were blonde, in tiny skirts and tight black T-shirts. They were extremely thin and practically naked. The patrons did not make a pretty crowd. The women were wearing jeans and mules, or high-heeled sandals and short skirts. Big pasty lips and big bad haircuts, the kind that are both too short and too long.

The music was loud, pulsing, echoing. It might have been raining men on the sound system but it wasn't working for the women in the room. The men drank beer and stared at the huge television screens. The women drank cocktails and went to the washroom to check their mascara and lipstick, staring glumly into the mirrors. No one was dancing.

Next: to Abbott and Hastings, the Lotus, a basement club awash in red plush. Men are admitted on some nights of the week, but tonight it was women only. It seemed the best-looking women in Vancouver were here, dancing with one another. They were beautiful, lean, muscular; there was definitely some steroid action as well. A range of distinctive choices in dress and style sent clear messages. Loose, crisp, pure white shirts. Short, tight white T-shirts tucked into jeans with wide belts. The leather and metal chain-and-stud types moved in grim packs. One Asian woman, with a sweet face and very short hair, sported bulging biceps under a sleeveless T-shirt. Possibly her breasts were bound.

The dancing was glorious, sexy and fun. The whole scene was fluid, lots of bare limbs twining, bodies meeting and separating, embracing and kissing. Great music.

Liza

A vivacious redhead, Liza, 39, is a filmmaker in Vancouver.

"You're actively looking for a relationship. How do you do that in the dyke community?"

"I went through a string of going to the bar, going to the bar. It makes me so depressed I've decided to take a break. I meet women totally through my art or my writing. I was the conference queen for a long time. That's where I was meeting a lot of women. Lesbian and gay film and video festivals are one of the best places to meet. Even the lineups are great."

"Is having sex quickly common in the dyke community?"

"Yeah, you know the line: on the second date you bring your U-Haul . . ."

"Presumably because, in many ways, the risks aren't there."

"Yes, exactly. Though if you engage in any kind of sado-masochism or piercing, or fisting, or anything like that, it's very dangerous. You have to know what you're doing. We're so confused, a lot of us. When do you use gloves? How come heterosexuals don't talk about dental dams, but lesbians talk about dental dams?"

"Because heterosexuals don't use them. I've never even seen a dental dam."

"Well, I'm not a big S-M girl at all, but I definitely wear gloves for fisting. I don't use the dental dam, but [one casual lover] I had, she had a wart on her vagina. I didn't use a dental dam with this gal. I told a friend a few nights later what happened, and she just yelled at me. There's so many levels of safe sex or unsafe sex, and there's mass confusion."

Secret Sex

One of the premises of *Sex and the City* is that when single women have good sex, bad sex, stupid sex, or no sex, they report it to their best friends over cocktails. That women will share with one another the most explicit details of their sexual encounters is true. But for a surprising number of single women, the only sex is secret sex, known only to themselves. This is most often the choice of women who are content being single and not actively looking for long-term partners. Some have double lives: a public life of work, community, family, and a seamless identity as a single; and a secret life behind closed doors with a sexual partner who could scarcely be imagined by their closest friends.

Cecilia

An accountant in her mid-40s living in Calgary, Cecilia has never married. She expects to be single forever and briskly organizes her life around her single identity. She enjoys a high profile in her community.

"He's married, with kids and all that . . . Yes, it's an affair, there's no question about it. But what's different about this relationship is that I am the beloved and he is the lover. I have more power in the relationship, in the sense that if he never phoned me again I wouldn't think twice. I might one day in passing say, Gee, I haven't heard from him in a while. But if he fell off the face of the earth tomorrow, I might not notice. Although I do enjoy my time with him.

"I'm quite open about it. He'd be mortified, the number of people who know that it's him. Far and wide across the land they know. Every Friday afternoon I come home and have sex with him. I've been doing that for a year and a half. My boss in Toronto knows. That's the big joke. I have 'meetings' every Friday afternoon. I'm leaving now! I've had enough for the day! Which isn't an issue at work really, but just a running joke, because that's when I see him.

"No jewellery, although he did bring me birthday presents, he did bring me Christmas presents; there's something to be said for that. He does take me out for lunch – not every Friday, but certainly we do go out for lunch. And he just worships me. Thinks I'm wonderful. Well, nothing wrong with that.

"I just think, Well, okay, it's sex, that's all it is, although we both have the same political interests, so we do have that common ground. That's how we met, at a fundraiser. But he's lazy, he's just horribly lazy. I find that a little bit difficult. Never finished university, and just does the minimum to get by. It's a good thing he's cute. This is the first relationship I can honestly say where I really have the upper hand. And it feels good. Very, very good."

Fran

In her mid-60s, Fran is divorced, with grown daughters. She lives in a modest apartment in Edmonton bursting with art, photos, and artifacts. She was once very pretty, she told me, and still has a warm, engaging presence. She is now suffering from weight gain caused by medication.

"I always had affairs with married men. I enjoyed sex for the sake of sex. I always had one for tennis, one for sex, one for this, one for that. I never had affairs with married men whose wives I knew. It was through classified ads, and I have no qualms with it. I probably helped their marriages more than anything. And they would have done it with someone else, is the way I looked at. It's not as though I stole someone away from anybody.

"'Middle-aged woman . . .' I'd say I was anywhere from 50 to 58. 'Young at heart. Loves dancing, politics . . .' I always got letters from married men or men in their 20s or 30s. And every time I went to singles dances, I always got them, because I really can dance. Always young men.

"You see, I can talk very openly about sex. And a lot of young guys like to. They need advice, and they just like that flow. A lot of men felt comfortable with me because of that. But it didn't mean that I went to bed with all of them. I'm selective.

"We'd meet in a public place. I was very sure that I drove, looking in my mirror, checking that they didn't follow me [afterwards], and I had a plan that if they did, I had a friend's place I'd go to. I wouldn't do it today, of course, maybe because I'm older or the world is scarier.

"The men aren't as interesting here in Edmonton. Oh, God, garlic breath, and they don't know how to dress. In Montreal, they were so adorable. Clothes turn me on and they were – oh, the French Canadians, and . . . well, those Hungarians. They were very well dressed and educated, and yet with a sense that they knew themselves – you know, classy. It is harder to find people out here that you actually want to go to bed with.

"I called the shots, so – Bingo, I need a change, just like a new café or bar. Six months, tops. It was almost like, Okay, I've kissed your bobo, you can go. I always needed that excitement, that living on the edge. It was always in motels or his place or the back of the car for a quickie. I would never bring a man into the house with my children. I would never bring a man into my bedroom.

"I never did use birth control. I hated those things. That's why I had four children; I didn't know how to put the diaphragm in. My tubes were tied when I was 37. I had great sex for years without worrying about it. In our time it was amazing.

"There's a fellow I meet at my friend's coffee shop, a little Italiano. He's short and I love short men. There's something about it, the two of us. I would go in and we would talk, laugh, you know. Whenever he'd see me, he'd come and he'd grab at me, and he'd make it a point to rub back and forth on me, and I just thought, That's fine. Go for it, you know. I've often thought of him, maybe I'll call him over one day to cleanse my sinuses, as I say. It would just be a finger and he can do oral sex on me, fine; I wouldn't do it on him, thank you. I never liked it much anyway."

Donna

"I've had an affair for nine years now. That's what I was doing in New York last weekend."

Donna is divorced, with three grown children, an insurance agent in Wawa, Ontario. She loves this man, whom she knew 30 years ago in Montreal. Now he lives in Vancouver. He sought her out nine years ago, and since then they have had an intense involvement. They take holidays together; he never takes holidays with his wife. "It's a relationship that we both enjoy, the kind of relationship we never thought we'd get involved in. I think probably we wouldn't have, if we hadn't had that time from years ago."

"Is the distance a good thing or a bad thing?"

"Actually it's a good thing. It doesn't interfere with my life. Every once in a while I get to take a nice holiday, and we talk on the phone maybe three times a week, or once every two weeks, depending on how busy each of us is."

"And is he happily married, or apparently happily married?"

"As near as I can figure out, it's a relationship that has been perpetuated for the sake of the children. At least that's the rationale. But they're also in a social and business circle in Vancouver where everybody is coupled. We have talked only a little about their relationship, but there is definitely a sexual incompatibility and an incompatibility with respect to how the children were raised. Those are pretty fundamental."

"Do your children know about this relationship?"

"Oh, yeah. That's something he's never quite understood. There's no way I'm going to deliberately deceive them. They've all met him. And they like what they know."

"Nine years is a long time to have an affair. His wife doesn't know about this at all?"

"Last Monday morning he dug out his wallet and said, I want to give you some money for the phone bill. Because he always calls me on my calling card, and he'll usually give me several hundred dollars towards the phone bill. He said, 'I'm only going to give you $100 this time, because I'm reluctant to take too much money out of the bank machine while I'm on trips. I don't do the family banking any more. And I get questioned about expenses.' And I thought, Why after 30 years of marriage is she suddenly getting involved in family finances? What's that tell you?"

"It tells me she's looking for something."

"It tells me that she's getting her information together, thank you very much!" She laughed, a little nervously.

"If his marriage ended, would the two of you end up together?"

"As far as I'm concerned, we would. We haven't discussed that, but I guess the big question would be, Would he be willing to come up here? Or would I be prepared to give up all I have here? He is probably the only person on the planet that I could ever imagine myself living with, man, woman, or child. [But] I very much enjoy my alone time. I don't get enough of it. And I have been living without anybody for probably eight years."

Iris

Iris is in her mid-70s, divorced since 1971, a freelance journalist, intrepid traveller, mother of two. She rents an apartment in downtown Ottawa. Iris is self-confident, almost exuberant in her singleness.

"One doesn't get out from under one relationship and say, Well, right, I'm never going to live with anyone else again. It's just a shortage of really good men at the age of 50-ish. You really have to be at the right place and the right time to snap up a recently widowed man. They seem to be the best ones. No baggage. I mean, you've got problems with your own life, you don't want to take on his! The other thing that used to irritate me so much with these men was they'd think, Ah, yes, she's divorced, she's separated, she lives alone. She must need sex. And I'm God's gift . . . And they are not! I mean, you're not so hard up that you're going to take anyone!

"The longer you live alone, either the more you like it or you get into a rut, the bar gets higher and higher for the sort of man that you would be likely to accommodate.

"It doesn't mean that I don't have a gentleman friend, but that's a different matter altogether. He's married. All the best ones are married. I've had a relationship for 20 years with someone who doesn't live here. We're as comfortable as I suppose it is possible to be comfortable. I don't see a lot of him, but it does something for the ego. It's a real charge when someone finds you attractive. It really is good for you.

"The relationship would never have matured if I had not been freelance. If he goes for a conference somewhere, I just pack up and take my work with me, and I go. He's very happily married and he's my age, and one doesn't rock the boat at that particular time. He does occasionally come here and stay. It's fine for three or four days, but I'm used to having this two-bedroom apartment to myself. I suppose if he ever was a widower, and we decided to live together, we'd get a large place so that we'd both have our own lives. With the best will in the world I would find it difficult to have him underfoot the whole time.

"Do I feel guilty? No, because I realize that men his age are not likely to go and throw their wives over. It is just that [the marriage] has become very boring, and their wives have become very demanding and so on. It gives him just a little bit of a feeling of excitement. It gives us both that sort of feeling.

"But I don't think you should ever go into that sort of relationship thinking that you're going to get much out of it. You're not going to see him at weekends. And if you start to say, Well, why don't you see me more often – you might as well stop. I suppose I should feel more guilty than I do. But I don't! I am not at all convinced that it does any harm to the marriage.

"When I was starting on the relationship I used to think, God, isn't there more to it than this? Then I realized that if I nagged . . . Because he's no good at lying, dear sweet man. He's no good at saying to his wife, I've got to go away to this conference, you know. He takes advantage of any opportunity that he gets, but he's not good at making opportunities. I think women are better at that.

"I am really glad that I have had it, and he's a wonderful letter writer, which is nice. I think it makes you still feel a woman. It's not that I don't have nice girlfriends and so on. But I find a man more stimulating. Even now."

Karen's Story

I arrived late afternoon on a Sunday after a five-hour drive. She had asked where I would be staying, and I said probably a cheap motel near the Trans-Canada. "Why don't you stay here – I have a spare room," she offered. She told me two other things on the phone: that she was a terrible cook, and that I could identify the house because it had red paint sprayed on the side.

The house was easy to find, her modest older car in the drive-way and the blur of paint a wide swath of uneven colour on the stucco siding.

Karen is 49 and has the straight back and broad shoulders of an athlete. Her thick black hair is flecked with steel grey and cut short; her eyes are dark. She was wearing a pretty, flowery dress because she'd been to a concert at the local seniors' home with Doris, an elderly friend with multiple sclerosis.

She suggested a walk, very welcome after the long drive. We circled around a long block. The sun was still high in the sky, but there were no cars on the street, no children playing. There was quiet but not serenity. We passed a large house, pale pink stucco, picture windows with vertical blinds firmly pulled, and surprisingly formal landscaping. "That house belongs to Cynthia, the principal at my school," she said, then added, "I tell you this because you'll hear more about her later."

We talked about the red paint as we strolled around. She had been away over Halloween, and when she came back, her wall had been sprayed with an epithet. Nobody knew or was saying who had done it, and more than six months had passed in this very small town.

When we got back to the house, she prepared dinner: potatoes, garlic bread, onions and mushrooms mixed, everything
hidden under foil during cooking; corn in the microwave, two big
steaks on the barbecue. I took over the grill work because she was
unsure of the timing. Salad and fruit, neatly arranged melon and
strawberries for dessert, were already on the formally set table.
She apologized repeatedly for her culinary shortcomings, for the
state of the unfinished kitchen, currently being repainted.

Over dinner she spoke of her childhood in a farm family and
her early dedication to sports. "We were dirt poor growing up.
When we moved into town, Mum made me two dresses for school,
a brown one and a green one. One day they were choosing sides for
teams, and one of the team captains said, 'Oh, I want her, the tall
one in the brown dress. Oh, no, she's wearing her green one today.'
I was mortified by that.

"I was at a national basketball team training camp after my
second year of university. I made it that summer and trained with
the team in the fall. Then in January, my first game back, I wrecked
my knee. I made some really foolish decisions. Put off having
surgery until after my exams because I didn't want to miss the
schooling. I had my surgery the beginning of May, and the next
training camp started the first of July. I didn't make the team. I was
out of shape and did further damage."

"So sport was always a big part of your life. And still is?"

"No, now I can't run. I used to do a lot of cycling and walking.
When I moved here, I took up golf for the first time and did quite
well. But I can't run." She described the joy of being physical,
playing sports, excelling at them. She unselfconsciously called herself
an elite athlete. It was the easiest thing she said about herself. This
she knew from the inside out.

"Did you imagine, when you were growing up, getting married
or being a single person?"

"I didn't think about that much. I remember once when I was little, I got the strap in school. I went home and thought, How am I ever going to tell my grandchildren that I got the strap? And then I remembered, I don't plan to have children! That's the only time I remember thinking about it. I wanted to go with sports as far as I could, and growing up on the farm, and pretty narrow-minded, I didn't want to be a farm wife, I didn't want to be any of the women that I knew. But I didn't know what else there was. Once I got to high school, I thought I either had to be a teacher or a nurse or a secretary. Not one of them looked very appealing."

"Was there pressure on you to get married, to settle down?"

"Well, from my uncles more than my aunts, I would say! I had one uncle who said, 'I'm coming back from the grave for your wedding, if you ever get married.' But he hasn't had to. My dad – not overt pressure, but I know he probably thought there was something wrong with me. He also felt he had to look after me because I didn't have a man to look after me. The others always said that I was the favourite. I don't know if I was, but I went farther in sports than the rest did, and my dad was very athletic, and I think he took some pride in that."

"Did you ever want to be married?"

"I don't think I thought about it a whole lot. It would be a lot easier. Society would be more accepting. [But] there are too many couples that I see and think, I don't want that. I've worked closely with kids all my life, and I hear what's happening in their homes, and it seems like there is so much abuse and so much dissension. Probably in my own home, my dad was pretty controlling. I don't know if I consciously thought, I don't want that. I didn't realize until a couple of years ago that people actually went out in search of a partner. I just assumed that if it's supposed to be, it'll happen."

"Have you ever had a long-term relationship or a live-in relationship?" I asked. She laughed nervously, then lapsed into silence.

She asked me to turn off my tape recorder before continuing.

There is a handsome square clock in the corner that ticks and chimes relentlessly, every quarter-hour. The clock is in a polished wooden case and has a plaque with her name and a citation on the base. It is surrounded by the wedding photographs of her family.

Karen's story came in bursts; some things poured out, others were said with difficulty. She did not cry.

In her late 30s, she had a love affair with a woman. It lasted five years. They were on the same basketball team and shared the same interests in photography and music. Then came the sex, which she told me she did not want at all. She felt at the time that it was wrong, that she was very naïve, that she was coerced into it. They lived together in Edmonton for several years. She spoke of it with shame rather than joy.

They returned to Lethbridge, and there the relationship ended. She quit the basketball team and she left teaching, taking a job at Canada Post, then as a real estate agent – anything but who and what she was before. She went back to university for an honours math degree. The male head of department tried to talk her out of it, suggesting it would be too hard for her. Her self-esteem plummeted and she carried the guilt of her affair.

She did well in math, brilliantly in fact, scoring 100 in some courses and above 90 in the rest. Then she moved to a small town in southwestern Manitoba to be a math teacher. No one there knew she had a past. She stayed for 14 years. At a counselling course in California, she talked for the first time to a therapist about her sexuality. She felt she had built walls around herself, terrified of who she might be. She had never had sex with a man then and still had not when we talked.

Back at school, she established a counselling program to help children deal with issues such as prejudice, racism, and sexuality. It drew the disapproval of a fundamentalist faction in town. She attended a question-and-answer session with some of the parents: What if your daughter came home and said, I'm pregnant? We'd say, We love you anyway. If your son came home and said, I'm gay? He would no longer be part of the family. Funding for the counselling program was ended. She was devastated and decided instantly to leave. Eight days later she signed a contract to teach in this small Alberta town.

She bought a house. "I hate this house. Since I moved in, I haven't been able to sleep. Last year I was sleeping less than an hour each night. The house was so dark. There were big brown overhead cabinets and I ripped them all out. There are holes everywhere and paint splatters. I'm sorry . . ."

She tried to do counselling again, teaching about prejudice and sexuality, even though she knew it was provocative and would make her own sexuality suspect. The school board allowed it, provided boys and girls were segregated. Parents could keep their kids out of the program if they wished. The parents complained, claiming those children kept out would be ostracized. The board defended her, saying it was better a child should feel ostracized than commit suicide.

She paused and looked at me expectantly.

I asked, "So, have you let the walls down? Have you made close friends here?" Then Karen told me about Cynthia, the principal at her present school.

Cynthia had grown children, grandchildren, and the imposing house down the street. She had been married to a lawyer who abused her; they separated. Cynthia confided in Karen about her marriage, and Karen confided in Cynthia about her past. She wanted that stuff to be up front. If it affected their friendship, so be it.

But clearly Karen was ambivalent, even confused about her feelings for Cynthia. Karen believed she was important to Cynthia when Cynthia was between men. She said Cynthia "treated her like a lover." But their relationship was not physical. Later, when a man came into Cynthia's life, their close friendship ended. A kind of shunning started. Karen was no longer welcome in the social circle Cynthia had introduced her to. She felt invisible and said so to Cynthia. Cynthia made some excuse. It was New Year's Eve, and the last occasion when they talked with any intimacy.

One night the following spring, she was taking a bath when a brick came through her bedroom window, landing in her bed, where she would have been sleeping not long after. She got out of the bath and went into the bedroom in her bare feet. The brick rested between two pillows, surrounded by shattered glass.

That September Karen was to be inducted into her hometown Hall of Fame for her sports accomplishments. It was a huge moment in her life, and her family was proud. The night before, she put on dark clothes and went out, walking and walking. She was ready to commit suicide. She had started taking Prozac two weeks before, and her doctor had warned that the medication might trigger a crisis. If it did, she was to get to a hospital right away. But she couldn't go to hospital because of the induction. She couldn't let her family down.

Her wandering took her to Cynthia's backyard, where she sat listening to the garden fountain. Somewhat soothed, she went to the front of the house. Cynthia was stepping through the door, talking on the phone. Karen backed into the shadows. Cynthia said, "Are you coming in or not?" Karen said, "No, I won't. I see you're on the phone." Cynthia responded, "Yes, I'm talking to my neighbour who's called about somebody loitering in my backyard."

Humiliated, Karen went home, somehow got through the night. The next day she drove to the induction ceremony. Afterwards, she checked into a hospital. She took a few months off, spending time in Lethbridge, Regina, and Calgary with friends – two of whom were lesbians, a word she can finally say without discomfort. She started taking reiki treatments and learned how to do them herself. It was while she was away that the red paint was sprayed on her house.

"Would you like a short reiki treatment before you go to bed?" she asked finally.

I felt it would be hurtful to decline.

The living room was transformed with candles and flute music. A small electric fountain burbled. I lay on the couch, one pillow under my neck, another under my knees. In the candlelight her features were softened, and she was animated and glowing. She placed a tissue over my eyes and started at my head. Her hands were trembling, but they settled gradually. When she reached my chest, I could feel my heartbeat reverberate against her hands, which were very warm. To the diaphragm and back and then feet. I drifted away, trying to keep her story in my head. Afterwards she asked me what I felt, and I didn't know what to say. But we were both comforted by sharing something other than pain.

My bedroom was in the basement beneath hers. I listened to her run the bath. Then the house was silent, except for the clock.

Karen believes she is asexual. She's always felt ambivalent about her passion for sport and what it says about her as a woman, even though this is the source of her greatest pleasure. She wonders if she needs to feel pain to know her body is alive. She craves companionship and friendship. She now does only career counselling at school.

She was pretty when she left for school the next morning; she has what used to be called a lovely figure and a spring in her step. I drove slowly away from her town. On the streets, there was superficial politeness, nothing more. This is a community in which maybe 75 percent of marriages end in divorce, where, Karen believes, fetal alcohol syndrome is the key to the problems of the children she teaches. It seemed to me a very cold place, an unforgiving and harsh and cruel part of the country.

Hormones: The Nights of Our Lives

Touch yourself; be touched by others. Easier said than done.

It is easy for single women to lose touch with their own sexuality when they are celibate for long periods. Will I ever get aroused again? What will happen if I have sex after not having sex forever? One of the impacts of celibacy over a long period is that it makes the possibility of sex intimidating. There is fear of failure, or of unexpected responses, especially from the late 40s onwards, when what you imagine to be your usual sexual responses may be altered by hormonal change. Single women joke about suddenly shaving their legs in anticipation of a sexual encounter; they don't readily admit to prepping themselves with vaginal creams, erotic fiction, and a few dry runs, so to speak, with a vibrator.

As with all aspects of female sexuality, the scientific literature is both inadequate and judgmental and clouded by pharmaceutical agendas. The medical profession provides lubricants or hormones and well-meaning advice but cannot even talk knowledgeably about what is "normal" sexual activity or a "real" orgasm for women. Recent panaceas being researched and promoted as the answer to a better sex life for women include estrogen supplements, testosterone patches, a nutritional supplement that contains ginseng and gingko, a common antidepressant, and even Viagra. Women and their physicians respond with ambivalence to such solutions. Some resent the medicalization of sexual activity, turning the vagaries and rhythms of personal experience into a medical problem that must be cured chemically; other women welcome the exploration and discussion of female sexual issues. All women are affected by these debates, but the single or celibate woman is typically ignored by the research, in which it is assumed that normal means having a partner.

The woman who lives alone is both an unwitting and an unknowing player in an entirely internal hormonal drama. She may not even clock hormonal surges and collapses. She may be unwilling to believe that regular masturbation is therapeutic. Or she may be alarmed by sudden, unbidden erotic urges, after weeks or months of complete sexual indifference – a testosterone rush. Or by a wash of uncontrollable sexual response to the casual touch of someone, like a cat in heat. Women prefer spontaneous arousal, to be overcome by desire, not just to succumb to the physical churn switched on in their nether parts by a pornographic video that at another level they despise as bad art or bad gender politics. But celibate women, living alone, come at sexual activity of any kind from relative isolation, a hormonal vacuum.

All women are familiar with the phenomenon of converging menstrual cycles – when two or more women live or work closely together, their periods often become simultaneous. Similarly, when people live as a couple, their hormones also cohabit in a sense, and they have some form of hormonal barometer. It may or may not be accurate, but it provides a reference point. Married women get to test their hormonal responses regularly. They know if they want sex or if they don't; they are able to respond to their own or their partner's desire, or not. And it is not even just about fucking. It is about a range of physical intimacies, both good and bad, pleasurable and repulsive. The woman in a long-term lesbian relationship and the woman who sleeps with a man most nights share daily intimacies of touch and talk, tenderness, even arguments. All kinds of subtle hormonal stews are simmering in the woman who does not live alone, even if she is having sex only a couple of times a month. She is functioning in a very different hormonal cocoon than the woman who lives alone, masturbates occasionally, and at best sleeps with her cat.

Fifty years hence, science may identify significant shifts in the hormonal makeup of single or celibate humans, which over time affect the reproductive capabilities and physical makeup of the species. The effect of long-term celibacy on hormonal balance is something that has yet to be studied, as far as I can determine. Yet it is probably more relevant to modern reality – because of the number of people, male and female, who live on their own for very long pieces of their lives – than, say, constructing elaborate theories around the history of polygamy to justify male mid-life crises.

Some single women, consciously or otherwise, develop strategies to compensate for the lack of regular sexual or even physical contact with other human beings: sports, massage, the spa. Others among us do not even recognize the need for such strategies or accept celibacy as a natural state. Anecdotal evidence supports the notion that single women recognize that their bodies are functioning differently than they were when they were sexually active. But this awareness is not expressed as something to do with substances as nebulous and unfamiliar as pheromones and sex hormones like dehydropiandrosterone (DHES). It takes the form of a thoughtful assessment of priorities.

Jasmine, 40, is a silversmith and artist who has lived alone for almost a decade in a salt-streaked cabin on a beach on one of the southern Gulf Islands.

"I'm not a strongly sexual person. For some people, their bodies pull them into relationships, when there isn't much else there, whereas with me that doesn't come up very often. I haven't been sexually active for about 15 years."

"What about the notion," I asked, "that if you are celibate, you are closing off parts of your body – that if you're not physically intimate with somebody, your hormonal balance is affected?"

"Oh, I think that's true. But I've been this way for so long. Maybe one way to put it would be, Every tree you look at is different, and it grows in a certain direction because that's where the light is. So it might be true that you miss things when you're not in a relationship.

"Sometimes if I meet someone I'm attracted to, it can be hard. When I'm really, really hungry. The last couple of times it's happened that the person has been in an unfinished relationship, so I have resisted it. Even if it's just a one-night stand, you bring that person's energy into you. And if it's good, then you're going to bond with them, and it's going to hurt you if you separate. If it's not good, it's like, *yech*. There's no such thing as casual sex, unless you're numb, and then what's the point?

"People use sex to satisfy a lot of different needs. I know I did – like, I'm valuable and worthwhile because people want me. Or not knowing how to communicate, and so using sex as kind of a communication device. We have this idea that you've got to be getting some, or you're missing out. Here on the island, there's a lot of sexual activity, people going from partner to partner. I see people all starry-eyed and in love, and then three years, five years down the road, it's bad news, and they're off with someone else, all starry-eyed and in love. I've done it myself."

"Do you have something in your life that replaces physical intimacy, or do you have a kind of emotional intimacy with some people?"

"Yes. I have friends. I have my connection with the earth. There's a month every summer I spend with a lot of people, and when I come back here, I am so lonely. I'm never lonely except then. And I go through about a month of grieving. But if I'm around people for a long period, I'll get exhausted. I just find it overwhelming, and I want to be by myself. I find dealing with people more scary than being alone."

Other single women desire and seek sexual encounters, but with very little guidance on what to expect if and when they have sex. Women construct their own theories and strategies from their own experience and those of others. One woman I met believes that her first sexual encounter after several years of celibacy so affected her body that she immediately had an exceptionally heavy period; it was as if, she said, all of her hormones roared to life like airplane engines. Another recounted the experience of having sex, again after a long period of abstinence: "It was fabulous, high-voltage sex; we really went for each other. And then I noticed this incredibly powerful aroma. At first, I thought it was him, some kind of musky aftershave or something. But I gradually realized, no, it was me. I was giving off this unbelievable scent; it was pouring out of me, almost like a liquid."

Or sexual reawakening might be more subtle, like a plant coming out of a long period of dormancy. Mona, in her mid-50s, is a traveller, sailor, skier, photographer, a vivacious, good-looking woman.

"I couldn't screw for years. Because it was painful. If I even touched myself or if any penis touched me, it was pain, burning pain, horrid pain. At the entrance to the vagina, at the back. I went on HRT for a while, because it is supposed to help with dryness, but I hated it.

"I went to this young gynecologist – 35 to 40, funny, neat, fun guy – and he said, Have you ever been forced? I said, Well, maybe when I wasn't lubricated. I said, I don't want to go back on HRT. He said, Now there is a wild yam cream, on prescription. So I started using the wild yam cream. Not that I was having sex or anything.

"And then – it was bizarre – last summer I went to a beach with a friend and her children. It's a nudist beach, she said, and I said, Fine, I'm a pantheist. I took off my clothes. It was a gorgeous, hot day, and this good-looking guy came along in his jeans and jacket and wandered along to a spot just past us. He took his clothes off and walked into the water, and my friend said, Look, he's got a hard-on, and I said, Oh yeah . . .

"Then he came out of the water, and he *really* had a hard-on. And my friend said, Oh, Mona, that one's for you! I laughed, but I watched him. He strolled back to his pile of clothes, towelled down very slowly, sat down, not looking at us.

"That was it, but it was the strangest thing. Thinking about him later turned me on to masturbate for the first time in my life. I finally felt horny. It was the most wonderful feeling. My husband never turned me on that way. Here I am, 54, and oh, God . . . I felt like a woman again."

Sexual activity for women over 50 is an issue linked inextricably to changes in their bodies that come with menopause. Because women fear that a decrease of sexual desire (and sexual appeal) might attend menopause, they start thinking about hormone replacement therapy as something more than symptom management. Guided by their reading of the latest literature, their doctor's advice (which can be purely subjective or ideological), their own medical and family history (especially concerning breast and ovarian cancer and strokes and heart attacks), and their own gut instinct and circumstances, they make a choice, one way or the other. How far to go along the road of ingesting chemically prepared hormones, while aging, is problematic. But it is a gamble that many single women are prepared to take.

Hormone replacement therapy is recommended to mitigate the symptoms of menopause, but it is also, like some medieval elixir, supposed to guard against aging. I once asked a female gynecologist about the wisdom of using HRT. She was in her mid-30s, a beautiful, recently married woman; for some reason, all of this caused me to doubt her expertise on menopause. She was an unequivocal champion of HRT. She told me about a male doctor who swore to her that he could tell in one whiff while conducting a gynecological exam of an older woman whether she was on HRT. He conjured up images of dead, grey, or decaying flesh in a woman who was not. For many women, one such anecdote would convert them into slaves to HRT for life, or until they read an equally vehement argument against it. The HRT scientific debate is often more polemical than factual.

What is rarely discussed in the HRT literature is whether a woman is single or sexually active. A single professional woman who has only her own income may feel she has more invested as she ages in looking attractive, looking young, than a contented, secure married woman. Single women feel they need to look young to get employment or stay employed. They need to look and feel youthful in order to attract potential partners for love or sex or both. They imagine with trepidation beginning a sexual relationship in their 50s and suddenly discovering they have dried up. Single women approach the HRT issue from the same perspective that female actors bring to cosmetic surgery. It is not just about looking pretty and youthful. It is about career and a sex life and maybe finding a long-term relationship.

All women, regardless of marital status, go through the alarming phase of becoming invisible, in their late 40s and early 50s, like ink that fades. The woman who is happily or safely ensconced in a relationship may become invisible to others, but she enjoys the loyalty and commitment of her partner. Even in a dysfunctional relationship, she *exists*. Some single women, admired and productive in their daily lives at work, say that from five o'clock on Friday to nine o'clock on Monday morning, they do not exist, in the minds or eyes of anyone else. This invisibility can be exacerbated by age.

The majority of older women I interviewed either were already taking HRT, or said they would do so. Women in their 60s and older had often been on a form of hormone replacement therapy (usually Premarin) for several decades, because of a hysterectomy in their 40s. This pattern will probably change as technology changes and fewer women have hysterectomies. But it surprised me that most of these women were not considering stopping HRT, had not even had such discussions with their physicians. Women in their 40s seemed to think they probably would use HRT, although they were bewildered by the literature and what the latest thinking is. Several women told horrible stories about starting on HRT, developing severe bleeding and other symptoms, and getting off right away. My own doctor told me it can take up to a year to get the dosage right, an indication of how precarious and contradictory the science is on HRT, and perhaps also an indication of how dramatically individual chemistries can vary.

The dynamics of their hormonal makeup is an aspect of the lives of single women that is confusing, even unnerving. While we feel we have acquired some understanding of the more obvious manifestations of hormonal activity – periods, pregnancy, menopause – we are adrift on a sea of misapprehensions and myths when it comes to the connections between our chemistry, our emotions, and both our mundane and intimate interactions with others.

From the Diary of a Single Woman

Grief unleashes a chaos of feelings: a shocking and overwhelming desire for physical closeness and sexual release. I want to be naked, and I want a lover to come and climb into my bed beside me, to put his arm around me so that I may cry into the warmth of his skin. He will hold me, stroke my hair, my breast, and I will be able to sob raw ugly sobs until one layer of pain has dissolved. And then our bodies will meld for that other release, deep inside. This happened to me once, when I learned of the death of my father. At the time, while feeling an overwhelming physical deliverance with my lover, I also felt that it was shameful to be having sex when my father had just died. But I know now it was not, that the deluge of tears and the torrent of hormones were healing floods. And that sex at that moment was purely and simply a gift from someone who loved me and whom I could trust.

In the grief that followed the end of my marriage, I could not bear to be touched. My whole body felt flayed or burned. Sex was a horrible invasion, a violation, more feeling than I could tolerate. I craved solitude, celibacy, and a time of healing.

When next I grieved, I was alone. Friends could and did offer solace, in many ways. But I cried alone, and felt, more than I do most days and nights, the absence of an intimate companion.

The Wild Women of St. John's

$\mathcal{M}$id-August, a steamy wet night in St. John's, Newfoundland. At my funky bed and breakfast in the area called the Battery, overlooking the harbour, I meet with three women in their late 30s. All have children and all have left marriages. They share a raucous rapport with one another, a connection that is, in their word, tribal.

"Recovery" is too small a word to describe the histories of these women. What distinguishes them from others I have met in their age group is a robust sexuality. They're not remotely cowed. They've all gone through difficult times with drugs, destructive relationships, poverty, and children in crisis. They are unsettled financially; two are living on the margins. But they live hard. They are survivors with attitude. Like others in isolated, resource-based communities, these women used men as their tickets out of the narrow expectations of their families and communities. They saw no other alternative.

Alison is 37, tall and statuesque, with dyed red hair and attractive features. She possesses a sexy confidence that allows her to be both a professional business person and a member of this close-knit sorority.

ALISON: I have been married once, down the aisle sort of thing, and in a long-term relationship once as well. One child from each. The children are 15 and 8, girls. I own my house, downtown. Since the divorce from my first husband. It was matrimonial property and I bought him out of the mortgage.

When I was younger, I did bar and restaurant work, hotel work. I loved it and I was great at it, and I made a lot of money, and I was single then too. You could live off your tips and bank your cheques, very few responsibilities. Then came the kids. I was going to university when I first got pregnant, and then I went back to university when she was six, and got pregnant again. So I gave up going to school and had my tubes tied.

Then I got scared, and I felt like the world was crumbling in on me, because I was in a relationship that was very oppressive. Drug abuse involved. I needed to get away from it, so I packed everything I owned in a 15-foot truck, left the kids with Mom and Dad, and made the journey across the "Great Water" to Halifax, where I struggled for six miserable months and became hopelessly entangled with that bastard again. I ended up coming home to save my house. That was a turning point, because that was when my girlfriend asked me to work for her in sales.

I sell advertising at the moment, but I'm in the process of coming into my own. In many ways. I think I could attribute that feeling of empowerment to being single, to feeling singular.

Patsy is 39 years old. She is wearing a spangled band around her forehead and a short petal-cut skirt and sandals. She's got great legs. She's bosomy and almost tough-looking. Edgy, nervous, her thoughts spinning off in all directions, she is the most vocal of the group. Still, she chooses not to tell all.

PATSY: I came into this world as one person and then became another. I was adopted into a really cool family. They were very involved with the arts . . . I had a very creative childhood. We got to dress up. We had theatrical makeup, wigs, everything. I've always been around thespians.

But when I was 18, I went the roller-coaster ride and got pregnant, and I had my daughter. That was the best thing. I nursed her for two years. I lived in New Jersey, I lived and worked in Calgary for a while. That was a wild bit of fun. Worked construction there. Came home, cut sod, took her with me. Holy shit, what a task! I had my son four and a half years later, different fathers, same general scenario as the lady over here. Our lives are very similar.

I've been through some turbulence, but I don't really want to go there because that's the past. It's there, it's yours, you're allowed to own it, but you've got to get on with it. It's not important, the details. I've been in abusive relationships, I'm everybody you've ever interviewed.

I'm a writer. I write erotica. I do erotic performance art. My erotica, it's about sensuality, right? It's our origin, you know? We defile our origin in our society, in all the societies of the world. I'm an artist most of the time. Everybody's trying to get used to that, although they all need me to be the other things they know me to be. I'm sick and tired of being called a ho because I have sensuality and that is my nature, my creature.

ALISON: Patsy stumbled, loaded drunk, into my life one night and made me wonder completely. She called the next day, because she was absolutely certain that the guy she was seeing at the time was doing it with somebody else – yours truly. And she knew that I knew!

PATSY: I was just checking my ass. I said, He's the peroxide lover, and she told me everything.

Lianne has a soft, drowsy voice and a sweet face. Blue eyes, hair pulled back into a bun, loose breasts, a post-hippie look. She smokes steadily, listens in silence, and laughs eagerly.

LIANNE: I have three children, a daughter, 15, a son, 13, and a daughter, 12. I'm from the Cape Shore, a tiny fishing community. I lived in Halifax for a couple of years when I was 18, and then I went to the States when I was 21. I was married to a guy from the army base in Argentia. We divorced about a year after we got to the States. I stayed there and met the kids' father and got pregnant really quickly. We lived in the States for 10 years, in Washington State and Wichita, Kansas. After Wichita, I moved back to Newfoundland, to the town I was born in. I brought my husband back with me. I was pregnant again with the angel Annie. We moved to Placentia, where we all shared the same bedroom. A wee space. I owned a coffee shop there for a couple of years.

[During that time] I got extremely bored and had an affair. After my husband and I separated, he just took off and never looked back. I'd say we've probably heard from him five times in five years.

I gave up the coffee shop and moved into St. John's, because I was heavily involved in the environmental project to stop the incinerator from going to Long Harbour. This obsessed me for three years. I was single then too, and I must say, it was the most powerful time in my life. I was working on something I really believed in. Constantly involved, dragging the kids to meetings at 10 o'clock at night, that kind of stuff.

I stayed in St. John's and went on welfare after I got out of the environmental work. Then I started bartending under the table, because of course you can't raise three kids on welfare. I started going out with the guy I'm still seeing, and I stopped bartending. I live with the guy; he has a child as well.

I'm not working now. Well, I'm working a lot, actually, trying to keep two families going. The big sucky boyfriend and four children. MBF: You describe yourself as single, but you are in this relationship. Would you ever marry again?

LIANNE: No. I just can't see any reason. Annie – she's 12 – was saying to me, Mom, why don't you get married? You and Lorne should get married. I said, Annie, why do you want me to get married? She said, Because I don't remember any wedding that I've ever been to in our family. I'm dying to go to a wedding.

ALISON: She just wants to get dressed for it and wear heels, Lianne. That's all.

MBF: Did you imagine when you were growing up that you would be the person you are today? Or did you have a different fantasy about how your life would unfold?

ALISON: Totally different fantasy. I wanted what my mother had: marry young, have babies, the guy does everything and pays for everything. I don't think I thought of my mother as a person for the longest time, but somehow I aspired to it as well. Although I must admit I don't think it took too long before I realized it's just not going to be that way. Then I started resenting her, I think. I felt that my illusions had been shattered.

LIANNE: I didn't want to have the life my mother had, but I didn't know what I wanted. Where I grew up, we were in an extremely isolated part of Newfoundland. I was 12 before we got electricity and 14 when we got telephones. I knew I didn't want that, but I didn't know what was out there.

PATSY: I always thought I was going to have an arranged marriage. According to the parents, they were primping me for just such an arrangement: a lawyer, or doctor, or such, and they would have felt accomplished. But it never happened that way. I was a great disappointment. I left town when I was 15. I learned that men were the highway to get out of my parents' house. Oh, damn right.

LIANNE: The first time I got married, it was like that. I'd come back from Halifax, and the hospital was after calling my family because I dropped acid, so of course I had to come home. I lived with various family members about a year, and then this good-looking Mexican guy comes around. I'm out of here!

MBF: So your first way of finding your identity was through men.
PATSY: I think women have to go through all this crap so they can find "self."
LIANNE: I think our children are facing the world with a much better knowledge of what's actually out there than I ever did.
MBF: How would you describe your relationship with men now? What role do they play in your lives?
PATSY: I'm of the opinion men and women should live next door to each other and visit often. It's so much more sane . . . I haven't been in a long-term relationship in about eight or nine years.
ALISON: But you have something neat-o happening now.
PATSY: I do. You tell the story. You were there.
ALISON: I don't know the whole story, but I know that Patsy is – what, 39, and she hasn't been in a relationship at all for years. And now all of a sudden, this really wild thing. This guy has shown up. And by all accounts he is really cool, a beautiful, beautiful man. I met him for the first time today, and he really is so beautiful. Twenty-two years old!
PATSY: He came courting me, let's be clear.
ALISON: I think that says something about the kind of men who are coming around . . .
PATSY: Men who women are raving about . . .
ALISON: Single women have raised those 22-year-olds.
PATSY: Yes! Young men have this bravery and honour and under-standing, right? The world is changing, and I'm just about where he is right now for the first time too! It's crazy, but he's sincere; I've never had that. I'm a grandmother and I've never known a sincere male heart.
MBF: Alison, you don't have a man in your life now?
ALISON: No, I don't.
PATSY: I know her pattern of migration.
LIANNE: Alison always goes back to the same guy, in the winter! Picks him up just before Christmas.

ALISON: I do? I guess it must be. It won't happen this year, though. And I've never said that before.

MBF: So do you have casual sex?

ALISON: Yes.

MBF: And how do you meet men?

ALISON: Bars.

PATSY: I haven't had casual sex in quite some time. Years.

ALISON: Actually, a couple of times I've been set up with men who worked out pretty good.

PATSY: A couple of times you've set people up.

ALISON: That's true too. We share lovers. We know each other's lovers.

MBF: How long do these things last – one-night stands, a couple of months?

PATSY: A season. Sometimes you meet again.

MBF: And are these guys married, or single –

ALISON: Usually single.

PATSY: Yeah. You've got to have some respect for the sisters here. That betrayal is the worst.

LIANNE: I can't stand that kind of stuff. I try not to bring bad karma on myself. And I think that's pretty bad karma.

PATSY: Amen. *Awomen.*

ALISON: I think I've finally decided that I really prefer not to live with a man. Even my eight-year-old daughter said to me yesterday, Mom, you are so much happier now that Dad is not here. I said, How does that make you feel? And she said, I'm happier too.

LIANNE: Lorne says to me, You're not single. I said, I'm not married. He said, Yeah, but you're committed, aren't you? I'm as committed as I can get, my darling.

MBF: Do you practise safe sex?

ALISON: I do.

PATSY: I do.

LIANNE: I do too. Always.

ALISON: I will admit there are times that I've slipped up, or ripped a condom off in the interests of a guy keeping a hard-on.

MBF: Would the 22-year-old use a condom?

PATSY: Absolutely.

ALISON: That's the difference between a 22-year-old and a 44-year-old or a 52-year-old.

PATSY: They think they'll lose it if they're not there in the flesh . . .

LIANNE: They bore me to death and they're all alcoholics. I don't want that in my life, boy.

ALISON: And they're really weird about oral sex.

PATSY: Yeah, I definitely have an attitude hanging off me when it comes to that stuff. I've cast my pearls before swine way too often. I cried for it and longed for it, because I knew I wasn't getting what I needed.

LIANNE: Well, I need to see this 22-year-old.

MBF: What's your long-term plan, Lianne?

LIANNE: In January I'm going back to school to finish an adult education degree. I would like to work in some kind of social justice area. I hope that in 10 years I'm financially self-sufficient. I'm still dependent on my partner to keep body and soul together financially, and I'm not happy with that part.

I'm really happy with the kids. Being single most of the time, raising the kids and raising the animals, I was wondering, What kind of decisions am I making here? And now, I feel like I did make the right decisions for the kids and I'm on the right track. They're strong human beings and good human beings.

MBF: What about you, Alison? How do you see your life over the next little while?

ALISON: Things are certainly changing for me now. I have made the decision to leave my very cushy job and take a leap of faith into publications and promotions. I'm looking forward to being my own boss, and I'd like to think that I'll be able to do that successfully and grow a thriving, successful business for myself . . . I see the extent of my experience melding together to form the person that I am now. I don't feel detached from what I have been, or the roles that I have played for myself. I still feel very much myself. In many ways I still feel very much the way I did when I was 18.

LIANNE: I don't. I feel I found out who I was only about 10 years ago, when I moved into the downtown here. I feel like I've been totally different people about four or five times in my life. There's parts of my life that I don't know who I was . . . Working with the environment and meeting so many people in the St. John's downtown community, I think we found safety and nourishment, and a lot of really earthy people who were doing stuff. It just blew me away. They were so accepting of me and the kids. It was just finding people who understood me.

ALISON: Your tribe.

PATSY: We are very tribal. We know where we all sit and what positions we sit in. Very matriarchal, I think.

ALISON: Our mothers were too. In Newfoundland history, I do believe men passed the money over to the women. They kept it in their bras. The men needed to go by Ma to get a few bucks. That's how the structure was underneath. They made like I'm the guy, I'm the head of the family, but . . .

MBF: You feel the loss of your community when you're not here, don't you?

LIANNE: Oh, absolutely. I feel like I'm totally off my turf. I'll do anything to avoid going off the reservation.

PATSY: Everybody's like a ship, each life is a ship, and you choose the direction you will float your ship, and the journey you're taking. Sometimes you get holes blown in your ship and you have to mend them, and sometimes you got full sail ahead and it's a beautiful thing. Somehow here there's a magic. There's a magic to this land. I call it the Rock of Eden. A lot of people stay here because they recognize this and then learn to flow with the island rhythm. We're very much island people.

MBF: How much of what you are and the journey you're on is a function of being a single person, as opposed to a coupled person?

PATSY: Oh, I am unable to function as part of a couple. I got too much to deal with just being here. In order for me to be a useful, productive person, it's necessary for me to operate as a single unit.

MBF: Why is that? What's wrong with living with men?

PATSY: They leave the fucking toilet seat up!

LIANNE: They never clean it either. Take that as a metaphor for all of it, you know?

PATSY: I think everybody craves their own space where they can just have their time with themselves.

MBF: But you all live with kids, right? How do you construct your own space if you're a mother? What's the difference between mothering and living with a man?

ALISON: I've never loved a man anything like I've loved my children.

LIANNE: There's never been a man in my life that I wouldn't leave if I wasn't happy, but I would never leave my children even when they drive me crazy. And yes, they drive me insane with their dirty laundry and all that shit. But I'd never leave them.

MBF: If your daughter came to you tomorrow and said, I want to get married in a church in a white dress and do the whole number, how would you respond?

PATSY: That's a good one! In all honesty I don't expect it to happen.

LIANNE: Oh, I think Annie will.

ALISON: Annie will, but Annie will choose him first, for many worthy reasons . . . Actually, I had a white dress . . .

PATSY: I wore scarlet!

CHAPTER 8

The Three Faces of Money

"Financially secure? Hah! Do I owe bills? Yes. Do I live from paycheque to paycheque? Yes. Do I own a home? No. That was a dream and a desire I would have liked to have fulfilled," said Valerie, a 45-year-old hairdresser I met in Edmonton.

"I make sure there's a little bit at the end of the paycheque to say, Val, you're going out and getting your nails done, or Val, you're going out with the girls tonight, and that gets me through. But do I have a nice savings account somewhere? No, I don't. Do I believe in the lottery? Yes, I do. No, I'm not hurting, I'm surviving."

The worst fear for single women – worse than having bad relationships or having no relationships – is having no money. A healthy income or some form of financial security is often what makes it possible to be happily unattached. Most single women, especially those who know they will be self-supporting for a foreseeable future, are acutely conscious of their financial situations. Many are determined either to never depend on a man for security or to never again be dependent. They are resilient and not afraid to downgrade, downsize, change directions if need be.

But money is not just a bank account, an RRSP, or real estate. Money – its abundance or its absence – is part of a single woman's identity and sense of self. For some, the achievement of wealth masks an emotional insecurity about being alone. For others, doing without is a badge of honour, a way of declaring freedom and independence in a consumer society. Quite often among the women I spoke to, it was clear that there was no boundary between their financial situation and their emotional state, their sense of security in being single. And there was usually a strong connection between their financial self-image and their physical surroundings, their homes. Women express their fiscal reality and objectives in the spaces they create for themselves.

Single women are in some sense subversive in their attitude towards money and security. A growing number of younger (30s and 40s) single women are comfortable financially. They often are aggressive spenders. Their career aspirations are not hooked to pension plans, and they do not see investment in real estate as a signal that they will be forever single. This group of women aspires to affluence in the traditional sense.

But other single women are stepping off the consumer fast track, which is a gentle form of subversion. They are not interested in conspicuous consumption or the stamps of affluence. They do not buy up as they get older. They scale back and down on big purchases and household embellishment. They invest cautiously, in RRSPs, not just by playing the stock market. They rent a downtown apartment instead of owning property, so they are free to travel. They move to rural areas and live modestly, indulging in one pleasure, again usually travel.

I found that single women fall into three distinct groups when it comes to resources and attitudes about money. At different points in their lives, women move from one category to another depending on other, non-financial circumstances. It is a descending scale: the moneyed (or upwardly mobile), the compromisers (down-wardly mobile), and the poor.

Moneyed

Women in this group have money, in some cases enough that it is the source of their power in the community and of their self-esteem as single women. Among them are those who are younger, in fast-track jobs, with their first houses or condos and investment plans in place before age 35. This is a relatively new demographic group, already identified as important consumers. Advertisers, banks, and mutual fund managers are very interested in these women, who will over time either solidify their own security or merge with an equally affluent partner.

In this group too are older professional women who are simply well off, having disposable income to spend as they like. Some of these are quietly wealthy. They might have a great deal tied up in homes or other investments, but outwardly they live modestly. This group thinks seriously about money, as suggested by Eileen, a Saskatoon stockbroker in her 40s.

I asked her whether she thought single women pay enough attention to their finances, to the reality of not being in a couple.

"When I think of my friends and associates generally, yes," she replied. "It's the ones who expect a comfortable marriage who ignore all that, because they think somebody else will handle every-thing. But a lot of us never bought into that, and maybe 10 years ago just said, 'I'm never going to get married. This is my life and I'm going to handle it, period.'"

Jean

"In my 30s, I desperately wanted to be married, but I don't agonize over it now. I have a very busy, very successful, very happy life. I'm fond of saying I've become the stereotype of every middle-aged woman who has never gotten married and never had babies, but did get the dog. And the nice thing about being middle-aged is, I don't care!"

It was a month before Christmas but there were carols playing, the smell of vanilla and chocolate, and trays of cookies in progress in the kitchen of a big beautiful house on the outskirts of a small southwestern Ontario town. Jean is also big and beautiful, a well-groomed, well-dressed woman, with shiny auburn hair, a lovely open face, and a beguiling voice. She is 50, an entrepreneur with interests in several businesses including real estate. An elderly barky dog "rules her life with an iron paw." She has an easy, glamorous affluence.

"I've been single all my life, I've lived alone all my life, and now I've gotten very set in my ways. I'm not nearly flexible enough any more to live with someone. I was on the leading edge of it being more acceptable to be a single woman, and I have been very successful. I also inherited what my parents had, which was fairly substantial, and I had no financial reason to get married. Fifty years ago that was why women got married.

"I'm an only child, and I'm the fourth generation in the family business. I bought another company last year and we doubled in size, and I'm just thrilled with it! I paid a great deal of money for it, and it will be paid off in three years.

"I've been seriously involved three times. The first of them, I was very young and that doesn't count. The next relationship died because I didn't want to leave this area, and he wasn't free to come here. The other one just ran its course. I fell in love with a gay man once, that was very self-destructive on my part . . . and as far as married men are concerned, that's difficult. It's a small town.

"My mother really wanted me to get married; she didn't want me tied to her apron strings. When she was dying, we had a conversation or two on that . . . Her comment was, I know you will look after your father, but who will look after you, dear? My mother was my best friend, and she died three years after a mastectomy. My father had a heart attack right after she died, and I supported him emotionally and ran the business for the next five years.

"Everybody thought my father was the nicest man, but he was very self-centred, very demanding, and set high standards. My mother had a difficult time. I'm not sure that if my mother had lived in my times she would have married. The last year of my father's life, I commuted every two weeks to Florida, where he lived with a housekeeper. When he died, my first thought was that I had done it: I looked after him properly and he died at home. My second thought was, I'm an orphan. I'm nobody's little girl any more.

"When I started working with my father, I lived at home, and my mother literally pushed me out of the nest. I think you should buy a house, she said, and my accountant said, Think of it as a savings account. So when I was 26, I had my own home. I was the first female to have a CMHC mortgage around here. We decided that I should never be without a mortgage, because I'm really good at spending money.

"Home is really important to me. After my father died, I moved back to the family home and renovated it top to bottom so that it was no longer the family home. It was my home. This new house is on the old site of the family cottage. Seven years ago, on a gorgeous March day, sun glistening on the snow, the river starting to open, I thought if I was serious about [building], I had better do it then. I moved in 10 months later. The design process was a nightmare; this house is Plan Five, Draft Three. I thought the architect was going to kill me.

"I do worry about getting old and sick. When they were about to pour the basement, they said, If you have any thought of having plumbing down here, speak now – so I had a kitchen and bathroom roughed in. It was the tradition for a certain class in a small Ontario town to have a housekeeper live in, and that's an option. The house is fully accessible, just one step coming in, so I thought of that when I designed it.

"I used to be very lonely, and then I realized everyone's lonely. One of my friends is in a very difficult marriage with difficult children, and she is far lonelier than I am. In my 30s my problem was that all my friends were married, having children, and had no spare money. Now I have friends who for one reason or another are single or free and do have money! I have a whole circle of people to travel with, to go to Stratford and Shaw, and that has changed my life. They're mostly men, which is odd when I think of it. Many of my women friends are married and preoccupied with older children.

"I'm a traveller, and it was a revelation to me that I could travel alone. It's a very selfish pleasure. I'm good at meeting people in those situations; whether those are long-term relationships, I don't know. I go to Europe every year; I once went for three months to cooking school. I go to Egypt, China, Ireland; it depends whether I feel like coping with the language or not. I'm very fond of lovely hotels.

"I've had my wings clipped with the house and the new business. But one of my friends is not very well – read 'terminal' – and I've thought lately, Time to get going again. You don't know how long you're here for. I've always lived that way. As long as I have enough money to live when I'm old, why shouldn't I spend it?"

Making Compromises

The second group of women is larger and more diverse in its assets and its attitudes. But these women share a deliberate intention to step off the upwardly mobile track and to live more modestly. For various reasons, these women organize their lives according to a rationale in which the acquisition of possessions or long-term financial security is not the priority. The most important value for such women might be the freedom to work when and if they please, or to travel when the spirit moves them; it might be their children's education, a rural form of self-reliance, or the liberty to be active in the community. Some women have to work very hard, physically, to sustain their choices, a way of life that might be considered borderline.

Achieving balance is the goal of others. Recently single after a long marriage, Louise is a science writer in Kingston. "Although I've worked for thirty-some years, I won't have a pension of any sort. I have an RRSP, but it's certainly not enough. I've come to the understanding that if you slow your pace totally, there is no need to stop working. We have this 65-year-old limit that we have to run like hell to get to, so we can sit down and do nothing. The best thing to do is pace yourself and imagine that you're going to have to go for the rest of your life. Maybe working two or three days a week.

"I don't work a very heavy schedule. I don't make very much money either. I get work by reputation. And I make a living, a modest living. But if I can keep making a modest living for the rest of my life, working at this pace, then maybe that's the answer. Then I won't need that pension. We tend to think we're going to need a great big bundle of money. I do have disability insurance, but it runs out even if you get disabled. I do still own half of the [marital] house and I have some small investments. But I try not to think about it very much. There's not a lot of value in thinking too far ahead. It's much better to stay in the present. The things you worry about are often not the things that happen. And the things that happen are often not the ones you've worried about."

Sybil

Quadra Island. Sun, silence, flowering trees, earth. The smell of the rich soil on her hands, Sybil was digging deep, pulling up buttercups. Squatting on a piece of cardboard. Funny old tennis shoes, purple shirt over a white T-shirt, hair pulled back, witchy-looking with her lean, narrow face. She is 39, sometimes haggard, sometimes serene. She didn't offer to show me her little house back up on the hillside, and she was afraid to be identified. She wouldn't say where she's from. She was careful, like a wild bird.

"I've been here 18 or 19 years. Until my son was seven, we lived on the outside; we squatted on beaches and we'd just go off in the woods and build a wickiup. He'd lived like that his whole life, and I felt he needed exposure to other kids, mainstream culture. There's a really good alternative school up the road here. My parents had been offering to buy me land, and though I don't really believe in land ownership, it just came to me, Yeah, I think I need to do it. I'm lucky, I don't have any mortgage to pay or anything, so I can really live my own lifestyle without having to come up with a lot of money to do it. These days you can work really hard when you're past my age just to get a place."

I sat on a log, watching her scratch at the hard spring soil. "So you have a son. Did you ever live with his father?"

"No, not really. We had a really strong spiritual connection. When we see each other, there's still this feeling of being connected. But on a practical level, we weren't really right for each other. He's quite an eccentric individual."

Sybil considered my questions with solemn thoughtfulness. "Marriage has always seemed kind of scary to me. My dad wasn't a healthy person at all, and so the thing of commitment, for better or worse – I got to see the 'for worse' side a lot. He was physically ill and emotionally ill and just not that great a person. He died a while ago when my mum had just blossomed.

"On the one hand, I was told marriage was the most important thing and the best thing that would ever happen to me. So I did grow up with that myth, but also I was told, Oh, you're too smart to get married. You'd waste yourself having a family. You've got to be a great scientist, you're just so smart. That's why I'm digging buttercups!"

"Does your son live with you now?"

"No, he's 25. I got pregnant with him when I was 14. We've always had kind of an odd relationship, I think, because I had him as young as I did. A lot of people put pressure on me to have an abortion. I had a social worker come right after I had him and try to force me to sign adoption papers, telling me she'd seen lots of mothers like me who had tried to kill their babies or have sex with them. Just after you give birth, you don't need to hear that. I strongly believed in the way that I was living, and so I felt like I was doing him a big favour by keeping him and bringing him up with the ideals I had. I wanted a lot of space."

"What do you think it is about you, intrinsically, that makes solitude right for you?"

She paused in her digging, squinting in the bright sun. "That's been a long process. I couldn't say it was a decision, more like adaptation perhaps. Like a cactus adapts to the desert. Initially I started living close to the earth because I had a strong vision that the creator lives in his creation, that the only way we have of praying is to live in a good way with creation, to live in a respectful way. So I've been passionate about wanting to find a harmonious and respectful way to live, growing all my food and living the way I live. That took me out of the cities, out of the mainstream. After I had my son, because of the hard time I had with social workers, I didn't want welfare, and so I went off in the woods and lived like that.

"There's not a lot of guys out in the woods. When I was younger, I'd want to be in a relationship because I was scared and I couldn't take care of myself. I'd end up taking care of somebody else, and I had good reason to be scared because they were violent. So it was a gradual evolution, just coming to a place where I felt much safer and much more complete and much more in control, just by myself."

"Do you think there's a connection between your solitude and your spirituality?"

"Definitely. If there were more people willing to live in connection with the earth, and walk instead of drive cars, and grow food that I could trade with, I'd probably have a lot more community around me and a lot more potential partners who were the same species as me. I'm aware of things that people don't even have time to think about or notice. There's rewards in everything, you know. There's costs as well. I'm not here to be independent. I'm here because it's really beautiful and I love the earth, and the times of deepest joy for me are when I look up and see something that's awesome. I feel a sense of oneness with that."

The pile of buttercups was slowly growing. This intensive weeding was hard work, requiring time and patience. "Is there anything that you regret? Are there moments when you imagine being somewhere else, doing something else?"

She smiled a little. "Sometimes I imagine being somewhere wild. Being able to make my own fire. But I don't have regrets. If there are good times or bad times, it's for a reason, just like there's a cost and a benefit to anything. The only way I could see myself getting together with someone is if that person was involved in doing some kind of humanitarian work or something that I admired so much that I wanted to support them and was willing to make the accommodation to support them. Otherwise, I see so many costs. So many risks.

"I've noticed that we get attracted to people who represent things we need to integrate into our own lives. I think one of the keys to happiness that I've found is feeling that things are happening for a good reason."

"Where do you think you'll be buried?"

She had no hesitation. "Oh, I want to be buried here. Then I will have seen both sides of things. I'll be looking at these buttercups from the other side!"

Some of the most contented women I met were women living on the edges, off the grid of conventional society. Island women, like Barbara and Sybil in the Gulf Islands, throwing bread to the seagulls, digging into the barely warmed earth of spring. Grace and her dogs in Newfoundland, walking the gorgeous beach down the road from her house. Marta, who loved her old farmhouse at the end of a dirt road in rural Ontario.

They showed a certain insouciance about money: if it's there, great; if it's not, life will be all right somehow. They immersed themselves in small sensual pleasures: the company of a cat, a Mason jar of wildflowers, a window box bursting with geraniums.

The Poor

The third group of women have crossed over the boundary into extreme poverty. They cannot see how they will escape, although some will. Many women fear this state: ever-dwindling resources, no job and then no prospect of a job, trapped in a bureaucratic net that cannot be untangled, becoming a bag lady. A few women, however, feel more secure with nothing: one is the street woman I met on Jericho Beach in Vancouver, who prefers to sleep in the woods, who has a shopping trolley filled with her possessions, who washes and changes every morning in the public washroom and then spends her days walking. With each small, careful piece of the ritual of her daily life, she is armoured against her addictions, enemies, fears. Others fight their way out.

Sharon

"If things don't turn around by September, I'm seriously considering just getting in my car and driving somewhere and changing my name and making sandwiches in a diner. Getting on with my life."

Sharon is 48, a slight woman with fading reddish hair, small enough to sit with her knees under her chin on a desk chair. Jeans and T-shirt, bare feet. Her cluttered one-bedroom apartment, stacked high with paper and books, smelled of stale food and smoke and dog. A panting German shepherd set his coarse-haired body firmly on my feet, begging to be let out onto the balcony. The apartment is small and dark, and it faces a bright green playing field that shimmers in the August heat. There's a cap-and-gown portrait of Sharon on the bookcase, taken only a few years ago; she is radiant, smiling, eyes and hair shining. She is still a woman of light and fire.

Sharon graduated from high school at 16 and has seen something of the world. In her 20s she drove from Toronto to Rio; on another trip she flew to Nairobi, then drove to London. She's had good jobs, and I can see why; she is smart, quick-witted, efficient in her movements and thoughts. When she came back from Europe, she got a job in a bank in Calgary. A man came in one day and declared he would marry her. He did.

"I was 25 when I got married. I should have known better. We were in marriage counselling the first year, and I worked at it for 13 years, not wanting to be a failure.

"I tried to leave several times. I kept leaving the relationship but going back to the lifestyle. I had a farm, I had horses, I had everything. We had three businesses and a fully operational farm. I worked 90 hours a week for 13 years. Sometimes I took really good jobs in Toronto, and after a certain amount of time, I'd find myself sitting at a desk in a tower thinking, Oh, my God! I've got 40 more years of this, I can't stand it! And go back to the farm.

"Finally, I left with just my car and my cat and my stereo. I used to say that when I left, at least I had my sanity. Now I'm not so sure I even had that. 'Cause I walked away from everything. I walked away from over a million dollars. And while I was trying to get myself together, he flew down to Vegas, and his business managers and accountants looked after everything. When he came back, he said he'd gambled everything away – when in actuality it was all stashed.

"Looking back, I think my failure was in not getting out sooner. When I was married, whenever I met a woman who was separated or divorced, I would ask them what it was like. How did they do it? When did they do it? What was the hardest part? As if there was some list of instructions – first you do this, then you do that, like a recipe – and I would then be able to leave. What struck me, and still stays with me, is the number of women who said the hardest thing was walking out the door. Once they did that, they couldn't believe that they hadn't done it sooner.

"I came to Peterborough. I didn't know anyone here, but because a friend suggested it, I filled in an application for Trent University. It was the first time in my whole life that I felt at home. The first semester I took a philosophy course. I thought I'd died and gone to heaven. So I did my undergraduate degree in philosophy. I desperately wanted to just go on and do a master's and a PhD in philosophy. But there's no money in it. After the BA, I knew I had to look after myself. It seemed that a bachelor of education, specializing in English as a second language, was the way to go. I felt there was something of value in that, something I wanted to do. But when I graduated, that was the beginning of the [education] cuts, and the first thing that went was ESL for new immigrants.

"I was trying to find something, some work that would support me and pay my student loans. I could find an entry-level job at $7 an hour, but it wouldn't pay my loan. They accumulate the interest, so it gets higher and higher. I got on a plane and went to Korea to find work teaching. I borrowed money to get over there, and it wasn't what it was cracked up to be financially. Then the exchange rate plummeted, and it was just a disaster! I went to Mexico to teach at a private high school, which was against everything that I believed in. I did not go into ESL to perpetuate the gap between the rich and the poor.

"While I was there, I was exposed to a bacterium found in chickens or pigeons, and I got sick and came home. The last little while, I've been doing some supply teaching, some freelance writing, some research assistant work up on campus. But none of it is enough to pay my student loan. I'm just able to pay my rent and my car insurance.

"See, no matter how bad things get, I can always escape. Even when I was on welfare, and it was $520 a month, I did everything I could to keep my car. So that if I had to, I could get in it at two o'clock in the morning and run away. I'm almost at that point now. September is coming up. Student loans are closing in. No one is willing to negotiate.

"A lot of my women friends are in similar circumstances. We went to university to improve ourselves, and student loans were the only way to do it. Some have declared bankruptcy on their student loans. Others have children from previous marriages, so they have support. Women in my situation are basically invisible. If I had kids, I'd get more on welfare. It's surprising how many of us there are. I'm constantly a month away from literally living on the street.

"I'm 48. I'm scared. Right now I want peace. I want quiet. What that means is I want money, and that's directly opposed to how I value life, and how I ultimately want to live it. But it's a necessity. I've got to get a lot of money, and I've got to get it fast . . . I find myself picking up shopping carts now, looking for ones that have good wheels. I look at one of the bridges, such a pretty bridge, with nice little ledges under it, I could live there . . .

"I bristle when people say, Go to a doctor and see if Prozac will help. I think, No, maybe talk to Mike Harris – I think maybe change the system a little bit, change the value system. If I were clinically depressed, I wouldn't still be looking for a way out of my situation. I'm still looking for it. Even if my only option now is to get into my car and drive up north and start a new life. That's something that would take a hell of a lot of determination and energy and desire, which I don't think depression allows one to do.

"There are times when I get really angry. The other day I was at the corner store, and I saw someone with a huge, big white brand-new Lincoln. And I just wanted to kick it. Isn't that awful? But I wanted to."

CHAPTER 9

End-games

$\mathcal{A}$s single women age, they become increasingly concerned about illness, old age, and dying. As early as their 40s and 50s, women are drawn into a series of confrontations with health issues as their parents, friends, or siblings age and fall victim to illness. Eventually their own well-being also demands attention.

Although in general single women eat well, exercise, and are informed about health matters, they do not always put their knowledge into practice. Very few have taken the steps they are advised to take: a disability pension, a health-care power of attorney, an up-to-date will, an executor. They are inconsistent in their attention to the basic medical checks: regular mammograms and Pap smears, bone scans for osteoporosis. It often takes a serious scare, for themselves or for a close friend, to get single women focused on their health. It is easier to attend to the health of others.

I do not know of many single women, except those who happen to have retired or who will retire on a company or government pension, who have arranged their affairs to provide for the possibility of their own serious illness. Many single women do not have long-term, full-time jobs. They are single mothers with part-time

work or divorcees with home-based businesses or freelance contracts. They are anticipating retirement with real estate investments
and RRSPs, but they are not prepared for the possibility of personal
incapacity. When I ask, Who will look after you if you get really
sick, few have a ready answer, and even fewer have a plan.

I wondered how Sybil, so close to the earth and so distant from
her family, would manage. She told me, "I was really ill a couple of
years ago. I had to have major surgery, and I had to set it up so that
I could take care of myself. Mum and my sister were totally off the
wall and they weren't helpful. I guess it was a pretty emotional
thing for them; my survival wasn't certain. But I didn't want to be
helping them cope. Friends dropped by, but they were just making
sure I had enough stuff in the freezer, and that I could manage.
They cleaned up my house really well. I live so close to the edge. I
live on between $3,500 and $6,000 a year. Somehow it just worked
out. It's incredible."

Marta, who declared herself "alone and happy to be so" in
her farmhouse, acknowledged that a serious illness could shake her.
"One of my fears is being alone and poor and out on the street.
One or another of my kids would probably be willing to help, but
it's not something I'd be willing to accept. I have a very dear friend
who does attendant care for people with disabilities. I've named
him in my living will as the person to determine what would
happen to me if I couldn't make those decisions myself. And he
knows that I would rather not be with my kids."

"Because you don't want to burden them?" I suggested.

"Exactly. When I see other people dealing with their parents, I
think I was lucky my parents died as young as they did. I don't
want to put that on my kids. They would be very upset to hear that.
I've named a lawyer friend as executor of my will, also attorney in
financial matters if I get incapacitated. If there's a need for hospi-
talization or chronic care, my other friend should interview people
and set things up for me. He's really good at that."

For Naomi, living with ovarian cancer, the prospect of needing care has become real. "I'm finding out that I have wonderful friends, and that we never realize how much we are a part of each other's lives," she told me. "There's a shop up the street where I've been shopping ever since I moved to the neighbourhood. Maria, who works there, was really upset to hear that I was sick, and is very clear that she could always come by at lunchtime and bring me stuff from the store. And neighbours who have dogs have offered to take care of the dog. There's community.

"Unfortunately, my parents are having to take care of me too, which is strange. I hate that my mother is coming in next week. But I've heard of relationships that end when one person gets sick. The partner can't cope. So that's not a guarantee, either."

"But in profound illness, you usually need one person who you rely on utterly, who will make decisions for you if necessary. Do you have someone who plays that role?"

"It would be Frank, even though he's in another city and the relationship is only a year old. I can't say it's because I'm in a relationship with him. It's because of who he is. Certainly in the past I would not have been trusting enough. I would not believe a man would be around for the long haul. That I would allow them that right. I think for the first time in my life, I'm letting go. I'm saying, You do it. It's an enormous relief."

From the Journal of a Caregiver

My friend Suzanne is dying. Over the past few days, she has become very thin but not fragile. Her bone structure is still that of a strong, tall woman. Her features are beautiful: high smooth brow, high angular cheekbones, straight even nose, graceful shoulders and collarbone, long, slender hands. Features obscured in health are illuminated in the process of dying. Her eyes are huge in her skull, her hair a light brown, baby-fine cap.

She lies regally on her big brass bed. The only sounds are her regular breathing, Debussy's wistful "Golliwog's Cakewalk" on the CD player, the click and whirr of the morphine cartridge tucked under her pillow, pumping a regulated flow of morphine to ease her pain, the quiet movement of a nurse, a friend, or one of her children. There is someone in the room at all times.

The room has been painted a deep orange-sherbet hue, and it wraps cheer and warmth around her. Dressers and tables are filled with flowers: irises and roses, big sweet-smelling lilies and bright daffodils and tulips, a pot of hyacinths. In one corner, a huge basket brimming with pale green orchids. It has been thus since her birthday a week ago and will be until her death. Scented candles are scattered around the room. Her son has put a small bird feeder outside the window; purple finches and cardinals perch there. Suzanne likes the window open, to hear the birds, smell the incipient spring.

These days, the front door of the house is always unlocked during the day. Friends come and go, bringing food, flowers, books, music, wine, candles, the good things of life that Suzanne loves. Someone comes from home care every morning to clean, to do laundry and dishes. For a month or so there were hospice volunteers and a nurse once a day; now there is always a nurse. There is a journal on the big wooden kitchen table that we read when we arrive. It is a record of medication, food, sleep patterns, pain, and the simple things that need doing or buying. Can someone pick up some jugs of water? We're out of garbage bags; we need more apricot juice. On the wall by the phone, a list of numbers, the friends in the city who are part of the care team, the friends in Vancouver, New York, Montreal, Ottawa, Chicago who call almost daily.

I did not know, when I became friends with Suzanne several years earlier, that I would become part of her care team in the last six months of her life, as she was swiftly overtaken by ovarian cancer.

End-games

Suzanne was a single mother with two teenage children, both, like her, tall, intense, and brainy with steely minds and chimerical emotions. She was one of the brightest people I knew; she had a solid academic intelligence coupled with a zany creativity. She was a social policy guru; she thought and wrote and spoke about family issues. She worked hard to push her generous ideas about children, family, women, and poverty into the minds and onto the agendas of people who could do something about the causes she cared about. Her optimism was boundless.

A year before Suzanne died, she hosted an Easter brunch at her house. She had not been feeling well, she was tired and aching, but her terrible diagnosis was several months away. There were eight or ten of us at brunch. We shared a certain sharp wit, but most of us did not know one another. We came from different corners, different periods in Suzanne's life. I remember a long conversation about the Finnish-Russian border with an archaeologist who was about to walk the entire length of that frontier.

Six months later, Suzanne asked virtually the same group of people to form her care team, and we came together again at her house one October evening to learn what that meant. We were guided through the stages of caregiving by June, a registered nurse from Trinity Home Hospice, a woman with a soft northern English accent, a gentle but firm manner, an apparently effortless way of securing our commitment to one day a week – a loose web of tentative okays that would turn into a carefully monitored roster of duties.

We did not, in the early days of this arrangement, talk about death. At first there was not much more than visiting once a week to cook a meal or bring one, to deliver videos, to take Suzanne's son to the supermarket. To drive Suzanne to the hospital for a blood transfusion or a radiation treatment or an X-ray, to clean the refrigerator, talk with the two children, sort through family photos,

257

paint the bedroom. Members of the team had their own strengths, and weaknesses, the things they were comfortable doing, the things they were not.

It was not until the final weeks that we openly acknowledged that, yes, our friend was dying and that, yes, we were somehow part of that experience. We accepted that she might die in our presence.

Death is not something we talk about easily. It is a potent word which, once uttered, can make dreaded things happen, it seems. Part of what we were being taught by June was to be ready for death, if and when it came. By being part of a team who came regularly into Suzanne's house, her bedroom, we became people who could embrace the idea of Suzanne dying, and help her through it. As Suzanne's condition worsened, as she needed more nursing support to manage bodily functions and monitor pain, our relationship became more intimate. There was a natural breaking down of inhibitors, like fear, ignorance, and the usual social reserve that exists between friends, the boundaries of touch and emotional expression that we do not easily cross. We began a journey in two dimensions: first, the quest for knowledge that would enable us to give Suzanne whatever she needed either to live or to die; second, the voyage into self-awareness and our own deeply held terrors and ignorance.

We were the family that Suzanne created for herself, a family of individuals who shared, in one way or another, Suzanne's values and her sense of what mattered. Just as Suzanne consciously chose and constructed her role as a single mother, so she constructed her family of friends. There was something pragmatic at the heart of this, although there was also love. The people Suzanne chose as her family were better equipped to help her move towards death than her birth family. Not because of knowledge – we had to acquire that. It was because we were receptive.

Wonderful phone conversation with Suzanne, clear and calm about her will, executors, insurance, about the legacy she would be leaving her children, not just money but her principles and hopes, values she may record as part of the will. She says in a matter-of-fact way that it's almost better if she dies. Of course it isn't, but there is no need to say that. But if she does not die, she may not be able to work. Her disability insurance and leave-of-absence arrangements with her current employer are not permanent benefits.

Suzanne can hardly sit without anguish, she cannot walk any more, the pain grows, and so too does the tumour, she believes. She goes to Florida for six days with a close friend, and then comes back, she says with a laugh, to ultrasound and ultratruth. She thinks there is nothing more that can be done. She is so grounded, even in her terrifying illness. This is one of many phone calls we have in the last months of her life. I realize she might not be able to have such conversations with some other friends. Those who have known her for a long time could not tolerate this train of thought without protestations and tears. But it feels completely right to speak the truth, with humour, with serenity, without denials. Maybe it would not happen face to face.

There is a connection between Suzanne's openness and transparency with her friends and the fact that she is single. She is both more vulnerable and more open, having to say things to us that she would not if she were part of a couple. There is no gatekeeper. It is also true that Suzanne orchestrated and planned her caregiving, just as she would have planned a conference or a communications strategy. In doing so she created a precedent for those who accepted the caregiving role, especially, I think, those of us who are without partners.

The care team met for a final session with June, but not at Suzanne's house. It was time for the questions people were reluctant to ask: How long, and how will we know? June talked about pain and distributed a slim booklet that outlined the signs of death. I read the booklet at Suzanne's kitchen table late one evening, the night after she had told her daughter she was not going to live, the night that signalled the beginning of her passage into death. The words I remember: coolness of the skin, and mottling, as blood is withdrawn to vital organs. Long periods of apparent sleep. Restless, flickering gestures of hands. The fact that people who are dying hear remarkably well, even when we think they are not conscious. The fact that death follows a logical sequence of events. I thought about the careful rituals of shutting down a cottage, or bedding down a garden, before the onset of winter.

Tuesday: Suzanne's best friend and I and one of the sympathetic nurses were there, late into the night. I fed Suzanne some stew, some yogourt, a sip of wine. She was noticeably weaker, quieter. She was in great pain and could not turn over. Knowing she was in agony was the hardest thing, worse than the notion of death itself. But we talked her through it: Breathe, Suzanne, just like labour, keep breathing.

Her skin was drying in places, as if it too had stopped breathing; I lathered her legs and feet as gently as possible with a lavender cream. The act allowed a closeness never offered or attempted in life. Perhaps this participation in death is one way our society can become more humane, achieve grace.

I can't do this any longer, she whispered.

One solitary orchid still bloomed palely.

Friday: I carried a bouquet of yellow tulips to Suzanne. I took off my shoes, climbed over the cat, a pile of pillows and quilts and bedcovers. I lay next to her on the bed and held the flowers out to her. She raised her head, a glimmer came into her eyes, her voice was barely audible. She reached out for the flowers and briefly held them, her eyes showing pleasure. Then she sank back onto the pillow, into the silence she had roused herself from. I could not reach her again. Are you sad or tired or both, I asked. No answer, but I knew. I knew that just as her body was gradually shutting down, so too was her consciousness. I sat with her awhile, my hand between her long, slim fingers.

Saturday/Sunday: Suzanne's strong, calm voice was still on the answering machine, already a voice from the past. The nurse called me back; maybe 12 to 24 hours, she said. Sunday morning was a bright, balmy day, and the children and closest friends were there. I said goodbye, good courage, good death to my friend, and I knew she heard this.

Monday: Suzanne died this evening, in the company of two friends, with her children each holding a hand. The heady fragrance of rerum lilies, and Gershwin's "Summertime" playing.

I have a photo of Suzanne, given to me and many of her friends by her children, after her death. Suzanne is standing in the bush, in winter. The snow is crisp white, her shadow sharp on the snow, the birch trees almost silver in their lustre, the woods behind dark and tangled. Suzanne is jubilant, long legs widespread in the snow, arms high over her head, holding her skis in a gesture of triumph. A big grin on her face: I did it, I have won, I am out there.

Grand Dames

Single women hope to live long and well. In my travels, I encountered many women who had done so. A few were especially memorable because they were living well, alone, with great verve and dignity, and because they shared an idealism, a sense that their role was to serve their community or their country in some way. They were women with vocations: doctors, teachers, social workers, civil servants. They lived comfortably, in interesting surroundings that reflected their means and their past.

These women had never married and were discreet about whatever relationships they had experienced. They had style, gracious manners, careful grooming, clear complexions, and sensible shoes. Their memories were like dreams, not always logical: some events sharp and clear; at other moments, dates and words beyond reach . . . no matter. Some had their twilight indulgences – one woman smoked constantly, another liked her whisky – but these were the deeply ingrained habits of long living. They signalled not weakness but an old-fashioned kind of fortitude.

Younger women may aspire to their longevity, more or less in good health, and to their carefully reserved solitude, and to their vehement determination to stay in their own homes as long as possible, because to leave, one woman said to me, is to begin to die. But few young women have that remarkable quality of being both selfish and selfless, which all of these women possess. It isn't a trait they would necessarily identify in themselves. They simply did what seemed right, and doing right did not include marriage and children.

In the 1930s and 1940s in Canada, there was honour attached to being a woman in public service. It was an honour bestowed on those who joined the armed forces, as several of these women did, and once given, it was not lost after the war. A significant number took their stints in the army as opportunities for further education, leading to careers. Now in their late 80s and early 90s, they have the stature of grand dames.

Geraldine

On the shores of a half-frozen lake in the northern prairies, I sat in the home of Geraldine, a retired doctor. A GP, she told me firmly; I am not a family doctor. She is thin, hard-wired, with short white hair, large glasses, brusque but cordial. She has built this house, a sprawling structure as close to the lake as it can be. The trees are strictly pruned, and there are many birdhouses.

Inside the screened porch, where we were having coffee, there were several large cats, glaring at the birdhouses. "The damn moose keep coming through the screen. We always had the odd moose, but now we've got them by the thousands. One clobbered me this fall at the turnoff. Wrecked my car. I was on my way in for my second cataract surgery, and the moose came out of that dip, where the road goes down there. It went right over the top of the car on to the other side of the road."

She pulled out her life story like a deck of cards, sometimes telling the same story more than once, in exactly the same words. Just as she has designed and built this house, she has built the story of her life.

"I had a choice when I graduated from high school. My parents said, We'll train you for a teacher; that took one year. Or we'll train you for a steno, that took six months. Train you for a nurse, three years. Nurses were getting about $50 a month, and three years is a long time before you get paid. Stenos were a dime a dozen, and you were lucky if you got a job. Teachers got $80 a month, and it only took eight months to train to be a teacher."

She taught for three years, in Alberta, then made plans to return to school. "But the war came along and they got me in the army, and I got my uniform and private's pay, which was $40 a month. I really wanted to be a vet. I looked into it, and the only place you could train was in Waterloo, Ontario. All my money would have gone in fare and I wouldn't have had anything to live on. So I decided I wouldn't be a vet, I'd be a doctor. You paid your own tuition. All the army gave you was your uniform, two for summer, two for winter, and $40 a month." She was happy to have the uniform because "it was clothes that you didn't have to buy."

When she first arrived in the North, "with $20 in my pocket," she was one of two doctors in a very large territory. It was 1947. She did everything, including surgery. "Hemorrhoids, hernias, tonsils. Tubal ligations. You know they were illegal for a while between

1947 and 1951. I used to do them anyway. If a woman was 35 and had eight kids, she didn't need any more. If she agreed, I did her tubes. Somebody reported me and I got called up by the college, but I fixed that. Thereafter the women always had 'appendicitis' on their second day. A poor woman with kids . . . it was just damn near criminal. But you had to be 35 and have at least eight kids. That was my criterion for breaking the law."

She practised for 40 years, part of that time serving as medical examiner and coroner, investigating every car accident and bush mishap. She delivered between 2,000 and 2,500 babies – just about everyone in town, she laughed, drawing to red hot on her cigarette.

For 23 years she was a town councillor. "I wanted to balance the budget and pay off the 1912 debt. I wanted recreation to be something besides baseball or hockey. The town housed a little library in its tiny office. I was quite interested in that. I sat on the library board for 45 years."

She still goes once a week to the library and clips newspapers for the archives. I suggested that women were a strong force in sustaining a community. She said, "They were the civilized persons. They were not regarded as community leaders, they just poked from behind, so to speak."

She was not prepared to talk much about her personal life; she had no time, no patience for such things. "Oh, I had odds and ends. There are several kinds of people, heterosexual, bisexual, homosexual, and asexual. I think I fit in that last category, because I was never interested in a man except as someone to go someplace with." She admitted to having had a sexual relationship with a man, but "I couldn't stand the interference. There's no way I was going to make it so they interfered with my life. Why would you ever get married? If you need sex, make an appointment . . . Why should I want to have children? I delivered a couple of thousand."

"Some women say that even though you don't want a child, you go through a period when the body wants one. Did you go through that?"

"No. Possibly because I started teaching school, and possibly because I was one of the brightest ones in the small backwoods where I was raised. I was always looking after the rest of the kids. So I never wanted any children. Never felt that there was any sense in reproducing my kind."

She said she had done "nothing" since she retired 13 years ago. I didn't believe her. She had read herself to sleep since she was four years old. "I don't think I know what loneliness is."

Minnie

On the South Shore of Nova Scotia, I met Minnie, a 92-year-old retired teacher. She owns her property, down a rough country road, overlooking a small flash of a lake, like a mirror thrown down in the bush. She lives in a converted trailer on land that used to be a sheep farm. The bush is thick and wild. "I was brought up on the prairie, and when my friends and relatives come from the prairie, they nearly have a fit to see the trees right outside. I'm going to have a few of these trees cut. My friends will come and cut them for me."

The trailer is attached to a long porch with a railing, and on the railing there were Mason jars filled with wildflowers. More inside on the dining-room table, which was set for lunch. There was an old upright piano, covered with sheet music. In the living room there was a sewing basket beside the chair and lots of knitted or crocheted pillow covers in bright colours. Stacks of books, about birds, the arts, Kierkegaard, Jean Vanier, and a map of the Yukon and Northwest Territories on the wall.

Her hair is dyed brown and coiffed around her head. She's very tiny and her neck muscles are like cords. Her body is a bit twisted, but she looks like an ancient dancer, very alert and agile. She's proud of being 92 and eagerly tells people her age, mostly to watch their response. One person said, I wouldn't have thought you were a day over 91. She was amused by that.

Minnie grew up on a farm and seemed destined to teach. "We were not rich people and there were six kids, and I don't ever remember giving it any consideration! A woman can be anything now, but not then. The only thing you could be was a stenographer or a teacher. Or a house servant. And I used to read, I read all kinds of books to my brothers and sisters. All the Zane Grey stories, and Dickens and Shakespeare and everything."

She began teaching in 1929 and taught for most of her life out west and in the North. When she retired at 65, she came east. "You know, we all have silly prejudices. I hate to say it now, but I thought that people here were kind of stupid and didn't know anything. I didn't want to go to the Maritimes. But there were some families here from the States, and they were starting up a school. Twenty-seven years ago the education program here was pretty abysmal. They were still standing kids in the corner, making them write words a hundred times. I don't believe in any of that nonsense. Never did. I was ahead of my time, and I was always afraid they were going to take my certificate away in Alberta, because I was reading the classics to the kids. They said it was a waste of time.

"So, these people came up from the States and found things so far behind in the Maritimes that they wanted to have a small private school. They couldn't find a teacher to run it. A friend of mine recommended me. They sent me the fare to come. I stayed two years, because by then I was 67 – and I loved children, but I'd been teaching from the time I was 21 years old. And I thought I'd better stop."

At some point – the chronology is uncertain – she realized she would not be a mother. She recounted it easily, but her mind drifted into a little bay of grief. "You see, you go along, you know how we go along, everybody else dies, everybody else has everything, and nothing happens to you. Well, I didn't realize until it was almost –" her mind skipped. "I didn't want a man. I never saw one that I wanted! I had all kinds of proposals. Every district you went to, you'd be about two years in a school and all the nice men – ranchers, farmers, very fine men, really, but I knew what I didn't want. I grew up on a farm. I knew I didn't want to be chasing chickens around. I wanted to see the world and to go as far as I could. So I didn't pay any attention to them.

"But I was very upset, very disappointed when I realized. I quit teaching for a while. I guess you'd almost call it a nervous break-down. You always think you'll have a child of your own, because I really like children. I just waited too long to –" She broke off. "There was a doctor in Calgary who had a child without being married and they took her credentials away from her. So I was in a place where . . . I was too busy teaching."

She remained in Nova Scotia but was ambivalent about this community she calls home. "I have to say that of all the places I've ever been, when I came here, this was the most unfriendly town. Just think, 27 years ago, they wouldn't build me a house. In the beginning they considered I was a prostitute or a lesbian, or some-thing was wrong. And buying land! How could she buy land, how's she going to pay for it? I was so surprised. They didn't want to do wells, they didn't want to do anything for me. I had an awful time. I think it was because I was a single woman. Married people don't realize that the mere fact that you have a man tagging along makes quite a bit of difference to the way you're received.

"Now they walk up to me and say that it's a privilege to know me. Really? I feel like slapping their faces. I belong to community groups and support all these things. But there's all kinds of people live near me, and it does seem odd to me that they never offer to do anything or call up to see how I am. If I phoned some of them up and asked them, well, sure, they'd say, Right away. But I'm not complaining. You have to look at things from both sides, really."

I asked her what would happen if she became ill. This was not something she wanted to contemplate. "I suppose I'd end up down in the senior citizens' home. It's very good, but I don't want to go there. I play music for them. My friend does volunteer work there; they told her, You know that woman who was here yesterday playing the piano? She's a liar. She couldn't play the piano like that if she was 92. See the idea they have? The minute you leave your own home . . . I'd just as soon die here as anywhere else. There's no place like home, it's sure true."

She had made a salmon loaf for lunch. She doesn't like to cook, but she said any fool can cook basically. Salmon loaf and squash, and then an angel food cake, with ice cream and tea. She gave me a little crocheted cushion that she'd made and a book about her life as a teacher. But she had a moment of sadness when she said her sister wrote to her a while back and said, We hope you don't imagine that we will look after you when you're old, because we won't. She felt very hurt by that.

She said it was only in the last year that she'd started to feel lonely. But she believes that being in your own home is the most important thing, being active and self-reliant. She has so many projects. "You get so you have to be by yourself after a while, because you just can't get anything done if there's anybody around. I can only stand to be around people for so long."

I wish that I had asked her to play the piano.

Elizabeth

Elizabeth greeted me in a large, comfortable apartment overlooking the river in Winnipeg. She was beautifully dressed in a well-cut wool dress, setting off a heavy gold locket on a chain. She sat perfectly still and released her memories, one by one, like balloons. Her diction was impeccable, and when she spoke of balls in Montreal in the 1930s, or the gallantry of officers on the base in Newfoundland, she brought a more gracious era to life. She was a recruiting officer in the army, then a social worker in Ontario. She is 94.

For many years, she lived with a woman friend. In Toronto in the 1950s, it seemed a sensible arrangement. Lisa was 15 years younger, an academic. They had known each other as graduate students in residence, Elizabeth having gone back to university after the war.

"When she left the residence, Lisa got a place and she kept phoning and saying, Can I come over for dinner? Sometimes it would be practically every night of the week Lisa was there. I like cooking and she doesn't, you see. So I said to her, I think you should be paying me for this. And she said, Well, perhaps I should. And I said, Unless we live together. She said, Well, that's an idea.

"What a time we had. It was awful. Because I'm so bossy, you know. I'm able to say that now. I was very bossy and I realized that, and she was very bright, a clever woman. She was the most untidy person in the world. I was terribly neat. She was at the Children's Aid then, but she went to the school of social work and became a professor there.

"We bought the house for no money at all. Lisa had $1,000. I put $100 into the credit union and got a loan of $1,000. We took a loan from the bank, and $7,000 we borrowed from her brother. We paid $22,500. We bought equally. In 10 years we had paid off everything with interest."

Their relationship took time to become what it finally was, a tender, loving friendship. "We had different friends. We liked different things. But we got to like each one of us better . . .

"Her family is very close to me. And my family was very close to her. When she died, we had a wonderful place in Kingston. I loved it. I would have stayed on there. She died in '95. By that time,

I had stopped driving a car. My eyes weren't very good." She was saying, a little crossly, that she had had to move back to Winnipeg, where her family is from, because Lisa was not there to drive any more. She was saying how much, still, she missed her.

"Was it unusual for two women to put their lives together like that?"

"I don't know. You mean, without being lesbians?"

"Yes."

"I don't know."

"You obviously had a great affection for each other."

"Oh, yes, we had great affection for each other."

"It does seem as if at some point you made a commitment to be together in some way."

"Well, until we got the house, we weren't sure, because Lisa was always talking about moving away. I think when we got the house, we really had committed ourselves to being together."

"Did people ever imagine that you had a sexual relationship?"

"I don't know what other people thought. Certainly my family didn't think so. I don't think any of my friends did."

"So it was an acceptable choice to make, to be good friends who lived together and shared a house."

"It was certainly economical. It was a good idea and . . . it was a very interesting life together. She was very much brighter than I was."

"Of course, we had planned it that I was going to die first, naturally. We had it all arranged, and she knew all about the things that I wanted done and where I wanted to be buried. I didn't know anything about her wishes. At the end I learned more. She'd been ill for about a year, off and on. She died of cancer. She was so angry. I think she was angry at me that I was still living."

"Where was she buried?"

"She was buried in Ontario, off Highway 15. Her parents are buried there, and her brothers. She always wanted to be buried there. It's a lovely place."

I asked her, "Where will you be buried?"

"Here. In Winnipeg. I want to be buried under a prairie sky."

I frequently asked women where they would be buried. It was a question that surprised them. Many had never thought about it. I asked because cemeteries, old-fashioned graveyards, can tell the stories of families and communities, and because the conventions of graveyards also reflect the tradition of women as belonging to one man or another. I asked as a way of examining changing ideas of what a family is and what defines it, and how this family or that, yours or mine, is a matter of personal and historical record.

The time when people were born, grew up, found work, married, bore children, and died all in the same community has almost passed. Graveyards are becoming anachronisms. On country roads one often sees a huddle of stones on a concrete pad in the corner of a farmer's field, alongside a plaque indicating that this was once the site of a church. Large city cemeteries now come with a crematorium wing, a room reminiscent of the mailbox wall at the local post office or the safety deposit vault at a bank, where the cindered remains of loved ones are stacked.

Very few women I spoke to had decided on a final resting place. Only one woman could say, "There are six spots in the family burial plot at the United Church. Five are filled and the sixth is mine." Another said her ashes could be used on icy sidewalks to prevent other old people from falling down. Many women thought in terms not of a resting place but of a locale where their ashes could be scattered to the wind, an act not so much of remembrance as freedom. This spot was most often a place that they associated with love, tranquility, a time of happiness in their lives.

I cannot answer this question myself. My father's parents, my mother's parents, aunts, and uncles, and many first and second cousins are buried in a small village cemetery in northern Michigan. Gravestones record their full names, their dates of birth and death.

Sometimes a small fragment of verse signals piety or sorrow. My parents were cremated, and we three children took their ashes into the Blue Mountains and scattered them at sunset in a grove of the wild rhododendrons that they both loved. My brother and sister and I are all single, so there is no plot of land that we will inhabit with a loved one into eternity. Our family name will survive only as the second name of some of our children.

This is one more piece of our lives that we are making up as we go along, one more example of the shift in ideas about family that marks the turn into a new century.

CHAPTER 10

Intervale Gardens

I spent three days in an inn that is truly a stone's throw from the Saint John River in New Brunswick. I love the river's black depths and sparkling surface, its meandering, slow course, the powerful Bay of Fundy tides that push high up inland and then turn, pulling the river out to the bay.

I was profoundly soothed by this river and by the little-engine-that-could cable ferry, chugging across it, back and forth, taking long, silent pauses in the night but ready and waiting should someone appear on one bank or the other. I lay on the wobbly wooden dock and felt the rhythm of the dark water beneath me, breathing deep of the musty, fishy smell of the marsh behind. There were pin cherries and sumac and wild apples hanging over the nearby narrow roads, and loosestrife, pickerel weed, and lilies on the ponds. Ducks panicked and flustered up into the sky, squawking.

The river wanders and spreads at several points, around low islands, into marshes, making secret channels known only to osprey and heron. The edges of the river are loosely defined in places: land that is sometimes under water, sometimes dry, depending on weather and tides and season, is known as the intervale. It is an unpredictable

273

terrain, where the soil is rich and where some optimistic people create gardens, so-called intervale gardens where they plant vegetables every spring.

Here I met a courageous woman. Shortly after turning 50, Glenna was in an accident on the river road. Her pelvis was broken in three places, arm fractured, heel smashed. Over three years of recuperation she slowly regained strength, exercising and bearing more and more weight in water. She has deep scars and deeper back pain. Otherwise, she is lean and tough, and she dresses provocatively, a chiffon camisole under a low-cut denim dress one day, a stretchy bustier and flowered skirt the next.

Her passion is old houses – a costly hobby, she said ruefully – and in particular the farmhouse she lives in and another that she bought with the idea of developing. It boasts a long waterfront where she has made an intervale garden.

It is the river that draws and keeps her here. She has a small wooden dinghy that she sails alone. She has cats, a perennial garden, and vibrant art and big dreams. Hers is the kind of place and life that makes you think, This is too much for a single woman – how does she do it? But she does. It was Glenna who told me about intervale gardens.

The lives of many single women are like intervale gardens. They are chancy, a little eccentric, and definitely not everyone's choice. They require much attention and hard work. They are always vulnerable to external forces but respond well to redesign and reinvention. It takes time to learn to cultivate an intervale garden. Sometimes they succeed, sometimes they don't, but when they do, the rewards are rich. They require resilience, stubbornness, fortitude.

Some would say an intervale garden is a foolish indulgence, a waste of time. Others wouldn't have it any other way.

I have spent a great deal of time on the road. I would fly into a major city, rent a car, and drive to meet people within a reasonable distance. This being Canada, that meant that one day I drove almost 800 kilometres for a single interview. At the end of such journeys, in isolated northern towns or along rural sideroads, I found strong women, living alone, scarred by relationships with husbands who are long gone, thriving in terrain that challenged their ability to survive on very thin soil. I also met women who had never married and who staked their sense of self on a profession or service to the community.

I have reflected on the traditional image of the spinster: a sense of being frozen in time, a girlishness that never fades, a womanliness never unleashed by sexual contact; I think of stuffed Victorian birds sealed in a bell jar or insects trapped in amber.

Canadian single women crossing the threshold into a new century are not trapped or frozen. They are notably resilient. They have often undergone remarkable transformations, more than once in their lives. Their hallmark is a continual remaking and redefining. They are works in progress.

Laura and Jennifer

I drove north of Edmonton for a couple of hours to meet Laura at a country store. We then travelled on in her car, a lumbering old blue Chrysler.

Laura is in her late 50s, medium height, softer in body than she was used to being. She has short, sensible hair, a pleasant face and voice, but also a no-nonsense demeanour. In October 1985, she left her home in Nova Scotia "with my two younger daughters, who were 14 and 16, in an old Pontiac Grand Am, heading across the country with a cactus plant and a hamster. The car made it and we made it." She was 43 and had never been west of Toronto.

A farmer's daughter from New Brunswick, Laura had once held a good job in administration in New York. She married a charmer who couldn't hold a job, then came back to Canada with three small

children. She continued to be the breadwinner; he was to be the
househusband. Not a term used at that time, I noted. "In the States
he lost his job every third month. When we came to Canada, he
decided to be self-employed, which gave him an excuse for doing
very little. I supported him from the time we came to Canada in '66
until our marriage split up in '78. Part of the deal was that he would
look after the children. But it never really worked.

"It was an excuse for him to sit and watch TV and drink beer.
He did fix the evening meals, and I did think he was looking after
the children well. In some respects he was, but we split when I discovered that he had been committing incest with my oldest daughter
for four years."

She was driving carefully, speaking calmly. We had been
acquainted for only a few minutes, and she had gone directly to
the most painful part of her life story.

"Back in the 1970s, that was not something people talked about
or even acknowledged," I said.

"Well, it was one of the crosses I had to bear. I never spoke to
my husband after I found out. My daughter never saw her father
again. He was charged, he pleaded guilty, he went to prison. Then
I had him deported back to the States. I was judged very severely
for that. Because at that time it was considered a family problem,
and the family should work together and make everything turn
out all right."

"Has your daughter healed from it?"

"No, she's 35, she's on her second marriage. We are estranged.
She would never get therapy. I feel very badly for her, but at 35,
there's not a lot I can do. If I had it to do over again, I would have
insisted on counselling when she was a minor. However, both the
doctor and the psychologist said, Look, she seems to be handling
things all right. Don't make a mountain out of a molehill.

"My daughter lives in a town about 20 kilometres from here,
and I rarely see her. When I do, she's cordial, but she has a very

controlling husband who doesn't want her having anything to do with family. I have more contact with my granddaughter through the first husband than I have through my daughter."

It was early spring, the frosted greys and browns were being eased and softened by tinges of colour, redbuds limned with bright green. We talked about the land, the long summer days of the North which make for a good growing season, the people. She admires the women especially, "because they do so much work on their own. They farm alongside their husbands as equals, and in many cases they run the farm while the husband's off in the oil patch. I just give them all my respect."

Laura is a hospital administrator. She went from a staff of three and a $200,000 budget down east to a staff here of 25 and a $2-million budget. After 11 years of dogged ascent up the corporate ladder in her previous job, she was squeezed out. "I almost had a nervous breakdown. I went on sick leave and then engaged a lawyer to pursue a settlement. We got a good settlement.

"One of the things I would love to study is what happens to women over 50 in organizations, particularly in bureaucracies. My casual observation is that it's okay to have up-and-coming women in the organization, but when you get near the top and you're over 50, you're not nearly as interesting. They'd just as soon hide you in a backroom someplace."

Laura is not the kind of person to be tucked way in a backroom. Being dumped in her mid-50s was a terrible crisis, the second major upheaval in her life and another blow to her sense of self. Although it happened three years before we met, the hurt was still fresh in her mind.

As Laura told me her story, I remembered a similar conversation with a woman in Vancouver named Jennifer. Very British in demeanour, speech, and appearance, she told me she had been a history and English teacher who then took a middle management job in education. In her early 50s Jennifer too was forced to retire – laid off, actually, with a severance arrangement that lasted her until after her 55th birthday. She had identified strongly with her career; it was a shock to be dismissed. "If I had gone when I was supposed to go, at 58, there would have been a retirement party. But as it was, we all just slunk away." She said she had no control over the whole episode, although control was obviously important to her. She used the word repeatedly in our discussion.

It wasn't until the end of the conversation that Jennifer revealed she'd been separated since 1984. She said she'd felt a kind of "honeymoon euphoria" when she was finally out of the marriage. Then she admitted, "Actually, my husband was – is – manic-depressive. It wasn't that he beat me, it wasn't that he was abusive to the children, it's just that I supported him for 17 years." She was still looking after him. "Sometimes I do it gracefully and sometimes not. He's in the same category as my aged mother. I get nothing from him, but I give him emotional and physical care, much the same as one would give to an invalid parent."

She had a long time to get used to the idea that the marriage would end. "I couldn't take it any more. It was finally a choice, a decision." But losing her job was devastating, at least in the short term. Now she's reinventing herself.

Jennifer worked for 27 years and, in addition to the severance, she has a good pension. She's always managed the household affairs and finds it even easier as a single person. Her new house is in her name; a friend, Moira, rents the upper floors. They met at daycare with their children and discovered they had grown up 50 kilometres apart and attended the same schools in England. Both wanted to be in a house, so they looked for an arrangement that would suit two families. They share all expenses and decisions about the house and garden. They imagine sharing other things as they age, including the care of each other.

Are you happy? I asked. "Unequivocally happy," Jennifer said with a big smile. Are you ever lonely? "Well, only fleetingly. If I look out the window and I see or hear something, or I read something, it would be nice to be able to turn to someone and share that with them. But it's just a fleeting thing. Nothing serious." She radiated energy but not restlessness. Like Laura, she is a woman who is not finished with the larger world but hasn't yet figured out what her next adventure will be.

It was thanks to their respective daughters that I met Laura and Jennifer. The younger women had used almost the same words: "You should talk to my mother if you want to meet a model single woman." They admired their mothers, working women who had supported their children alone. In addition to the long, drawn-out suffering of alcoholism or abuse or mental illness, there was the added responsibility of protecting the children, of being the one who was reliable and resilient and able to fix or alleviate some of the damage. It may be that women are trained from girlhood to handle emotional crisis, but where is the preparation for the loss of income and dignity that comes with the unexpected end of a career?

Laura and I drove on. This is the kind of empty northern highway where you are as likely to meet a house being transported down the road as anything else. There are long intervals between vehicles, the signs of habitation few. Laura now lives on the outskirts of a good-sized town, in a converted schoolhouse. Her new job demands a lot of travel time.

"What's it like being a single woman in a community like this?"

"Actually, it was extremely difficult when I first came. It's difficult almost anywhere, because our society is so coupled. I didn't know anyone, and I didn't have any family here. To find a niche was difficult, because the community revolved around youth activities and church. If you didn't go to church and you didn't have kids involved in swimming or Girl Guides, then you didn't have a vehicle for meeting people. Hospital people are a bit strange anyway. It was a rough few years until my daughters married into the community. Then I began to find a network. In a smaller community, I think everybody is accepted for who they are."

"People can't afford to be judgmental."

"No, there's not enough people around."

We were in town by then, and we had lunch at the best restaurant, which, as in many northern towns, is family-run. It is a cheery establishment, and people stopped to talk to Laura about a forum she had organized. She enjoys the status of a well-liked, well-established professional. But she has few close friends: "This has been true ever since I came out here 15 years ago. If I have something really earth-shaking to share, I have to call long-distance to Montreal or Toronto, or Wisconsin, or Regina. But the time I would spend building friendships I devote to my children and my grandchildren instead."

"Have you ever been lonely being a single woman?"

She laughed, or rather grimaced. "During the first few years I was single, I felt as if I was between husbands. Sometimes I would feel quite lonely and unwanted because nothing seemed to be happening on the romantic front. But I was never one to wallow in self-pity, or to inflict my self-pity on friends or relatives. I have a little mental exercise: I look at my acquaintances and I say, Would I like to trade places with her? Or with her? Or with her? I never did find a woman in my circle of friends that I particularly wanted to trade places with, so I figured I wasn't so bad off after all.

"The other thing I always keep looking for is the 'normal' family. I'm not sure it exists. Certainly I don't see much evidence of it. I asked one of my girls once if she ever felt deprived because she had only one parent. And she said, No, she felt better off than other kids, who always talked about their parents fighting and about how they manipulated their parents one against the other. She said, Life is so much simpler and more straightforward with just one parent. You know where you stand, you know what the rules are.

"When you're single, you have to be more honest with your kids. I saw other parents raising their kids and teaching them things I knew they didn't believe, that I knew they hadn't lived. It's like they had licence to be hypocritical about extramarital sex and premarital sex and things like that. When you're a single parent, you have to live what you teach."

Laura's house is nondescript. She had been in it only a year or so, and she admitted it was not a priority. She is not especially domestic, except that she knits. One daughter, Ginger – we stopped in to visit at the gift shop she owns – tried to be charitable about her mother's indifference to cooking. "I remember that we had just a few dishes, frequently rotated. When I married, my husband complained that I had to vary my menu!"

Laura was unperturbed by this small revelation. "There were two things that were really important to me in the kitchen. One was that my kids always had homemade cookies. Somehow I clung to that as a symbol that I was being a good mother. The other thing was that I always baked their birthday cakes."

"And you put money in them," recalled Ginger. "Foil-wrapped money. One time we tried to make cookies when you were tired and sleeping on the sofa. When I asked if we could do some baking, you said, As long as you don't need any help!"

Laura is like a pragmatic pioneer woman, one who packs up the family and moves as necessary, who reconstitutes her life after profound shock or disaster, who more than makes do. She stitched her family of daughters back together as best she could after her husband's betrayal. She has not forgiven him, but her emotions are ordered and channelled into making things work. She does what she has to do. She manages.

From the Diary of a Single Woman

A summer evening. Katherine and I are sitting side by side in the gossip chairs on the back deck, looking at the moon. A perfect half-moon. Honeysuckle and nicotiana scents hang heavy in the air. The citronella candle casts a yellow glow on the wisteria.

She tells me that for the first time, on her 25th birthday, this year, she imagined conceiving and giving birth. The possibility of something slowly growing within: as she tells me this, her hands move down her body, curving to describe a pregnant belly, then flowing outwards. I tell her I have yet to imagine being a grandmother. I don't tell her how clearly I can still see her as a newborn infant, her face already intent and curious, as it is now.

She is proud of her independence, her emotionally uncomplicated life, the space to create herself. I can't picture the big romance, the lifetime union looming in front of me, she says. It's not something I'm working towards. I like not being on a roller coaster. And also not settling.

The romance in my garden is cast in stone. It is Katherine who first made up this story four years ago, and it is retold every summer. At the back of the garden is a small fountain in the shape of a pelican, its long pale beak the spout, trickling a light stream of water. On the deck, there is a large Canada goose, clearly male, carved from soapstone. High on the garden shed is a small Canada goose, just as clearly female, and she is facing a point midway between the other birds.

The pelican is Cyrano, making music, Katherine says, wooing in his way. Christian sits silent, handsome but inarticulate. Roxanne is torn; she looks with one eye at beautiful Christian, but she hears the music of Cyrano.

Here at least the love story remains unfinished.

Of course I don't want to hit 30 and turn into a cougar, she says. What's a cougar? I ask.

You don't know cougars? she says. Slightly trashy, desperate, tight leather pants, hunting for a man. Everybody knows cougars. Nobody wants to be one.

I ask if her ideas about marriage have been affected by the marriage of her parents, ending after 20 years.

No, she is clear, that's a cliché. You don't want to think about the ending at the beginning or you would never begin. And there is nothing wrong with something good ending after 20 or so years.

It is 10 years this summer since my marriage to her father ended. It has taken most of that decade for me to acquire equilibrium and tranquility as a single woman. To become fully at ease with my place in this city. To redefine, reshape my body to move with grace and lightness over the next decades. This is a surprise. So too is the happy discovery that my sexual self can be ignited after prolonged dormancy. I have embraced, as the eldest child of three, my role as matriarch in my family, a family in flux and reconfiguration, through couplings and uncouplings, deaths and births. And I am learning that although time is precious, some things cannot be rushed.

We watch the moon. A cat watches us.

Epilogue

In my journey across the country and into the lives of single women, I of course found many cats and dogs, no men, and only a few babies. I did find women who were able to articulate who they are, why they live the way they do, what they love and hate about being single. I did see sorrow and anger and frustration; I also saw serenity and contentment and, most of all, resilience.

I was struck often by the balanced ambivalence with which people live their lives, on two parallel tracks. Some single women flip almost daily from a sense of serenity or triumph into complete despair and unresolved lust. I suppose this is no different from the love/hate perspective many married women have, except that married women rail behind the curtain of respectability and apparent security. The ambivalence of single women is more exposed, more naked when you ask the questions, even though often the same piece – engagement, emotional intimacy – is missing from the lives of both single and married women.

I heard over and over again this lament: women have liberated themselves from being mere baby machines bereft of opportunity and education and freedom. But men over 30 have not evolved at all! Women are eager to try creative, equality-based versions of marriage or relationships. But men are terrified, reluctant, or unimaginative and passive. I also heard repeatedly the affirmation that women will not settle for an unsatisfying relationship. They are happier alone than in bondage. They prefer to live alone rather than to live badly or in misery with a man. A joke, but also true: a man has to be really, really good to be better than no man at all.

The backlash flaps on, with books counselling women to adore their men and be submissive, to remain virgins until marriage, to give up their own aspirations for the sake of the marriage, to marry early and breed. (Men never get this advice.) There are some who think the liberal phase in social convention has peaked and that the next generation will revert to white weddings and stay-at-home motherhood. I did not see this in the women I spoke to, although there will always be a segment of society following a more conventional track.

My daughter is 25, and she has been to only two or three weddings. Her friends think in terms of relationships, not marriage. When I asked, "Is it still better to have married badly than not at all?" I was told, "It's not about marriage. But it is better to have loved badly than not at all." These young women are not yet committed to having babies. This may change, but in the meantime, a surprising number of young women quietly have abortions. Women closer to 30 may have a focused image of man, home, baby in their sights, but they are not always in a rush.

Women in their early to mid-20s are also openly experimental with their sexuality, floating with ease from flirtations with both lesbian and heterosexual choices. There is less division between the worlds of straight and lesbian women, especially where there is convergence between issues of sexuality and other issues, political or cultural. It is not possible to say whether this will result in an increase in the number of women who statistically count as lesbian. For some young women it does appear that lesbian chic (being a

LUG, lesbian until graduation) is a safe, cool place in which to experience sex.

However, in more covert ways, I found that single women of all ages are flexible in their sexual activity. They can imagine sex with women and often wish for a long-term relationship with a woman, if only because it seems practical. Women are easier to live with, they say; there are more attractive single women out there than there are men. But just as these women are not out beating the bushes for men, they are not actively seeking relationships with women.

At the same time, single women of all ages, except the very young, are subversive or reckless when it comes to practising safe sex. I found the same insouciance among close friends as I did among strangers and especially among women over 40. I found this attitude among savvy health professionals, middle-class conservatives, and party girls. The reasons are pathetically simple: men over 30 hate condoms. Women would rather take the chance than not have sex at all, especially if a rare opportunity presents itself. Women under 30 are more likely to practise safe sex, because men under 30 will. Or if they are careless, they go to STD clinics more casually than they go to the dentist.

For many women, the act of becoming single, or the moment of realization that this is who they are and that is just fine, is often a process of reinvention. They look back on this moment as climactic, as significant as giving birth, as a rite of passage. It is not a rite of passage honoured and celebrated by ritual. It is, however, recognized by women themselves, and by those who love them.

A decision to be single, to marry, to divorce is more than a private one. It is attached to a raft of laws, contracts, and transactions. For centuries the institution of marriage was the instrument for controlling the rights, persons, and property of women. In the words of the 18th-century English jurist Sir William Blackstone, "By marriage, husband and wife are one person in law." That one person was the husband.

That principle informed English-Canadian law and was only slowly, painstakingly unravelled through the efforts of women, beginning in the 1850s with a number of provincial acknowledgments of a married woman's right to property and then to earnings. Then came the right to vote, the right of widows to inheritance. Divorce was easier for men until 1925, when adultery became the only cause for both men and women. There have been challenges to and erosions of the tax system that penalizes people on the basis of their marital status, and to the definitions of eligibility for pensions. Divorce statistics in Canada reflect changes in divorce legislation, with sharp rises in the number of divorces after the liberalizing Divorce Acts of 1968 and 1986.

In February 2000, the federal government introduced the Modernization of Benefits and Obligations Act, which gives to gay couples the rights and responsibilities already enjoyed by common-law couples but maintains a hard line between gay and common-law relationships on one hand and heterosexual marriage on the other. Because, said Justice Minister Anne McLellan at the time, "the definition of marriage has not changed . . . [It] relates to an institution that is of fundamental and longstanding religious and historical significance." In the legislation, marriage is defined as "the lawful union of one man and one woman to the exclusion of all others."

The legal definition of marriage may not have been affected by this legislation, but the reality of marriage has changed dramatically. The people who embody that institution, or challenge or cease to honour its conditions, have changed. Yet the word, its definition, is treated as sacrosanct. Editorialists and politicians feel obliged to stand by marriage as untouchable, holy, indivisible, and, of course, heterosexual – an eternal verity of Canadian life.

Which it patently is not. People form a range of partnerships and lifelong commitments and do not marry. The energy that goes into protecting the definition of marriage, as opposed to its reality, might better be spent ensuring the economic, educational, and legal rights of the children who are the often unfortunate, unprotected outcome of unreliable unions between men and women, including legal marriages. But as long as the spectre of this sacred union is the standard by which Canadians are deemed to be good, better, or best citizens (the more "married" you are, the more credit you get, literally), it remains very difficult for individuals to make alternative choices and feel validated in those choices.

This is not to deny the traditions by which people celebrate their choice of one another. People may say what they like to each other when they come together in a contractual, loving partnership, to celebrate their affection and devotion with family and friends, to engage in age-old rituals of union. This is surely not the business of anyone other than the individuals, except where there are children or financial implications. For these conditions, there must be contracts. Both the mother and the father of a child must accept responsibility for the children they create. If one person's contribution is to take the burden of caregiving, that should be balanced by the financial support of the other.

There have been sea changes in Canada in our ideas of equality: shared parental responsibilities and rights, an unhooking of divorce from adultery, and the acknowledgment of the rights of all children, conceived under the umbrella of marriage or just any old umbrella. But there remain injustices and bureaucratic bunglings and laws that are anachronistic.

I would argue that we must bring legislation and public posturing into line with reality. Marriage is no longer sacred, if indeed it ever was. The term "to the exclusion of all others" is not a definition of marriage, it is a definition of commitment, which any two people might make as steadfastly or frivolously as two people who choose to call such a commitment marriage. The term itself glosses over its intended true meaning, which is two people who never have sex with anyone else, a condition surely as often broken as kept.

A "legal" union is nothing more than a piece of paper signed by someone designated by the government – a Unitarian minister, a Catholic priest, a Salvation Army major, or a justice of the peace – as having the authority to declare two people "married" at that moment in time. Instead of trying to force the infinite range of possible living arrangements – sexual or nonsexual cohabiting – into good boxes and bad boxes, marriage and unmarriage, we should find other, true-to-life bases for taxation, pension benefits, and contractual obligation.

For example, in assuming that people have one job for life and retire at 65 on a pension, the retirement pension system is blind to the current reality of people's lives. Most of us change jobs, are not lifelong employees, are freelance, have one or two or three part-time jobs, work from home, run small businesses, do not have pensions, and may never retire. The definitions of marriage and family that form the basis of relevant legislation, and the social expectations attached to them, are equally anachronistic.

In some cases, there is a political or ideological agenda attached to resistance to change. Often there is not. As a society, we are not engaged in a rigorous reassessment of priorities, assumptions, and the legal apparatus we have cobbled together over time to support these things. We go through periods of crisis, analysis, critiques that grow into movements and counter-movements. We struggle as individuals to find our own way in accordance with or in defiance of what is happening around us, what our parents did or did not do. It often comes as a surprise that choices and decisions we have made have simultaneously been made by others.

The choice to be, to become, or to remain single is arguably subversive, a form of revolt. Not always a loud, large sign, but a way nevertheless of saying, I am not conforming. I will make my way in this society as something other than a wife. I will define myself by what I do, not by my attachments. I may choose not to be upwardly mobile in order to realize other ideals. I will absolutely fulfill my obligations as a mother, but I want to construct family life on a less rigid model.

Is society weakened by this choice? I think not. Single women, not locked into the demands of a nuclear family, are available to society at large. They are the tireless caretakers of aging parents and siblings. They are conscientious about community engagement. Are these bad people, unfit for marriage, not morally or emotionally up to the challenge? No, no, and no. Many single women do not want to be forever single. But they want to be in relationships that are not constrained by traditional notions of duty or configuration or hierarchy. They want to transform the rules of the game.

For Further Reading

Abbott, Elizabeth. *A History of Celibacy*. Toronto: HarperCollins, 1999.

Angier, Natalie. *Woman: An Intimate Geography*. New York: Houghton Mifflin, 1999.

Anderson, Bonnie S., and Judith P. Zinsser. *A History of Their Own: Women in Europe from Prehistory to the Present*. 2 vols. Oxford: Oxford University Press, 2000.

Backhouse, Constance. *Petticoats and Prejudice: Women and Law in Nineteenth Century Canada*. Toronto: Women's Press, 1991.

Blum, Deborah. *Sex on the Brain: The Biological Differences Between Men and Women*. New York: Penguin Books, 1997.

Clements, Marcelle. *The Improvised Woman: Single Women Reinventing Single Life*. New York: W.W. Norton, 1998.

Christie, Nancy. *Engendering the State: Family, Work, and Welfare in Canada*. Toronto: University of Toronto Press, 2000.

Cook, Ramsay, and Wendy Mitchinson, eds. *The Proper Sphere: Woman's Place in Canadian Society.*

Crenshaw, Theresa L. *The Alchemy of Love and Lust: How Our Sex Hormones Influence Our Relationships.* New York: Pocket Books, 1996.

Ehrenreich, Barbara, and Deirdre English. *For Her Own Good: 150 Years of the Experts' Advice to Women.* New York: Anchor Books, 1983.

Faludi, Susan. *Backlash: The Undeclared War Against American Women.* New York: Anchor Books, 1991.

Ignatieff, Michael. *The Rights Revolution.* Toronto: Anansi, 2000.

Jeffreys, Sheila. *Anticlimax: A Feminist Perspective on the Sexual Revolution.* London: Women's Press, 1990.

Jeffreys, Sheila. *The Spinster and Her Enemies: Feminism and Sexuality 1880-1930.* Melbourne: Spinifex Press, 1985.

Little, Margaret Jane Hillyard. *'No Car, No Radio, No Liquor Permit': The Moral Regulation of Single Mothers in Ontario, 1920-1997.* Toronto: Oxford University Press, 1998.

Luepnitz, Deborah Anna. *The Family Interpreted: Psychoanalysis, Feminism, and Family Therapy.* New York: Basic Books, 1988.

Mandell, Nancy, and Ann Duffy. *Canadian Families: Diversity, Conflict, and Change.* Toronto: Harcourt Brace, 2000.

McGoldrick, Monica, Carol M. Anderson, and Froma Walsh, eds. *Women in Families: A Framework for Family Therapy.* New York: W.W. Norton, 1989.

Phillips, Roderick. *Putting Asunder: A History of Divorce in Western Society.* Cambridge: Cambridge University Press, 1988.

Prentice, Alison, Paula Bourne, Gail Cuthbert Brandt, Beth Light, Wendy Mitchinson, and Naomi Black. *Canadian Women: A History.* Toronto: Harcourt Brace, 1996.

Siggins, Maggie. *In Her Own Time: A Class Reunion Inspires a Cultural History of Women*. Toronto: HarperCollins, 2000.

Vicinus, Martha, ed. *A Widening Sphere: Changing Roles of Victorian Women*. Bloomington, Indiana: Indiana University Press, 1997.

Woodman, Marion. *Bone: Dying into Life*. New York: Viking Penguin, 2000.

Acknowledgments

$\mathcal{M}$y thanks go to the many, many women who gave generously of their time, wisdom, thoughts, and afterthoughts, who sent me handwritten notes and e-mails, who offered me a bed, a meal, and their own community of single women friends.

Katherine Lochnan and George Yost, Caroline Orr, and Mary Link offered extended hospitality during the research and writing of this book, and women across the country gave me shelter as well as their stories.

Friends listened to me, talked to me, suggested ideas about our similarities and differences as single women, especially Suzanne Peters, who happily encouraged me to tell her story.

Lannie Messervey and Erica Fram were dedicated, engrossed transcribers of tapes.

I thank my agents Jan Whitford and Jackie Kaiser of Westwood Creative Artists; Rona Maynard, editor of *Chatelaine* magazine, for generous access to the *Chatelaine* archives; the librarians at the Ontario Institute for Studies in Education, for friendly advice and a helpful introduction to the excellent women's studies collection; and

Acknowledgments

the Banff Cultural Journalism program and the Ontario Arts Council for creative support during and specifically for this project.

Thanks also to Jan Walter, for moral support and editorial brilliance, and to Sarah Swartz and Barbara Czarnecki for their patience with my long sentences, big paragraphs, and innumerable semi-colons.

I am grateful to my sister, Sara, and my daughter, Katherine, for curiosity, tolerance, laughter, and occasional glasses of wine.

During the research for and writing of this book, my brother, Dave, was very ill, first with chronic progressive multiple sclerosis and then with melanoma. Yet his interest in this book, his patience with my absences, his good-natured encouragement of me even as he failed were unflagging. He died the week the galleys came back from typesetting. He was a strong, stalwart man whose ashes we scattered on a northern blackwater lake.

The text of this book was set in Sabon, Jan Tschichold's interpretation of Garamond, originally released in metal by Stempel in 1964 and later digitized by Adobe. Renaissance letter forms and large x-height make Sabon ideal for book setting.

Book design by Terri Fong

Developmental editor: Sarah Swartz